The Films of
James Cameron

The Films of James Cameron

Critical Essays

Edited by
MATTHEW WILHELM KAPELL
and STEPHEN MCVEIGH

McFarland & Company, Inc., Publishers
Jefferson, North Carolina, and London

ALSO OF INTEREST: *Star Trek as Myth: Essays on Symbol and Archetype at the Final Frontier.* Edited by Matthew Wilhelm Kapell (McFarland, 2010)

LIBRARY OF CONGRESS CATALOGUING-IN-PUBLICATION DATA

The films of James Cameron : critical essays / edited by Matthew Wilhelm Kapell and Stephen McVeigh.
   p.   cm.
Includes bibliographical references and index.

ISBN 978-0-7864-6279-7
softcover : 50# alkaline paper ∞

1. Cameron, James, 1954– — Criticism and interpretation.
I. Kapell, Mathew.   II. McVeigh, Stephen.
PN1998.3.C352F57   2011
791.43023'3092 — dc23   2011033689

BRITISH LIBRARY CATALOGUING DATA ARE AVAILABLE

Front cover design by David K. Landis (Shake It Loose Graphics).

Manufactured in the United States of America

McFarland & Company, Inc., Publishers
  Box 611, Jefferson, North Carolina 28640
  www.mcfarlandpub.com

For our wives Catherine and Amy,
without whom we would accomplish little

and

For our colleague and friend, C. Scott Littleton,
who passed away shortly after finishing
the essay that appears here

Table of Contents

Acknowledgments　　ix

Introduction: Persistence of Visions—Approaching the Films of James Cameron
　STEPHEN MCVEIGH AND MATTHEW WILHELM KAPELL　　1

Surveying James Cameron's Reluctant Political Commentaries: 1984–2009
　STEPHEN MCVEIGH AND MATTHEW WILHELM KAPELL　　15

Fighting the History Wars on the Big Screen: From *The Terminator* to *Avatar*
　ACE G. PILKINGTON　　44

"She's a goddamn liar": Perspectives on the Truth in *Aliens* and *Titanic*
　ANDREW B. R. ELLIOTT　　72

Art, Image and Spectacle in High Concept Cinema
　BRUCE ISAACS　　90

"You have to look with better eyes than that": A Filmmaker's Ambivalence to Technology
　ELIZABETH ROSEN　　109

"So, what's your story?" Morphing Myths and Feminizing Archetypes from *The Terminator* to *Avatar*
　DEAN CONRAD　　124

Between *Aliens* and *Avatar*: Mapping the Shifting Terrain of the Struggle for Women's Rights
　ELISA NARMINIO AND MATTHEW WILHELM KAPELL　　146

Terminators, Aliens, and Avatars: The Emergence of Archetypal Homosexual Themes in a Filmmaker's Imagination
　ROGER KAUFMAN　　167

"I see you": Colonial Narratives and the Act of Seeing in *Avatar*
   JOHN JAMES AND TOM UE   186

Gonzalo Guerrero and the Maya Resistance to the Spanish
   Conquistadors: A Sixteenth Century "Avatar" of *Avatar*
   C. SCOTT LITTLETON   200

Conclusion: Seeing the Films of James Cameron Mythically
   MATTHEW WILHELM KAPELL AND STEPHEN MCVEIGH   216

About the Contributors   221

Index   225

Acknowledgments

We are deeply thankful to the many people who have aided in the production of this volume. It was Zoe Sluka-Kapell who first said "why don't you do a book on that guy who made *Avatar*," and this book was born. Our wives, Amy Kapell and Catherine McVeigh, watched and re-watched more James Cameron movies, more times, than should be required of anyone. They listened sympathetically, criticized constructively and improved immeasurably the work you are now holding. Among their enormous and various contributions, thanks especially to Catherine for coffee and blankets and to Amy for her ability to figure out what a certain very evil Seattle computer company was thinking when they updated their word processing software.

Our contributors, who worked under deadline, accepted feedback graciously, and reworked entire sections to meet our needs, have our greatest appreciation. Guernsey Kapell offered feedback on many of the chapters, often offering his insight before we had even read them ourselves. The Department of Political and Cultural Studies at Swansea University, Wales, UK, was supportive of the project, especially colleagues in the programs in War and Society and American Studies. Nancy Greer, acting as our North American project manager, made it possible to get all documentation to our publisher on time. Without her this book would have been late.

Our especially heartfelt thanks to Mary Ann Littleton who, in a manner more heroic than any of Cameron's imagining, made sure that her husband's work was finalized for this project after his untimely passing.

Introduction: Persistence of Visions — Approaching the Films of James Cameron

STEPHEN MCVEIGH *and*
MATTHEW WILHELM KAPELL

The films of James Cameron are dominated by his concern with vision, whether they are visions of the past or the future, of strong women and driven men, of heroism and villainy, of apocalyptic scenarios and human endurance. Film scholars have had a long romance with the now generally discredited theory of the "persistence of vision" which they have used to explain how motion pictures convey the perception of movement. In that theory the moving image is created for the viewer because of a flaw in the human perceptual system, allowing rapidly shifting images to be processed by the brain as motion. David A. Cook described "persistence of vision" as the "optical phenomenon [whereby] the brain retains images cast upon the retina of the eye" long enough to provide the illusion of movement.[1] The theory fits nicely with Modernist film studies in that it requires, as Joseph and Barbara Anderson have put it, "a passive viewer upon whose sluggish retina images pile up."[2] This technical explanation of how the human eye or the combination of the eye and the brain work together to decode what the filmmaker means works perfectly if one assumes that the filmmaker — that is, the author — has a specific truth to impart, and the audience's job is merely to passively receive that truth.

This notion of persistence of vision, though, neither explains why it is movies seem to be in motion, nor does it explain what we mean by this approach. The essays herein recognize the fundamental importance of the active audience as well as the active filmmaker. The contention of each of the contributors to this volume is that, simply, James Cameron has registered such seismic impact on his contemporary culture and society because the visions presented in his films have been consistent and resonant visions of the contemporary zeitgeist. An important implication of this approach is that the audiences for Cameron's films have not passively accepted his visions over

1

and over, but have continuously interacted with them until they have become part of the collective cultural landscape.

The original theory of persistence of vision is one in which the brain and the eye work to retain one image long enough for a newer, slightly altered image in the next frame of film to be processed and retained, thus creating the illusion of movement. The inference here for this collection is quite the opposite. Contemporary culture has retained images, ideas, motifs, and themes from the films of James Cameron as he has moved forward with new projects. The new "frames" do not replace the old, but rather reinforce, extend or speak to those that came before. The persistence of the vision here is not the illusion of motion, but the suggestion that Cameron's visions have become a persistent feature of our culture. The brain may not retain the previous image as it moves to process the next, slightly different image to create the illusion of movement. But culturally, we have retained the images of James Cameron's films, and those images have persisted for significantly longer than the work of the majority of filmmakers.

This longevity and relevance is a central concern of this book. James Cameron is a persistently visionary filmmaker, bringing to the screen meticulously constructed worlds which tie together art, science and technology. Furthermore, his cinematic visions have persisted in global culture, thrilling audiences today as they did upon their initial release, extending genres and influencing subsequent generations of screenwriters and film directors. Vision is fundamental to Cameron's work. He has been exploring ways of seeing throughout his career. His detailed visualizations of aspects of history, his stylized depictions of the present and his renderings of grittily authentic human futures have shaped our imaginations over a span of 25 years. Behind his efforts to show the audience things never before seen lies an intersection of art and technology. His revolutions in special effects technology have seared themselves into the cultural lexicon, forever altering what cinema is capable of. Imagery that is at once visceral, challenging and unforgettable is Cameron's stock in trade. The Terminator removing its eye, a woman encased in the loader fighting an alien mother, the morphing beauty of the T-1000, a romantic kiss against the backdrop of an atomic explosion, the terrifying last moments of RMS *Titanic* or the luminescent biodiversity of Pandora are all pivotal waypoints in the evolution of film effects technology and are part of the imaginary landscape of countless millions of people. It does not matter that the idea of the persistence of vision no longer explains human interaction with film. Its implications offer an especially evocative way of thinking about Cameron's oeuvre.

It is perhaps surprising to note, given his primacy in the Hollywood firmament, that Cameron's reputation is based on a relatively short list of movies. Between 1984 and 2009 he has directed only seven feature films, three documentaries, executive produced a television show and written screenplays turned into films for other directors.[3] This volume focuses primarily on the seven full features. It is a measure of how rich and deep these films are, how culturally significant, that such a small number of texts can support the wide-ranging and conceptually diverse analyses here collected.

Dreamer? Futurist? Blockbuster Auteur?[4]

Christopher Heard's *Dreaming Aloud*, Rebecca Keegan's *The Futurist* and Alexandra Keller's *Routledge Film Guidebook: James Cameron* all follow to some degree a similar pattern of making Cameron himself their subject. In this way, Heard and Keegan function as celebrity biographers for whom the films are employed to explicate some aspect of Cameron's character. They discuss the entire sweep of the filmmaker's career, sometimes without the necessary nuance (for example, they both talk about *Strange Days* as a Cameron film, even though he only wrote the screenplay). It is not surprising that both Heard and Keegan subtitle their efforts "The Life and Films of James Cameron," as it is Cameron's "life" that tends to come first in their analyses. Keller's book goes beyond this sole focus on Cameron to provide an academic overview of the kinds of analytical perspectives and readings that can be applied to his films. This collection, then, is a deliberate attempt to move away from such spotlighting of the filmmaker. Cameron is still clearly a prominent dimension of this volume but whereas the works by Heard, Keegan and Keller privilege the author, this collection gives priority to the texts and their interactions with wider social, political and cultural contexts. To put it another way, this book is about the films of James Cameron, not James Cameron's films. However, the issues that surround the question, "What kind of filmmaker is James Cameron?" are important. These other books answer this question by singling out a feature of his character and subsequently processing his films through that lens. And while these portraits of Cameron as an imaginative technician or as hybrid of company man and individual artist do figure as elements of his character, they are clearly partial or selective. Their titles do capture the sense of a filmmaker caught up in a world of fantasy and the imagination and working within heavily prescribed lines of industrial film production. They do not necessarily offer a means of appreciating his oeuvre. Of the labels, it is Keller's articulation of "the blockbuster auteur" that is most useful. She makes some interesting observations about Cameron's credentials as an auteur, not least of which is that, even in this realm, Cameron is once again a force of change and innovation. Observing that the Academy Award for Best Picture which he received for *Titanic* marks the moment Cameron, the "master, even genius technician," was transformed into the artist, she remarks: "To talk about James Cameron as an auteur is to acknowledge how very far film culture has come from the original usage of that term. To talk about Titanic as a blockbuster is to speak about how the film has profoundly changed what that category means."[5]

That Cameron can claim the status of auteur is undeniable: his films contain recurring patterns, themes, visual and narrative signatures and motifs. He has consciously or otherwise extended the range and possibilities of mainstream cinema. He locates himself, in his role of director, at the very center of his productions. If there is an impediment it would seem to be that he works in the milieu of the blockbuster, which is by implication a formula and resistant to such artistic considerations. If however one accepts that, since the late 70s, the blockbuster has evolved beyond its meaning as a big production and become a genre in and of itself, Cameron's status as auteur is unarguable.

To accept Cameron at face value then, to see only the massive budgets, the enormous popular appeal and staggering box office figures is to miss much about a serious filmmaker working in a popular entertainment medium. His high visibility and deeply impressive statistics belie a risk-taking innovator with a seriousness of purpose, a distinctive intellectual engagement and an uncanny knack for capturing the mood of his audience. Cameron's is a profile that seems incongruous in an industry that tends to play safe, creating formulaic product for the sole purpose of maximizing profit. Perhaps this is Cameron's key strength, his ability to function perfectly inside the system while simultaneously transcending it, playing outside of it or subverting it from within.

Since the release of *The Terminator* in 1984, Cameron has become one of the most consistently bankable of Hollywood directors. He shares the rarefied heights of such A-list directors as Steven Spielberg and George Lucas, directors who work in the similar generic and commercial landscapes of the action-fantasy blockbuster. While not quite of the same generation as Spielberg and Lucas (the Movie Brats, as they have been described, including such figures as Martin Scorsese, Francis Ford Coppola, Brian DePalma and John Milius[6]), Cameron evinces something of the same spirit and approach to cinema. In common with Spielberg, Cameron makes big budget and profitable blockbusters, harnessing state of the art special effects in pursuit of universal, human stories. Indeed, it could be argued that without Spielberg there would be no Cameron. The former's breakthrough movie, *Jaws* (1975), inaugurated the dominance of the blockbuster in the contemporary Hollywood formula, a style of filmmaking Cameron would make his own. It is fun to note that this dominance impacted upon Cameron early in his career. *Piranha II: The*

Spawning (1981), Cameron's first shot at feature directing, albeit a fraught and unsatisfactory one, was a cheap and exploitative emulation of *Jaws*.

There are significant differences between the two, though. Spielberg is prolific by comparison, with some 24 feature films in a similar timeframe. Perhaps more importantly, Spielberg's movies have demonstrated a greater range of styles and voices. For every blockbuster there are a number of more personal or intimate films, more seriously intended films, literary adaptations, and realistic historical dramas. Although Cameron has at times in his career toyed with undertaking similar, smaller projects, he has been consistently drawn to the epic blockbusting event movie.

Another distinction between the two can be made in their role as cinematic innovators. Spielberg's innovations rest upon his position as a director with the power and influence to have what he wants. He is not a writer, nor is he directly engaged in or responsible for pushing the boundaries of technology. When he wanted "real" dinosaurs for *Jurassic Park* (1993), the movie that heralded the arrival of photorealistic digital effects, he hired existing companies and talent to work out how to make it happen. Cameron's approach is much more hands on, extending his involvement to the entire filmmaking process, from writing and directing to inventing new equipment and techniques. In this way, he more closely resembles the figure of George Lucas. Similarly restrained in terms of output (only some six features directed since 1971), Lucas has had enormous impact upon American cinema in two key areas. *Star Wars* (1977) guaranteed the permanence of the kind of blockbuster filmmaking that *Jaws* originated. It also established science fiction fantasy as a dominant narrative vehicle for the form, a style of cinema and a generic landscape that Cameron has repeatedly revisited. Science fiction lies at the core of his urge to make films. A viewing of Stanley Kubrick's *2001: A Space Odyssey* in 1968 had a profound effect upon Cameron: "It was really exciting intellectually, but mystifying and powerful visually. It was everything I thought I liked, but it didn't really have the answers. But I felt viscerally that I knew what the answers were."[7]

The film *2001* turned his interest in film-going into the ambition to be a filmmaker. *Star Wars* was similarly influential. *Xenogenesis*, his experimental short film, was an attempt to emulate the success of that film. Cameron subsequently wanted to turn the short into a feature and in the pursuit of financing he took the short to Roger Corman's New World Pictures, using it as an illustration of his developing skills in model building, special effects, lighting, and camera techniques. His arrival coincided with the start of work on *Battle Beyond the Stars*, another attempt to jump on the *Star Wars* bandwagon. After a screening of *Xenogenesis* he was hired as the model builder for the movie. From this role, where he was required to produce the maximum visual impact at minimum cost, Cameron began to establish himself as an up and coming talent. Other features of Cameron's approach began to emerge. He increasingly brought more and more responsibility into his orbit, feeling that no one could do it as well as he could. This experience with the Corman style of filmmaking, of experimenting and innovating, lies at the core of another connection between Cameron and Lucas: their relationship with technology. Both have found that their imagination has run beyond the capacity of the immediate generation of effects technology, leading both to either invent new processes or to sit on projects until the technology catches up. As a consequence, apart from *Star Wars*, Lucas' legacy will likely be the variety of processes and techniques he has been involved in creating, whether that be the effects company Industrial Light and Magic, Skywalker Sound or THX theatrical projection systems. Cameron similarly founded an effects house, Digital Domain, and his work on *The Abyss*, where his innovations in diving equipment made it possible to capture performance and sound while underwater, generated five patents. Likewise, advances in working with motion capture and 3-D processes in *Avatar* have led to more patents. This innovation has been the engine driving technological advance in film.

And yet despite some ringing similarities with the likes of Spielberg and Lucas, Cameron remains unique, not of any generation except his own. It is fascinating to consider how, in a system that would seem to stifle such individuality, he has maintained such impressive autonomy. He is an artist/technician with a unique vision and an affinity with the mindset of his audience. Cameron has changed the face of contemporary American film and captured the imagination of a global audience. And yet his work and his mission, his impact and longevity require further scrutiny. The essays that make up this volume provide such an investigation.

Ordering Cameron's Visions and Ordering This Volume

There are many visions in the films of James Cameron, but those visions persist because they also complement each other. The American scholar of myth William G. Doty has suggested that networks of myths "embody ideas of wholeness, or order replacing chaos."[8] The organization of this volume is an attempt to offer the same, at least metaphorically, for the films of James Cameron. The authors in this collection approach the full range of themes contained in James Cameron's oeuvre and the essays assess not only the construction of his films but the broader social, cultural and political impact and implications of this singular body of work. As Doty again notes about myths, "they are regarded as expressing lasting nodal points of human significance

[that] continue to evoke emotional participation."[9] This volume maintains a similar position about James Cameron's oeuvre: his visions persist because they have evoked for viewers emotional participation. As a result each chapter is an examination of such a nodal point, and the collection as a whole is intended to provide interlinked examinations of Cameron's lasting network of points of significance.

McVeigh and Kapell provide in the first instance a survey of the political dimension of Cameron's filmmaking. However, given that the filmmaker and his critics have been happy to ignore this dimension, the essay provides a range of contexts against which to interrogate Cameron's evolving narration of American political culture. Arguing against Cameron's suggestion upon the release of *Avatar* that it is his first foray into political filmmaking, the authors demonstrate that he has been consistently and sophisticatedly political since his earliest films. The essay exhaustively demonstrates that Cameron has repeatedly used politically historical contexts as a backdrop to his stories. His success commercially speaks to an unerring ability to connect with his audience and is a clear indication that his messages have been timely and relevant. The essay argues persuasively that what's new about *Avatar* is not the fact of a political core and content, but that the content is self-reflexively political. He has moved from reflecting the zeitgeist to actively shaping the terms of the debate.

Moving from the strictly political to conceptions of history, the essays by Ace G. Pilkington and Andrew B.R. Elliott each confront Cameron's use of history more centrally. First, Pilkington argues in his essay that the primary reason for Cameron's success has been his ability to use history as a structure for his films. Even though most of his work has been in the genre of action-fantasy-science fiction, history has underpinned all of it, whether that be internally or an external resonance with actual real world events. Pilkington argues that Cameron's approach to and use of history is particularly powerful because he equates it with Truth. In this conception, Pilkington sees Cameron's characters as historians, seeking data, developing an understanding and working to impose the validity of their own interpretations over other competing ones. Given Cameron's predilection for apocalyptic stories, the consequences for those who fail to impose their truth are grave. For Pilkington, this may be what Cameron's films are all about: A promise of redemption for humanity, not through fantasy, though that may be found along the way, but through asking honest questions and finding accurate answers.

Andrew B.R. Elliott also examines Cameron's ongoing debate between "truth" and "history" in the next essay, but with a far more pragmatic approach. He argues that the popular appeal of Cameron's films can be understood by reading them as resisting the nature and implications of postmodernity.

Elliott's argument is that Cameron consistently creates narratives with a choice of perspectives, all of which are equally valid, but which are ultimately reconciled by an underlying truth which confirms one or other of these perspectives and offers a clear narrative resolution. This he argues is symptomatic of a director who is at once visionary but working within a rigidly industrial system where any ambiguity must be ironed out to appeal to the widest audience and in so doing generate the maximum profit. In that context, he suggests, the Real, single truth sustains its credibility by supporting the perspective of his protagonists. And, for Elliott, it is precisely this inviolable sense of the Real which explains the continued appeal of Cameron's films, for each contains a conflict of perspectives, a fiery clash of opinion which is ultimately smoothed over by a fixed belief that the Truth will out. Amid the multiplicity and confusion of postmodern life, it is perhaps reassuring to audiences to find that there are still moments in which we can separate out the truth from the lies.

Of course, when considering questions of Truth and Reality, how Cameron chooses to represent these concepts in his films becomes itself important. Bruce Isaacs turns to this very topic in his essay and extends a consideration of Cameron's seemingly contradictory nature in the areas of art and industry and in so doing offers an insight into the importance of what we see and how we see it in Cameron's films. Isaacs argues that Cameron's aesthetic orientation is located at the intersection of the two competing interests of the Hollywood blockbuster: the individual artist and the product. The auteurist vision subsists in the attempt to "invent cinema," to make cinema new through the exponentially advancing technologies of the spectacle. For Cameron, vision is more than a medium for the conveyance of "reality." The special effect is never purely the depiction of the "real," but is actually transformative. And it is on these terms that Cameron's auteurist credentials rest: Cameron's High Concept auteurism is founded upon his use of the technology of cinematic spectacle. Each new Cameron film is a landmark in the advancement of the technological spectacle. And, for Isaacs, each new technological spectacle presents a new way of seeing.

If Isaacs is correct in treating Cameron as an auteur of filmmaking technology, then how Cameron represents technology in the narratives of his films is of central import as well. Thus, Elizabeth Rosen concentrates on that recurring element in Cameron's films. Rosen argues that there is ambivalence in his use of technology that in turn makes his films ambivalent on other levels. In agreement with Isaacs, she argues that Cameron is clearly the technological director par excellence. However, his films tend to evince an anti-technological, perhaps even technophobic, stance. His cinematic visions all project the idea that technology will be the means of our destruction. *Avatar*, she suggests, is particularly problematic in this way. A film made upon the cutting edge of cinematic technology demands that the audience sympathize with a primitive, pre-technological culture wherein technology is presented as militarized and repressive. Rosen suggests that Cameron has taken a wrong turn, then, with *Avatar*. She sees in his earlier films depictions of the possibilities as well as the dangers of technology, and considers those films more thoughtful and meaningful disquisitions on the dangers and benefits of a dependency upon technology.

As much as issues that seem large, like politics, history, or technology, dominate Cameron's films, other issues are also present. While themes of gender seem more narrowly defined than the previous topics, gender actually looms larger in his films than almost any other topic. As a result, the next three chapters discuss gender from three different perspectives. Dean Conrad moves on to consider Cameron's relationship to gender on archetypal levels. Cameron's representations of strong heroic women have long been the subject of critical praise and academic discussion. Conrad argues that there is a danger in considering these representations of heroic women as a collective whole and that there has not been sufficient analysis directed towards the evolving function of Cameron's female characters as his career has progressed. Such attention shows that all of Cameron's women are not fully of the same archetype, or if they are, the subtle, and not so subtle, differences chart ongoing shifts in Cameron's priorities as a filmmaker. Conrad identifies such changes emerging from personal experiences, from the maturing mind of the creator or as reflections of shifting cultural and political climates; or perhaps a symptom of ballooning budgets and the need to appeal to as wide an audience as possible. From these perspectives, he suggests that Cameron's female narratives have suffered. Neytiri may be the model of the powerful woman, as Ripley and Sarah Connor before her, an Amazonian warrior woman, with a visceral femininity, and although she does save Sully's life on at least two occasions, *Avatar* is clearly Jake's story, and not Neytiri's. Despite arguably being an amalgam of residual elements from Cameron's women — smart, sassy, sexy — she must be all this from the sidelines.

In the next essay Elisa Narminio and Matthew Wilhelm Kapell chart a similar course in considering Cameron's female characters, but place that course alongside the trajectomy of academic feminism. Narminio and Kapell specifically account for the distance between Ripley and Neytiri as the distance between the aims and objectives of second and third wave feminism. They argue that as feminism has become institutionalized, it has lost its dynamism and radical dimension. As a result the possible readings of Ripley in *Aliens*— which for many at the time seemed radical — made for both an excellent narrative and one that the audience could, perhaps unexpectedly, latch on to. In some ways they suggest Cameron can be seen to have betrayed the strength of his 1986 representations with *Avatar*. But Narminio and Kapell also point out that the less effective aspects of third wave feminism on popular culture mean that there was less reason for Cameron to try to make a similarly radical female hero. By combining the threads of both feminist discourses in the academy and the shifting roles of Cameron's female characters the essay leaves open which of these two is more to blame but suggests both Cameron and academic feminism might have some issues to resolve.

Roger Kaufman takes that theme one step further in his essay. A practicing Jungian psychologist, Kaufman looks to Cameron for underlying themes of gay sexuality. In part, his essay mirrors his previous work on *The Lord of the Rings*, *Star Wars* and *Star Trek* where he uncovered similar gay-centered themes. More significantly for this work, Kaufman's practice specializes in working with gay men and lesbians, and in working with Cameron he does something that might not be fully expected: he finds subliminal themes that allow even the most hetero-normal of films — of which Cameron's certainly are — to have real world applications. As so much of the major productions of Hollywood appear convincingly "straight," it is very important that this kind of gay-centered reading can still be found within them. Not only does such a reading indicate the ability to take the unfortunately still too often marginalized voices and bring them to the center of analysis, but it also shows that for those struggling at those margins there are ways of looking at popular culture that have a real-world resonance.

Gender and sexuality are prominent ways in which Cameron has approached issues of "difference" in his work, issues he has also dealt with in terms of "otherness." Thus, the final two essays in the collection deal with issues surrounding colonialism and postcolonialism. John James and Tom Ue explore in their essay the implications of the central concept of "seeing" in *Avatar* in terms of the colonial experience. They argue that seeing is not merely a passive act, and that someone — the one doing the seeing — is always privileged, while that which is seen becomes objectified. Thus, the narrative structure of *Avatar* may encourage us to sympathize with and overlook the central focalizer Jake's ethical flaws but those flaws still remain. For James and Ue the gap between the privileged and the objectified becomes increasingly salient when the human–Na'vi relationship is considered in terms of colonizer and colonized, for that is precisely the social process beginning to take place on Pandora. When the seer becomes the objectifying colonizer, the seen takes up a position of cultural, economic and racial subservience. *Avatar* stands out, however, in the protagonist Jake's adoption of indigenous morals, which he uses to defeat his own culture. Yes, indigenous values are championed but Cameron's use of a human liberator, let alone a white male, illustrates the insistence of the West on Eurocentric racial and cultural power structures. However, for James and Ue *Avatar* is a step in the right direction; Cameron does not condone the colonial process taking place on Pandora. James and Ue thus offer a reading that confronts the way Cameron allows the audience to accept the heroism of a colonizer without accounting for their own behavior in such a process in the real world.

The next essay looks to this adoption of indigenous morals in that real world and takes this approach in a historical direction by suggesting a strikingly similar historical antecedent for *Avatar's* narrative. This is not simply recognizing the surface similarities with *Dances with Wolves* or *The Last Samurai* or *Pocahontas*. C. Scott Littleton investigates a 16th century encounter between advanced and primitive cultures with significant parallels to Cameron's films and illuminates *Avatar's* colonial context as a consequence. Littleton depicts Gonzalo Guerrero, one of a pair of Spanish sailors who were shipwrecked off the coast of the Yucatan in 1511, as a version of Jake Sully, the renegade Marine. Guerrero, and Geronimo Aguilar were captured by local Maya chiefs just prior to the onset of the Spanish colonial conquest of Central America and Mexico. Aguilar remained loyal to his culture and religion, and gladly joined Cortez when he showed up on Cozumel in 1518 en route to Veracruz. However, Guerrero's story is entirely different. Like Jake with the Na'vi, he fell in love with Maya culture, and more importantly, with the chief's daughter, eventually becoming a chief himself, and later led his adopted people's successful resistance to the Spanish in the early 1530s. Indeed, it was only after Guerrero lost out in a power struggle and died in exile in Honduras in 1536 — to the end, leading a band of Maya against his former countrymen — that the Spanish finally managed to conquer the Yucatan in 1542. Littleton's observations about the ending of the two narratives provide a profound comment upon the nature of depicting colonization in contemporary film. Where in *Avatar* Sully's intervention sees off the colonizer's threat, the Maya were not as fortunate: the Spaniards' victory effectively destroyed an entire culture. History, unlike Cameron, does not provide a Hollywood ending.

This volume serves two purposes. In the first place, the essays collected herein are intended to accord James Cameron a level of critical and intellectual attention he has only partially received to date. In this mode, the book seeks to redress the balance in his portrait as Hollywood's "King" of the blockbuster, which veils the depth and consistency of his thematic range. Its second function is broader, grander than the concern for an individual filmmaker. The contributors all illuminate in multiple contexts the ways in which Cameron's films repeatedly capture, with sophistication and nuance, portraits of America in her passage through the late 20th and into the 21st century. In this way, his films are not merely the films of a Hollywood employee, albeit a very special employee, but are the films of a visionary filmmaker. They are not merely the films of a talented manipulator of well-worn formulae for popular consumption but a true innovator and artist, with coherent visions and messages. Thus, this work provides insight into just how it is that James Cameron has expressed "lasting nodal points of human significance" that viewers, again and again, find worthy of their "emotional participation." And perhaps this is the ultimate ambition for this book: the opportunity to provide a series of challenging and illuminating new visions on the work of a filmmaker who had seemingly already shown us everything there was to see.

NOTES

1. David A. Cook, *A History of Narrative Film* (New York: W.W. Norton, 1981), 1.
2. Joseph and Barbara Anderson, "The Myth of the Persistence of Vision Revisited," *Journal of Film and Video*, 45:1 (Spring 1993), 4.
3. Cameron produced and directed the documentaries, *James Cameron's Expedition: Bismarck* (2002), *Ghosts of the Abyss* (2003) and *Aliens of the Deep* (2005). He was creator, producer and occasional writer for the TV series *Dark Angel* (2000–2002). He was involved in writing the screenplays that became the movies *Rambo: First Blood Part II* (1986), *Point Break* (1991), and *Strange Days* (1995).
4. Christopher Heard, *Dreaming Aloud: The Life and Films of James Cameron* (New York: Bantam, 1998); Rebecca Keegan, *The Futurist: The Life and Films of James Cameron* (New York: Crown, 2009); Alexandra Keller, *Routledge Film Guidebooks: James Cameron* (New York: Routledge, 2006).
5. Keller, *James Cameron*, 2.
6. See Michael Pye and Lynda Myles, *The Movie Brats: How the Film Generation Took Over Hollywood. London*: Faber & Faber, 1979.
7. Quoted in Keegan, *The Futurist*, 10.
8. William G. Doty, *Mythography: The Study of Myth and Ritual* (Tuscaloosa, AL: University of Alabama Press, 2000), 60.
9. Doty, *Mythography*, 61.

WORKS CITED

Altman, Rick. *Film/Genre*. London: BFI Publishing, 1999.
Anderson, Joseph, and Barbara Anderson. "The Myth of the Persistence of Vision Revisited," *Journal of Film and Video*, 45:1 (Spring 1993): 3–12.
Biskind, Peter. *Easy Riders Raging Bulls*. London: Bloomsbury, 1998.
Cook, David A. *A History of Narrative Film*. New York: W.W. Norton, 1981.
Doty, William G. *Mythography: The Study of Myth and Ritual*. Tuscaloosa: University of Alabama Press, 2000.
Heard, Christopher. *Dreaming Aloud: The Life and Films of James Cameron*. New York: Bantam, 1998.
Keegan, Rebecca. *The Futurist: The Life and Films of James Cameron*. New York: Crown, 2009.
Keller, Alexandra. *Routledge Film Guidebooks: James Cameron*. New York: Routledge, 2006.
Neale, Steven, ed. *Genre and Contemporary Hollywood*. London: BFI Publishing, 2002.
Pye, Michael, and Lynda Myles. *The Movie Brats: How the Film Generation Took Over Hollywood*. London: Faber & Faber, 1979.

Shone, Tom. *Blockbuster: How the Jaws and Jedi Generation Turned Hollywood Into a Boom-Town*. London: Scribner, 2004.

Stokes, Melvyn, and Richard Maltby, eds. *Identifying Hollywood's Audiences: Cultural Identity and the Movies*. London: BFI Publishing, 1999.

FILMS CITED

The Abyss. Directed by James Cameron. Twentieth Century–Fox, 1989.

Alien. Directed by Ridely Scott. Twentieth Century–Fox, 1979.

Aliens. Directed by James Cameron. Twentieth Century–Fox, 1986.

Avatar. Directed by James Cameron. Twentieth Century–Fox, 2009.

Battle Beyond the Stars. Directed by Jimmy T. Murakami. New World, 1980.

Dances with Wolves. Directed by Kevin Costner. MGM, 1990.

Jaws. Directed by Steven Spielberg. Universal Pictures, 1975.

Jurassic Park. Directed by Steven Spielberg. Universal Pictures, 1993.

The Last Samurai. Directed by Edward Zwick. Warner Bros., 2003.

Piranha Part Two: The Spawning. Directed by James Cameron. Saturn International Pictures, 1981.

Pochahontas. Directed by Mike Gabriel and Eric Goldberg. Walt Disney Pictures, 1995.

Rambo: First Blood Part II. Directed by George P. Cosmatos. Tri-Star, 1986.

Star Wars. Directed by George Lucas. Twentieth Century–Fox, 1977.

Strange Days. Directed by Kathryn Bigelow. Twentieth Century–Fox, 1995.

The Terminator. Directed by James Cameron. Hemdale Films, 1984.

Terminator 2: Judgment Day. Directed by James Cameron. Carolco Pictures, 1991.

Titanic. Directed by James Cameron. Twentieth Century–Fox, 1997.

True Lies. Directed by James Cameron. Twentieth Century–Fox, 1994.

2001: A Space Odyssey. Directed by Stanley Kubrick. Warner Bros., 1968.

Surveying James Cameron's Reluctant Political Commentaries: 1984–2009

STEPHEN MCVEIGH *and*
MATTHEW WILHELM KAPELL

On the morning of September 11, 2001, James Cameron and his crew of submariners dove from the Russian vessel *Keldysh* to RMS *Titanic* in an effort to rescue a stricken ROV. An hour into the descent to the Atlantic floor, a message was received from the *Keldysh*: "Terrorist activity: World Trade Center. Air travel stopped." The crew asked whether they should abort the dive but were advised to proceed. Quickly, events above them were forgotten as the rescue mission commenced. Acting with a tenacity and ingenuity often attributed to Cameron, the mission was a success and the damaged ROV was recovered. They returned to the Russian ship, ecstatic at their success but they were "surfacing to a changed world." Cameron and his crew were given the terrible details of the day's events in New York, Washington, D.C., and Pennsylvania. Rebecca Keegan records Cameron's response: "All of a sudden everything we're doing means nothing. It felt like it was so trivial. You're interested in your own fantasy, feeling like it's life or death, and then you realize it's stupid, it's juvenile."[1]

It is a revealing statement and offers a provocative lens through which to consider the creation of *Avatar*. For many, including the filmmaker himself it would seem, *Avatar* is Cameron's first political movie. Cameron has spoken explicitly about the politics of *Avatar* in ways he has never even hinted at concerning his previous films. While he identifies issues of the environment and ecology or humanity's capacity for orchestrating its own destruction in his work, on more direct political matters he remains largely ambiguous. In 1986, for example, explaining the differences in his script for *Rambo: First Blood Part II* and the film as released in 1985, Cameron put it this way: "I was trying to make a semi-realistic, haunted character ... not a political statement."[2]

And yet, Cameron's oeuvre is consistently political. His Terminator films and *The Abyss* could not exist narratively without the framing context of the Cold War. His sequel to Ridley Scott's *Alien* differs in scope from the source film, but also in political emphasis: where *Alien* is an exercise in cross genre film-making, *Aliens* centers its narrative on a historically resonant depiction of the military-industrial complex. *True Lies* can be read as Cameron's search for a new enemy, for a new set of political interrelations at the close of the Cold War, the context that had dominated his previous work. Even *Titanic*, which seems to stand apart from his other films, has at its core concerns consonant with the landscape of American political culture in the 1990s as it suffers the "End of History." This essay will argue that *Avatar* does not in fact represent a new political motivation or sensitivity in Cameron's filmmaking. Such dimensions have been consistent features of his life and films.

Thus, *Avatar* is not a departure. It is as consistently political a film as the rest of Cameron's major works. As a consequence, *Avatar's* distinctiveness lies not in the presence of politics but with the self-consciousness of those politics. To put it another way, in *Avatar*, Cameron has for the first time made a film that is reflexively political but it is by no means the first time Cameron has made a film that *is* political.

Recalibrating Cameron's Political Vision

A feature of the critical response in the wake of the release of *Avatar* in 2009 is the observation that James Cameron has seemingly added a new, political dimension to his filmmaking. This requires some examination. There can be no doubt that he intends this to be a film with a message, perhaps several messages. And, just as clearly, a message has got through. Among all the talk of 3-D technology and astonishing box office performance, the most interesting aspect of *Avatar* may be its reception. *Avatar* was released at time of flux and division in the United States, when the nation was dealing with the downsizing of the idealistic vision of Democratic president Barrack Obama, and a simultaneous resurgence of conservatism; with the fallout of the global economic recession that is consistently traced back to American banking practice; and with a war that is expensive and unpopular. If Cameron is critiquing this historical moment, his sympathies openly chime with a more liberal sensibility. Not surprisingly then, the conservative response was as vocal as it was vehement. However, there is much that is odd about Cameron's political movie. Like *Titanic* before it (a film dealing with class and presenting something of an anti-rich tract that cost upwards of $200 million to produce and made a small group of individuals somewhere in the region of $1.8 billion),

Avatar's location on the political spectrum is not absolute. Its perspective on contemporary events is clearly left leaning, and this is the main point of attack for the conservative critics, its "liberal tell." And yet it should not go unnoticed that *Avatar* was produced by Rupert Murdoch's 20th Century–Fox. John Nolte's review for the *Big Hollywood* website is representative.[3] Under the slightly hysterical headline, "Cameron's *Avatar* is a big, dull, America-hating, PC revenge fantasy" he proceeds to offer a fascinating reading of the film's political message and context. Although he begins framing his analysis in the traditional film criticism areas of narrative and structure, complaining that this "sanctimonious thud of a movie so infested with one-dimensional characters and PC clichés that not a single plot turn — small or large — surprises," he soon moves to his real objection to the film. For Nolte, *Avatar* is quite simply un–American: "Set in 2154, *Avatar* is a thinly disguised, heavy-handed and simplistic fantasy/allegory of America from our founding straight through to the Iraq War." There is a paranoid excess in the tone of the review that is frequently replayed. John Podhoretz, in *The Weekly Standard*, writes that the film asks "the audience to root for the defeat of American soldiers at the hands of an insurgency. So it is a deep expression of anti–Americanism-kind of." Such reviews have a scattershot approach, attacking every conceivable element of the film. Podhoretz, after suggesting that Cameron had produced a film with a political perspective, even if it is one to which he is diametrically opposed, changes tack unconvincingly:

> The thing is, one would be giving James Cameron too much credit to take *Avatar*— with its mindless worship of a nature-loving tribe and the tribe's adorable pagan rituals, its hatred of the military and American institutions, and the notion that to be human is just way uncool — at all seriously as a political document. It's more interesting as an example of how deeply rooted these standard-issue counterculture clichés in Hollywood have become by now.[4]

Putting aside some of the more troubling aspects of this argument (for example, the suggestion that thinking of imperialism as problematic is somehow counter-cultural) it is worth noting the contradiction is represents: if *Avatar* was so obviously a cliché ridden and hollow spectacle, why is he and other similarly minded critics taking it so seriously? Perhaps the answer lies with the right's impression that Cameron was "one of them." As Tom Shone puts it, "Once you've gotten over your shock at seeing James Cameron pilloried as a typical Hollywood liberal — dude wrote *Rambo II* for heaven's sake!— the first response to this is: What took them so long?"[5] The question can be usefully asked of Cameron and his perceived new political standing.

At an industry Q & A session following a screening of the movie, Cameron outlined the dimensions of *Avatar's* political statement. He explained his motivation "as an artist ... to say something about what I saw around me."

What he sees is conflict: "This movie reflects that we are living through war... There are boots on the ground, troops who I personally believe were sent there under false pretenses, so I hope this will be part of opening our eyes." Such a statement makes explicit Cameron's didactic intent. A feature on the film website *The Wrap* reporting the session was framed with the headline, "Yes, *Avatar* is a political film."[6] It is curious that this should need such explicit confirmation. At a basic level and for any number of reasons, it could be argued that all film is political, so why should *Avatar* be any different? Furthermore, *Avatar* is full of references to war and pre-emptive strikes, shock and awe, the military-industrial complex and Haliburton-esque companies, all in relation to the excesses of a specifically American imperialism desperate to secure vital but scarce resources. Perhaps the surprise implicit in the headline can be more usefully interpreted as a response to the fact that James Cameron has made this political film. Indeed, such an observation would seem to run counter to Cameron's perceived reputation. In the most general terms, his films are genre pieces, deliberately tooled for mass consumption and built to perform to generic expectations. Perhaps more importantly, much of what makes a James Cameron film a James Cameron film is the spectacle, the sheer technological ambition of the movie. His reliance upon special effects and his pushing at, and successfully extending, the boundaries of effects technology are hallmarks of the Cameron style. However, such features necessarily keep the audience at a surface level. A sense of depth, whether in terms of character or narrative rigor, is an issue in his movies. Cameron is capable of "doing emotion," but more often than not it is of a melodramatic variety, with *Titanic* the most telling exemplar. And he can spin a thrilling story, but they often do not withstand closer scrutiny. That is not to say that his films lack serious merit or purpose. His representations of female heroism have rightfully received significant amounts of scholarly attention. Elsewhere however, elements of his work that could potentially offer themselves to some deeper reading are often dismissed as narrative expediency rather than an attempt to proffer an opinion or elucidate an argument. Stephen Prince, in an analysis of *The Terminator*, makes precisely this judgment: "Cameron proves himself to be an adept manipulator of the zeitgeist while lacking the ability or the inclination to probe critically at the social roots of the popular fears he manipulates."[7]

However, such a dismissive evaluation is inadequate. Among those elements of the zeitgeist are his recurrent visions of an apocalyptic future of natural collapse predicated upon humanity's tendency to war and connected reliance upon technology. His application of this theme is consistently framed in a system of recurring structures. He constructs narratives built around a combination of technology, representations of the military, corporations, systems of authority or government and an "everyman" or "blue collar" hero, usually a civilian or outsider. Even such a preliminary observation leads simply to the conclusion that his films are indeed political.

The Birth of a Political Filmmaker

Rebecca Keegan's journalistic biography of Cameron, *The Futurist*, reinforces this image of Cameron as a filmmaker who has only recently become politically aware. In the aftermath of *Titanic*'s extraordinary success, Cameron took an extended sabbatical from commercial film-making and pursued his interest in exploration. Among a number of projects he was involved with in this period, the most ambitious was a return to RMS *Titanic* to gather unprecedented footage from the wreck using two miniature robotic vehicles or ROVs, the development of which he had funded. Keegan recounts how on a dive in September 2001 one of the multi-million dollar ROVs malfunctioned leading Cameron and his crew to attempt a difficult rescue operation and how the elation at its success was dwarfed by the gravity of the changes wrought by the events of 9/11.

Keegan's construction of this event is dramatic. In her conception Cameron almost physically emerges from a self-absorbed world of fantasy into a new political era, a new geopolitical landscape of threat and conflict. The reader is given nothing less than Cameron's political awakening at its first moments. It is a useful point of origin for *Avatar*'s overtly political tendency. *Avatar* is his first film since this literal and metaphorical emergence and it is a film littered with references to 9/11 and its iconography, to the War on Terror and to the subsequent wars in Afghanistan and Iraq. However, there is much about this portrait of Cameron's acquisition of a political sensibility and its subsequent impact upon *Avatar*'s agenda that is disingenuous.

Much of Cameron's political sensibility was acquired growing up in Ontario, Canada. For Cameron, as recounted by Keegan, the defining feature of his early years was the threat of nuclear apocalypse. She suggestively pinpoints Cameron's transitional moment from childhood innocence to adult awareness. When Cameron was eight years old he found on a table in the family home an instruction manual detailing how to construct a civilian fallout shelter. Cameron celebrated his eighth year in 1962, the year of the Cuban Missile Crisis, so the sense of imminent apocalyptic threat is understandable. Once again, as she does with 9/11, Keegan uses the discovery of the pamphlet as a moment of epiphany, after which nothing is the same. The safe world of childhood became an illusion and the terrifying prospect of nuclear war captured his imagination. His parents were both in differing ways concerned with the Cold War and amplified his sensitivity to the contemporary situation. His mother, Shirley, who had won countywide competitions with her striking designs for the covers of war bonds, joined the Canadian Women's Army Corps, where her son witnessed her "happily trooping off on weekends in fatigues and combat boots to assemble a rifle while blindfolded and march through fields in the pouring rain." Though they were Canadians, his parents were very aware that they lived only a mile or so away from Niagara Falls, a major source of power for the United States as well as Canada and consequently a legitimate target should the Cold War turn hot. In this environment, Cameron developed a fascination with nuclear war: "I realized that the safe and nurturing world I thought I lived in was an illusion, and that the world as we know it could end at any moment."[8]

In his films, this biographical detail has frequently recurred and has evolved. As both an historical frame and an image system, his use of certain elements resonant with the Cold War, however abstract, is a common motif. This biographical detail underlines the tensions in the depiction of the military-industrial complex in the *Terminator* films, the analysis of the mythologizing of the Vietnam War in *Aliens*, the simplistic and anachronistic depiction of the Cold War in *The Abyss* and to an extent the prophetic vision of the possible location of a new war, the successor to the Cold War, in *True Lies*. It is incorrect to argue that Cameron simply utilizes the Cold War as a context only insofar as it is useful as a pre-fabricated narrative frame, one predicated upon threat, anxiety and conflict, to house his latest blockbuster spectacle. It is immensely rewarding to revisit his earlier work from this political perspective and, upon doing so it becomes evident that Cameron's recent claims to a new found and purposeful political awareness ignore a series of politically engaged movies. In this way, although the historical and thematic context may have evolved, *Avatar* emerges as a logical step in a progression rather than a step in a new direction.

The Terminator, Terminator 2: Judgment Day *and the Nature of the Military-Industrial Complex*

In *The Terminator*, his first directorial effort proper released in 1984, Cameron established a set of concerns and themes that would recur throughout his films up to and including *Avatar*. The film is clearly a reflection upon its own historical moment, a specific point in the late Cold War. In 1984, the specter of nuclear annihilation remained a frightening possibility. The 1980s are replete with movies reflecting various kinds of Cold War anxiety, such as

WarGames (1983) and *The Day After* (1983). The United States of *The Terminator* is presented as a nation fully in the grip of the Cold War, the fear of which leads to the development of an artificially intelligent defense system, Skynet. At some point in the future, Skynet achieves sentience and calculates that the eradication of humanity is in its own best interests. On a simple level, Skynet and the machines it produces to destroy humanity can be read as a conventional Cold War metaphor. Soviet communism had long been portrayed in film as a model of society that lacked emotion and human feeling, that it was a model of society that created virtual automatons. In 1950s science fiction classics such as *Invaders from Mars* (1953) and *Invasion of the Body Snatchers* (1956), normal Americans are turned into such unfeeling robots. This reading of the film is reinforced with the appearance of Arnold Schwarzenegger's terminator: his European features and Austrian accent are in broad terms suggestive of the otherness that constituted America's binary adversary.

However, Cameron's comprehension of the back-story is subtler and more sophisticated than a simple, metaphorical Cold War morality play. At the heart of *The Terminator* is a representation of the military-industrial complex and an imagining of the farthest consequences of America's unquestioning acceptance of its existence. The representation of the military-industrial complex is crucial, as it is a feature, whether explicit or otherwise, of the majority of his films.

The term, though common, is a vexatious one in some ways. Its most renowned use appeared in President Dwight Eisenhower's Farewell Address in 1961:

> But now we can no longer risk emergency improvisation of national defense; we have been compelled to create a permanent armaments industry of vast proportions. Added to this, three and a half million men and women are directly engaged in the defense establishment. We annually spend on military security more than the net income of all United States corporations. This conjunction of an immense military establishment and a large arms industry is new in the American experience. The total influence — economic, political, even spiritual — is felt in every city, every Statehouse, every office of the Federal government. We recognize the imperative need for this development. Yet we must not fail to comprehend its grave implications. Our toil, resources and livelihood are all involved; so is the very structure of our society. In the councils of government, we must guard against the acquisition of unwarranted influence, whether sought or unsought, by the military-industrial complex. The potential for the disastrous rise of misplaced power exists and will persist.[9]

Its employment here represented a way of understanding the power structures that had emerged in the United States in the aftermath of the Second World War and at onset of the Cold War. It suggested an integration of agendas that potentially posed a problem. President Eisenhower argued that linkage of war and industrial production was a dangerous one. However, this was not the first time the complex had been observed or had its implications discussed. In this way then it must be noted that Eisenhower's conception of the military-industrial complex was quite limited. Eisenhower's broad contention was that there could emerge a hybrid of military and business or economic interests which might seek to further their agendas with the potential to damage the country, its peace and security as well as its core values. This contention contains two immediate flaws, one that has no bearing upon Cameron, another that most certainly does. Eisenhower is clearly suggesting that this is an issue for the future. However, that there existed already by 1961 some form of military-industrial complex is inarguable. C. Wright Mills, noted in the epochal sociological text *The Power Elite* in 1956 that the military had achieved since World War II "decisive political ... relevance"[10] such that military leadership was from that point a segment of the ruling elite, along with the political and the corporate elites, dominating the organization of American society:

> American capitalism is now in considerable part a military capitalism and the most important relation of the big corporation to the state rests on the coincidence of interests between military and corporate needs as defined by [the] warlords and the corporate rich.[11]

Eisenhower's warning could be seen then as a very public airing of the concerns articulated by Mills about the increasing dangers to peace posed by coalescing interest groups. In his speech, however, Eisenhower offers only a partial vision of the military-industrial complex. In his conception, the term refers only to military/corporate interactions, excluding a group crucial to Mills' thesis (and to Cameron's evolving depictions): governmental authority. That Eisenhower should not wish to associate the government with a concept he was presenting as a potential threat to American society is not surprising. However, most other thinking on and definitions of the military-industrial complex locate a governmental aspect as an integral component, one third of a triumvirate.

Cameron adheres to Eisenhower's model of the military-industrial complex in *The Terminator* rather than that of Mills. His use of the complex is no mere reflection but rather functions as a critique. Among the literature there are those who consider the military-industrial complex an essential component in the organization of American society. In *The Terminator*, and its depiction of the human future brought about directly by the military-industrial complex, Cameron is clearly articulating the dangers of such thinking. This commentary is expanded upon in, and central to the sequel *Terminator 2: Judgment Day*. The apocalypse on the horizon at the end of the first movie is a direct consequence of an American military seeking power and dominance through technologies developed by Cyberdyne, a civilian corporation.

It is often overlooked that Eisenhower's warnings were not restricted solely to a military-industrial complex. In the address, he also makes special mention of a possible scientific-technological complex:

> Akin to, and largely responsible for the sweeping changes in our industrial-military posture, has been the technological revolution during recent decades. In this revolution, research has become central, it also becomes more formalized, complex, and costly. A steadily increasing share is conducted for, by, or at the direction of, the Federal government. Today, the solitary inventor, tinkering in his shop, has been overshadowed by task forces of scientists in laboratories and testing fields. In the same fashion, the free university, historically the fountainhead of free ideas and scientific discovery, has experienced a revolution in the conduct of research. Partly because of the huge costs involved, a government contract becomes virtually a substitute for intellectual curiosity. For every old blackboard there are now hundreds of new electronic computers. The prospect of domination of the nation's scholars by Federal employment, project allocations, and the power of money is ever present — and is gravely to be regarded. Yet, in holding scientific research and discovery in respect, as we should, we must also be alert to the equal and opposite danger that public policy could itself become the captive of a scientific-technological elite.[12]

In a sense, such concerns are not surprising given the distrust of education and research that were a feature of his early, pre–Sputnik presidency where there was manifested a distinct anti-intellectualism. However, it does identify an important element of the military-industrial complex. In *T2*, running parallel to the machinations of Skynet's efforts to kill John Connor before he can become a threat, there is a parallel narrative strand dealing with Miles Dyson, the lead researcher on the project that will ultimately make Skynet possible. The dialogue and the evolution of the character's comprehension of his role in the unfolding apocalypse once more presents a filmmaker not merely reflecting a socio-historical context but critiquing it.

At the climax of *The Terminator*, Sarah Connor crushes the cyborg terminator, shorn of its human skin and stripped back to its skeletal frame, in an industrial metal press. In *T2*, the audience learns that some of its remains were recovered and are being reverse engineered. In a problematic time loop, this technology is central to the creation of Skynet and as such, Cyberdyne becomes a target for Sarah Connor. Connor decides to go to Dyson's home and kill him as a means of preventing the coming war by stopping the research. Though she is unable to kill Dyson, the dialogue between the two is revealing. Cameron uses the sequence to lay bare for the audience, via Dyson's gradual awakening to the magnitude of the "truth," his assessment of the implications of the military-industrial complex. The decision not to kill him necessitates an explanation of events, past and future, to secure his help.

> (voice over) Dyson listened while the terminator laid it all down. Skynet, judgment day, the history of things to come. It's not every day you find you're responsible for 3 billion deaths. He took it pretty well.

Upon hearing this, Dyson's first reaction is ignorance and incredulity: "You're judging me on things I haven't even done yet. How were we supposed to know?"

Connor's response is interesting in its attack upon those civilian innovators who have their research co-opted by the military:

> Yeah, right, how were you supposed to know? Fucking men like you built the hydrogen bomb. Men like you thought it up. You think you're so creative. You don't know what its like to really create something, to create a life.

However, Dyson very quickly takes responsibility and vows he will not finish the project and will leave the company. Connor tells him this is not good enough and the project must be destroyed so no one else could follow his work and complete the reverse engineered microprocessor designed from the remains of the first terminator. He agrees and identifies the files, computer drives and technology at Cyberdyne that will need to be destroyed. In the face of the scale of the danger posed by the military-industrial complex, Dyson, a family man and civilian scientist is motivated to take up arms and act. Although he is killed in the process of destroying the lab and the research, Dyson's trajectory should be read as fundamentally political. The character arc is an opportunity for Cameron to articulate his own thoughts on the nature of the military-industrial complex and further, Dyson's development clearly conveys a message to the audience advocating awareness of the dangers inherent within it.

The Terminator films then demonstrate that from the earliest point in his career Cameron had an opinion, that Cameron was politically expressive. However, the military-industrial complex is only one feature of that expression.

Aliens *and the Vietnam War*

A somewhat different version of the military-industrial complex is portrayed in *Aliens* (1987). In this sequel to Ridley Scott's 1979 original *Alien*, Cameron moved away from the haunted house horror style of the former and produced, for all intents and purposes, a war movie. The change in narrative direction is exemplified in the taglines for the two films: from "In space no-one can hear you scream" to "this time it's war!" Ripley, the only survivor of the crew of the *Nostromo* from the first film is recovered in deep space and returned to Earth. The company which owned the *Nostromo*, Weyland-Yutani, has since established a colony on LV-426, the planet where Ripley's crew encountered the aliens. The centrality of the company in the narrative is a crucial element of this film and a clear evocation of the military-industrial complex. Weyland-Yutani is depicted as more than a business, its logo is everywhere, and there is little sense of traditional corporate competition. It also has the resources, the influence and the power to enlist the aid of American marines to investigate the loss of communication with the colony that sets a reluctant Ripley against the "xenomorphs." The company is portrayed as monolithic and faceless, but it is given human dimension, in the character of Burke. His evolution, from his seeming concern for and interest in Ripley to the "villain" focused solely on "dollar value" and who attempts to secure the return of an alien to Earth for military research purposes by orchestrating, albeit unsuccessfully, the impregnation of Ripley and/or Newt, is similarly evocative of Cameron's perspective in this area.

However, there is another dimension to *Aliens* which aligns Cameron and other aspects of the Cold War and further cements his credentials as a politically sensitive film maker. His depiction of the conflict at the core of *Aliens*, the "war" of the tagline, is a representation of the Vietnam War, arguably one of the most vivid consequences of the Cold War and the military-industrial complex. Tim Blackmore was among the first critics to explore this dimension of Cameron's film in his 1996 essay, "Is this going to be another bug-hunt?"[13] The article identifies the way in which Cameron clearly utilizes the language and imagery of the Vietnam War and uses this approach to reinterpret that film, to move away from the "condemnation" directed at it by critics who fixated upon questions of gender and patriarchy. However, this kind of analysis lends itself to an expansion into the realm of the political.

In his previous film, Cameron had already utilized aspects of the popular understanding of the Vietnam War. In *The Terminator* he deploys references to the conflict and devices associated with narratives about the war to give shape to the future war against the machines and specifically to the character of Kyle Reese. Reese is portrayed as a war veteran, scarred physically but also mentally. His experiences have damaged him and the film uses the trauma as a device to flashback (forward) to important events in Reese's war. The film also draws other analogies. In the future war as depicted, the humans (read Americans) are fighting a war of insurgency and employing guerrilla tactics. The machines are depicted as technologically superior. This reversal of the historical reality of the United States' role in Vietnam is suggestive of Cameron's purpose and is similar to the approach taken by George Lucas in *Star*

Wars, of pitting a band of rebel heroes against the evil Empire, as an antidote to the defeat in South East Asia.[14]

In *Aliens* Cameron presents a coherent and sustained discussion of aspects of the Vietnam War. That Cameron should use the war is not surprising. One of the lesser known items on his resume was the scripting of *Rambo: First Blood Part II*. Although it is a film from which he maintains a distance as ultimately released, the research that went into his draft clearly informed the projects that surrounded it. Indeed, Cameron worked on the scripts for *Aliens* and *Rambo II* simultaneously, and both films bear the imprint of his Vietnam research. *Aliens* does not intend, however, to present a detailed appraisal of the war itself. Rather it seeks to explore the impact of the war upon the American psyche. The decade of the 1980s saw a wealth of material emerge on screen as well as in print wrestling with the war's meaning. *Aliens* (like the *Star Wars Trilogy* before it) can be usefully read as part of this process of absorbing the war.

The terms of the conflict in Southeast Asia (technological excellence versus primitive warrior) represent a starting point for this approach to *Aliens* then. Cameron depicts the marines and their weaponry in almost fetishistic detail. They have access to an arsenal of devastating military technology, from communication equipment to armor to the vast battleship carrying them to LV-426. This technological superiority generates a distinct sense of hubris. As Bill Paxton's Private Hudson colorfully puts it in a scene from the extended special edition of *Aliens*:

> I'm ready, man, check it out. I am the ultimate badass! State of the badass art! You do not want to fuck with me. Check it out. Hey, Ripley, don't worry. Me and my squad of ultimate badasses will protect you! Check it out. Independently targeting particle beam phalanx. Wham! Fry half a city with this puppy. We got tactical smart missiles, phased plasma pulse rifles, RPGs, we got sonic electronic ball breakers. We got nukes, we got knives, we got sharp sticks...

As is the case with most war films, the enemy is presented in anonymous terms, a faceless horde to be slaughtered with impunity. That they are nonhuman resonates with the derogative labeling of the Vietnamese as "gooks," a means of rendering the enemy as something less than human. The differences between the two forces are evocative. The aliens are a versatile force with absolutely no technological aspect. Their vicious skill as warriors is constituted by the ability to wield the tools biology has provided them (acid for blood, a razor sharp, slashing tail, a projectile second mouth) and to exploit their environment, where they can effectively camouflage themselves almost in the open and can climb walls and scurry across ceilings. This lack of technological weaponry is mistaken for weakness by the marines. Their understanding of the enemy is that of an animal, primitive and instinctual, and so easily overcome. The marines describe the mission as a "bug hunt," a clear expression of their perceived superiority. This aspect resonates most strongly with the historical conflict. The parallels with history, with the arrogant belief that U.S. forces could enter a sovereign state and bend it to their will while not taking stock of the single-minded commitment and environmental advantages with which the opposing force would protect their space, are purposefully intended. This arrogance does not survive the first encounter with the enemy and the reversal is clearly articulated in the transition of Hudson's "bug hunt" to his call to "bug out."

The constitution of the platoon offers another example of the urge to revisionism in representing the war. The platoon is led by a black sergeant, hard-edged but respected. The rest of the squad is constituted of honorable and professional soldiers. Within the mythology of the Vietnam War though, the incompetent officer was to become commonplace. In part this is a consequence of President Reagan's revisionism of the war. It was certainly a feature in Oliver Stone's *Platoon*, released the same year as *Aliens*, via the character Lt. Wolfe. Like Wolfe, Lt. Gorman's indecision and inexperience causes the deaths of several members of the platoon. This reflects not only the scapegoating of the administrators, which was central to Reagan's revision, but also endorses the new found sympathy for the soldiers. Where, upon their return, Vietnam veterans had been reviled and called "baby killers," Reagan recast them as the real heroes whose defeat was not a consequence of any failing on their part, but a consequence of bad civilian management and inadequate leadership. In an important exchange, Burke, speaking after Gorman has been trivially incapacitated, registers his disdain of Ripley's observation that Corporal Hicks is next in the chain of command and should decide how to proceed: "He can't make that kind of decision, he's just a grunt." This corporate figure, interested only in material worth of the colony is depicted as an impediment to the real soldier, attempting to frustrate his ability to perform the job for which he was trained and at which he is clearly adept. In the film, unlike in history, Hicks ignores such poorly considered directives. Presenting the grunt as a victim of mismanagement and consequently, as a victim of the war, is an astute encapsulation of Reagan's efforts to turn the war from national disaster to noble cause.

However, Cameron is not simply allowing America a victory on celluloid that it was unable to achieve in reality. Throughout the film the aliens are superior, despite the technological superiority of the marines. Only a few of the characters escape, and while they seemingly destroy the aliens, they do so only at the cost of vaporizing the colony, by deploying a nuclear weapon, (a measure discussed in relation to the prosecution of the war to a victory). It is also an action resonant with one of the abiding rationalizations of the war, that "it became necessary to destroy the village to save it."

Cameron's presentation of the implications of the Vietnam War is not merely an appropriation of the zeitgeist then. Similarly it is not a means, like *Rambo: First Blood Part II*, of giving America a safe victory. In the final showdown, he seems to add an important dimension to this analysis. Much has been made by critics of gender of the fight between the two mothers, Ripley to protect Newt, and parallel to that, the Alien Queen's fight to save her children. For Cameron presenting Ripley as a mother gives her struggle a purpose, something arguably missing from America's war in Vietnam. Wars for power, influence, resource or profit, the spurs to conflict in the film are illegitimate, he seems to argue. What comes over most strongly is the sense that Cameron, in his revisioning of the Vietnam War is demanding that there must be legitimate and clear reasons to go to war, human reasons, something he believes the Cold War was demonstrably unable to provide, and an idea which will find resonance in *Avatar*.

The Abyss *and the Late Cold War*

The Abyss occupies a peculiar place in Cameron's oeuvre. It was the first of his films to perform poorly, relatively speaking, at the box office. It is also, at least in its theatrical cut, a curiously structured narrative which loses much of its well crafted tension in the final third, largely forgetting about the real world implications that the kind of alien contact depicted in the dénouement would create, given the proximity of U.S. and Soviet forces. In its extended version however, *The Abyss* represents Cameron's most obvious and direct political commentary. Central to the narrative tension is the Cold War and the likelihood of standoff escalating into Armageddon. The film begins with a U.S. submarine, *Montana*, coming into close contact with an alien vessel. The contact results in massive malfunction aboard the *Montana*. News reports suggest that the sinking was caused by a Soviet fast attack sub. The American military rush to the location above the wreck, off the coast of Cuba, and so too do trawlers and other vessels, presumed to be operating as Soviet intelligence gatherers. The escalation in Cold War hostility generates much of the narrative's dramatic energy. The military send a SEAL team to a civilian underwater exploration platform, Deep Core with orders to retrieve the *Montana*'s nuclear warheads and put the stricken submarine beyond the use of the Soviets. With a hurricane approaching and the escalation of tensions above the surface and with the leader of the SEALs, Lt. Coffey, increasingly displaying the effects of pressure sickness and the implications of alien or Non-Terrestrial Intelligence (NTI) contact below, the narrative generates an impressive, multifaceted sense of tension. In the course of the narrative, the deranged SEAL leader is killed and the nuclear device falls into the eponymous abyss.

Bud Brigman, the platform's foreman, dons an experimental suit and falls into the abyss to defuse it. The amount of oxygen needed for the drop means that it is a "one way ticket." The device defused and his oxygen running out, Brigman sends a message to his estranged wife back on the platform: "love you wife."

As he waits for the inevitable, one of the NTIs collects him and takes him to an enormous vessel. At this point, the two versions of the film diverge markedly. In the theatrical cut, the aliens make contact simply because Brigman's final message was a statement of love and a demonstration of heroism and sacrifice. However, the special edition, the version closer to Cameron's vision, is far more opinionated. Once aboard the vessel, the aliens communicate by showing Brigman newscasts of the escalation above the surface and footage of giant waves approaching land around the world. Brigman asks, "why are you doing this?" They respond by showing more images, this time of nuclear tests in the Pacific. The aliens have been watching and are passing judgment on humanity, the giant waves a means of quite literally wiping humanity away. Brigman pleads against the NTIs pre-emptive attack, asking how they know that mankind will use such weaponry. Once again, they project a series of images, images of war atrocities, many of them from the Vietnam War, as well as examples of environmental destruction. Cameron cuts back to tsunami waves approaching shore, but as they reach their zenith, they stop and slowly recede. The aliens project these images too and Brigman asks, "Why didn't you?" The reason for the stay is once more the message sent to his wife, the messages of love and sacrifice. As an opinion on the Cold War, this is all direct enough, but Cameron has more to say. To the surprise of the crew of Deep Core, Brigman announces via the text messaging device, that he is still alive, refers to the "friends" he has made, and provides a version of the message they wish to convey: "They've left us alone but it bothers them to see us hurting each other. Getting out of hand. They sent a message. Hope you got it. They want us to grow up a bit and put away childish things. Of course it's just a suggestion."

If the point had not been made emphatically enough, a character aboard Deep Core's support vessel turns to a member of the military and says, "It looks like you boys might be out of business." The message is as simplistic as it is pedantic, an attempt to force the audience to consider the absurdity of the Cold War. At least it is in the special edition. In the theatrical cut, such a message is missing and what remains is saccharine and shallow. Such a hollow ending may explain *The Abyss'* more reserved box office performance. However it is also worth noting that released in 1989, it found itself on the cusp of the post–Cold War world, leaving the film's message already out of time. For these reasons, *The Abyss* is not remembered as a political film, and perhaps why Cameron and his critics can claim some kind of political awakening with regard to *Avatar*. The changed geopolitical landscape of the post–Cold War world would however lead to a very interesting political film.

True Lies *and the Coming Clash of Civilizations*

Were one still unconvinced about Cameron's credentials as a politically aware filmmaker, the underlying political context of *True Lies* forces a re-examination. The film is generally discussed in dismissive terms. Its central depiction of Islamofascist terrorists is considered at best simple opportunism or, at worst, an example of longstanding xenophobic stereotypes. Evelyn Alsutany reads *True Lies* in this way:

> Before 9/11 Arabs had predominantly been represented variously as villains, oppressed veiled women, exotic belly dancers, rich sheiks with harems and most remarkably, as terrorists... Over the past four or five decades, the majority of television and film representations of Arabs and Muslims have been as terrorists, seeking to elicit a celebration from the audience upon their murder (e.g. *True Lies*...).[15]

Unquestionably, Cameron does not intend the film to be a realistic portrayal of Islamic terrorists. The depiction of Salim Abu Aziz, the leader of Crimson Jihad, is for the most part, comic book. However, this is not Cameron's purpose. This is not an attempt to understand the mind of the terrorist but rather a film that understands the minds of its American audience and their need for an enemy.

Whatever else the Cold War generated, it generated a sense of identity, a consensus to challenge the opposing binary of Soviet communism, most graphically illustrated in the concept of "un–American." George Kennan's X-article, "The Sources of Soviet Conduct" published in *Foreign Affairs* in 1947, argued that such a binary conflict was a positive thing insofar as it allowed Americans to test and challenge their national institutions, ideals and character.[16] At the end of the Cold War, with the Soviet Union in collapse, America found itself bereft of an enemy. It is in this lacuna that *True Lies* can be best understood. In one way, it can be read as an affirmation of traditional American values. Harry Tasker (Schwarzenegger) confronts the terrorists simultaneously as a family man and traditional American hero, imbued most obviously with the qualities of the cowboy. But the film's political intentions go further than that.

True Lies is in many ways the least like a James Cameron movie he has made. Apart from the astonishing budget and the appearance of Arnold Schwarzenegger, this film represents a number of new directions for Cameron. This is not surprising. Given the importance of the Cold War as a framing device for his narratives, the end of the Cold War meant that he is without is usual narrative scaffolding. Read in this way, the film can be seen on one level as a conscious attempt to locate a new narrative voice for the changed times. That he was looking for such a voice is apparent from the other possible film projects to which he was attached before proceeding with *True Lies*. Rebecca Keegan notes that after *T2*, "his fourth science fiction movie in a row, Cameron was ready for a new challenge — maybe a character drama or a comedy."[17] It was around this time that his name was attached to a screen version of *Spiderman*, that we worked on the script that would become *Strange Days* (and though he would produce, Kathryn Bigelow would direct) and a screenplay, *The Crowded Room*, a version of Daniel Keyes' book *The Minds of Billy Milligan*. However, at Schwarzenegger's suggestion, *True Lies*, an adaptation of the French film *La Totale*, became his next project.

The film is a high concept concoction of James Bond–like spectacle, 80s action movie and romantic comedy. Half of the film is largely inconsequential. These elements of the movie which deal with Harry Tasker's domestic situation as a husband, father and supposed computer salesman as it increasingly clashes with his work as an operative for a shadowy federal agency. The other half though is fascinating, especially viewed from the other side of the events of 9/11. If Cameron's stated intention for the film was to establish a new, non-science fiction narrative terrain for himself, another objective is to identify a new political context. *True Lies* utilizes a new enemy and creates a backdrop of threat and conflict that in 1994 was quite fantastical but which was to be immensely prescient. Aziz' group, Crimson Jihad, is a terrorist organization that is operating on U.S. soil and has acquired a number of nuclear devices. The terrorist threat is not then the traditional external threat of a nation-state; the terrorists have infiltrated American society. Such a depiction was certainly resonant after the first attack on the World Trade Center in 1993. The nature of their operation, their stated aims and their media savvy all prefigure the events of 9/11. In one notable scene, Aziz presents the explanation for the actions of his group direct to camera:

> You have killed our women and our children, bombed our cities from afar like cowards and you dare to call us terrorists. Now the oppressed have been given a mighty sword with which to strike back at their enemies. Unless you, America, pulls all military forces out of the Persian Gulf area immediately and forever, Crimson Jihad will rain fire down on one major U.S. city each week until our demands are met.

Although the seriousness of the monologue is undercut by the cameraman's awareness that batteries are running low, Aziz' words constitute a concise and surprising indictment of the implications of American imperialism.

Indeed it is provocative to imagine Cameron, polymath and genius, at least according to his biographers, reading a *Foreign Affairs* article published in 1993, and written by Harvard professor Samuel Huntington. The article, entitled "The Clash of Civilizations?" and subsequent book *The Clash of Civilizations and the Remaking of World Order* (1996) were instantly reverberative and they provide a close match to Cameron's presentation of his new enemy:

> The underlying problem for the West is not Islamic fundamentalism. It is Islam, a different people who are convinced of the superiority of their culture and are obsessed with the inferiority of their power. The problem for Islam is not the CIA or the U.S. Department of Defense. It is the West, a different civilization whose people are convinced of the universality of their culture and believe that their superior, if declining, power imposes on them the obligation to extend that culture throughout the world.[18]

There are undoubtedly problems with Huntington's thesis, and they have been discussed at length elsewhere, but in terms of cultural impact, the binary it suggests, "the next pattern of conflict"[19] it portends resonated with American society and provide a means of reading the film.

The critical reaction to *True Lies* has emphasized the problem in envisioning Huntington's paradigm by drawing attention to the racist portrayal of the Islamic terrorists of the film. This is precisely what film scholar Alexandra Keller does in describing the film, noting "Schwarzenegger plays an American secret agent single-handedly battling hordes of generic, hysterical Arab terrorists [in a way that] offends like few films since *Birth of a Nation*."[20] Like many film scholars working toward a simple classification of Cameron's work, Keller falls prey to the same critique she uses against Cameron, thus making *True Lies* merely an example of "generically" racist films. As a result *True Lies* is often listed with other films as merely another example of the racism inherent in the representations of Middle Eastern characters. Canadian media education scholar Ibrahim Abukhattala has taken this a step further, placing *True Lies* in his list of films that "portray, with absolutely no justification, *all* Arabs and Muslims as being at war with the West."[21]

Abukhattala is obviously wrong in his details, even if not in his main point. In *True Lies* itself, all characters that can be read either visually or culturally as Arab or Muslim are most certainly *not* villains. Cameron has seemingly gone to some lengths to make sure that the team of "good guys" that Schwarzenegger's Harry Tasker leads includes a member named Faisil (Grant Heslov), whose name, alone, suggests a Middle Eastern heritage. And it is through this character that the issues surrounding Huntington's thesis are both made apparent and, in the end, not solved in a convincing fashion within the narrative. Early in the film, after an operation run by Schwarzenegger's Tasker fails, the team debriefs with their leader, played by Charlton Heston. Considering the careers of both the actors Heston and Schwarzenegger, between the two of them they must operate as convincing symbols of Huntington's notion of "Western civilization." In the debriefing scene there is a significant level of banter about the mission and Tasker's teams' failure or, as Heston's Spencer Trilby puts it, the fact that they, "screwed the pooch." Attempting to enter into the spirit of the banter Heslov's Faisil begins attempting jokes as well, prompting a quick reply from Heston's character. "You're new on Harry's team, aren't you?" Trilby asks. When Faisil answers in the affirmative, Trilby then retorts, "So what makes you think in any way the slack I cut him translates to you?"

On one level Trilby's statement to the youngest member of Harry's team can be read as simply humor. Indeed, Faisil is young and presumably less experienced as a result. Yet on another level this exchange captures the very essence of Huntington's thesis. In confrontation with Huntington's "Western Civilization" the options are stark. Faisil's option is the option of Islam as a whole: be adopted as a junior, probationary member — and hopefully one day some "slack" will come along as well. The only other option in Huntington's post–Cold War world, in the world of the Clash of Civilizations, is the one taken by terrorist leader Salim Abu Aziz.

By the climactic scenes of the film it will be obvious how Faisil has chosen in this regard. Infiltrating the high rise building held by the terrorists he will take part in the ultimate defeat of the terrorist cell, the saving of his team leader's daughter, and foil a plot to destroy Miami with a nuclear weapon. One would imagine that such an act — and his character literally kills a number of the terrorists, presenting the image of one visually "Middle Eastern" character killing others — would allow Faisil to finally be allowed some "slack." Yet, as the credits for the film begin to roll later Faisil is exactly where he began the film: in the back of a van, acting as support for Schwarzenegger's Harry Tasker. Cameron's previous films work against him in *True Lies* simply because his previous films had delighted in finding the ostensibly "other" (usually women) and providing them the narrative structure to become part of the heroic structure of the society the films depict. The Clash of Civilizations, however useful it might be as a descriptor of post–Cold War political reality, does not make for good narrative closure nor does it allow for "the other" to easily become central to the heroism of the film's narrative. In the character of Faisil, at least, the closure does not work in the way that the actual Cold War did in Cameron's earlier films.

Titanic *and* The End of History

If *True Lies* captured, consciously or otherwise, the tenor of Huntington's Clash of Civilizations, *Titanic* represents another artifact of post–Cold War filmmaking that sees Cameron searching for a politico-historical narrative frame. This time Cameron is less concerned with a possible new world order and the conflicts it may generate, and more concerned with an End of History. The other major interpretation of the new global political situation at the ending of the Cold War, Francis Fukuyama's essay, "The End of History?" and the subsequent book, *The End of History and the Last Man* presented a singular and provocative argument in favor of liberal democracy.[22] As such, it saw the Cold War not merely as the end of a specific historical period, "but the end of history as such: that is, the end point of mankind's ideological evolution and the universalization of Western liberal democracy as the final form of human government."[23]

At the time of its release *Titanic* seemed to be a departure for Cameron. The filmmaker known for working with science-fiction and action spectacle elements in all of his films, *Titanic* was reviewed as an historical epic and a romance. Yet there are clear lines of connection. Like his previous work, *Titanic* is concerned with technology, the effects of technology upon the people who interact with it and with the capacity for technology to lead humanity inexorably to destruction. *Titanic's* significant departure lies firmly within the political frame of the film. Where Cameron had previously dealt with the Cold War, with the Military-industrial Complex, and even with the possible "Clash of Civilizations" of *True Lies*, *Titanic's* main concern is the class system.

This emphasis on the class system in less Fukuyama's End of History than it is the French philosopher Jacques Derrida's critique of Fukuyama in his *Spectres of Marx*.[24] For Derrida the main failure of Fukuyama is his failure to recognize that, regardless of the apparent victory of liberal democracy, injustice is still dominant on the planet:

> Instead of singing the advent of the ideal of liberal democracy and of the capitalist market in the euphoria of the end of history, instead of celebrating the "end of ideologies" and the end of the great emancipatory discourses, let us never neglect this obvious macroscopic fact, made up of innumerable singular sites of suffering: no degree of progress allows one to ignore that never before, in absolute figures, have so many men, women and children been subjugated, starved or exterminated on the earth.[25]

Such a perspective can be discerned in Cameron's approach to the political core of the film. In a film dripping with nostalgia and the authentic reproduction of even the smallest of historical detail, *Titanic* never loses sight of its class consciousness. Katha Pollitt, writing in the American news magazine *The Nation*, described *Titanic* as a film that managed "to have filled the need for mass ritual and emotional fulfillment in a period of relative aimlessness: the ideological vacuum of post–Cold War civilization."[26]

As difficult a project as the making of *Titanic* was, it was not a daunting task to make the actual ship work as a giant, floating metaphor for the class system of the West. But making a film that filled the post–Cold War vacuum was a far more difficult undertaking than making the film itself. Cameron did this in a way that the working class passengers in the film, as on the real ship, found themselves lost in the maze of the lower decks. When the inevitable tragedy of an iceberg strikes those on the lower decks — and thus of the lower classes — would be left to die. Those lucky enough to be bourgeois passengers found themselves on the upper decks, attended to by the petite bourgeoisie of the crew. Framing his story around a free-spirited artist who won his steer-age ticket in a card game and a first class debutante fiancé from Philadelphia, the entire film acts as a metaphor for the class system. In his witheringly neg-ative review, *Time Magazine's* Richard Corliss summed up the film's main point simply by calling the film's characters "a caricature of class, designed only to illustrate a predictable prejudice: that the first-class passengers are third-class people, and vice versa."[27] This was not an issue lost on Cameron. Quoted in the *New York Times'* review of the film by Janet Maslin, Cameron wryly noted that thematically, "we're holding just short of Marxist dogma."[28] Maslin agreed, describing *Titanic* as a film that "pitilessly observes the different plights of the rich and the poor."[29]

At the same time the issues of class are not as simplistically rendered as critics have made out. The distinctions between "new money" and "old" are on display in a number of scenes. As Kathy Bates' Molly Brown instructs Jack as he joins the first class passengers for dinner, "remember, they love money so act like you own a gold mine and you're in the club." Those passengers in first class who can be categrized as *nouveau riche* are rendered distinctly from those born to wealth throughout the film. The character of Rose is defined by her desire to interact with the ship's designers and engineers as much as by her love for Jack and her dislike of her rich but non-productive fiancé, Cal.

Titanic is something more than simply a film undermining notions of class privilege in predictable ways. As with his earlier films, *Titanic* presents Cameron's characters as stereotypes, but stereotypes he believes his audience can relate to. So, when Leonardo DiCaprio's Jack describes his situation and his place in the world by saying to Rose, "I'm not an idiot, I know how the world works. I've got ten bucks in my pocket, I have nothing to offer you and I know that. I understand," Cameron is deliberately appealing to the lived experience of much of his audience. They are meant to fully understand the personal ramifications of being from the lower classes. And, in the end, Jack is dead. But at the same time the stereotype of upper class unhappiness, Rose, lives to reject her class and adopt the ideology of her savior, the steer-age-traveling Jack.

Thus, it may seem like blatant disregard to describe *Titanic*, a film about what was, at the time, the largest ship ever put to sea in what became, at the time, the largest grossing film ever made as transitional — but *Titanic* is exactly that. It remains a politically transitional film between the concerns of the "Cold War Cameron" and the "eco-political Cameron." And, like *True Lies* before it, *Titanic* is an attempt to identify an alternative source of narrative energy now that the United States no longer has the motifs of the Cold War to draw upon. There can be no surer sign of disaster for a storyteller like Cameron than Fukuyama's notions of an End of History and the "universalization of Western liberal democracy."

The American philosopher Richard Rorty, like Derrida, offered a critique of Fukuyama that pointed to all the problems Cameron would have adapting the End of History to his filmmaking. Rorty's concern was how Fukuyama's thesis undermined the use of intellectuals, but where he cited the intelligentsia he could as easily have been thinking of Cameron's films. For Rorty Fukuyama, "sees nothing but boredom ahead of us ... once we have admitted that bourgeois democratic welfare states are the best polities we can imagine."[30] If Rorty is correct about the End of History there is little left besides nostalgia for the past for Cameron to build his films upon. Cameron's notion of "history" prior to *Titanic* had been a fantastic image upon which to build his narratives. Rorty had seen history in much the same way, before Fukuyama. He noted, "history [has been] an object around which we intellectuals can wrap our fantasies" in the same way Cameron had made his films.[31] If Fukuyama is correct where does a James Cameron find a usable source of narrative conflict and meaningful villains of seemingly world-historical import? The answer, as the American film scholar Alexandra Keller has noted, might be a nostalgic history. The filmmaker that had been obsessed in his early films with notions of time, in reaction to the end of the Cold War, turns to history itself. He becomes, instead, "obsessed with history."[32] In *Titanic* Cameron need not "be worried about ... the end of history ... and thus the romance of history,"[33] because he can try to ignore it by looking for a meaningful thesis in the class structure of the ship and a personal romance in the past. But in attempting to either capture or ignore that End of History Cameron is also left with the emerging realization that with Fukuyama's thesis comes the knowledge, again in Rorty's terms, that his "old large blurry fantasies are gone, and we are left with only small concrete ones."[34] For a filmmaker with the aspirations of a James Cameron such limitations might make possible a single film like *Titanic*, but inevitably a return to a grander politico-historical narrative would become necessary.

Avatar *and America After 9/11*

When his films are considered in continuity, *Avatar* no longer represents such a departure for Cameron, but part of an evolution of themes and perspectives already well established his oeuvre. Much of *Avatar's* politics have antecedents in his earlier work. At the core of the film is another representation of the military-industrial complex. This is not a general observation, but a stated narrative frame. In a presentation to the Electronic Entertainment Exposition in 2009, Cameron articulates the premise of the story in specific terms:

> ... our main character, Jake Sulley, who was a marine who was wounded in combat, paralyzed, goes to Pandora, and in his avatar body of course he can walk, he can run, he can live again. As the story develops he finds himself caught between the military-industrial complex from earth and the Na'vi on the other hand who are increasingly threatened by the human expansion on Pandora.[35]

However, this is not the limited model described by Eisenhower in 1961. The premise of the movie hinges upon the needs of a future United States to colonize, at enormous expense, faraway planets to harvest an essential resource, unobtainium. The future Cameron imagines is suggestive. The human operation on Pandora is a fully functioning example of an integrated military-industrial complex including the corporation, the military, the scientists and, although veiled, the government. The company responsible for the extraction of the precious element is designated the RDA, the Resources Development Agency. There is some suggestion in the film that the USA and the RDA are synonymous. The level of detail Cameron demanded in the creation of the world of *Avatar* has been noted. One such detail is illuminating. A poster designed for the back story displays the RDA logo in a provocative modification of the stars and stripes. This sense that the country is governed by a super-company is even more apparent in the third iteration of the movie, a DVD-only collector's edition, which begins on Earth and details the moment that Sully is approached to take his brother's place in the avatar program. Two figures in dark suits, the embodiment of company men, approach Sully in an official capacity. They are not presented as businessmen looking to sign a deal, but rather government employees recruiting a specialist. In such details, Cameron's concept of the military-industrial complex finds a connection to a definition offered by Mark Pilisuk and Thomas Hayden, as

> an informal and changing coalition of groups with vested psychological, moral, and material interests in the continuous development and maintenance of high levels of weaponry, in preservation of colonial markets and in military-strategic conceptions of internal affairs.[36]

Cameron knowingly employs differing models of the complex: where the issue in *The Terminator* was the role of the military-industrial complex in the ultimate annihilation of humanity, its deployment in *Avatar* suggests that it is the engine of imperialism. It is certainly worth noting the reviews that have connected the RDAs exploits on Pandora with the similar exploits of Halliburton in Iraq. There are other real-world analogies. The hubris of the organization and the sense of technological superiority outweighing the primitive resources of the Na'vi is resonant. Cameron shows the RDA actions on Pandora as being a replay of the current war in Iraq. The same mistakes made through the same assumptions and the same recurring arrogance. That the war in Iraq, a similar imperial war for resources, has been referred to in terms redolent of the Vietnam War, specifically the employment of the loaded rhetoric of the "quagmire," cements these connections. The Na'vi too are portrayed in familiar ways, as technologically backward guerrilla warriors, fighting an insurgent war motivated by the attack upon their territory.

The critique of American imperialism is perhaps the most controversial aspect of *Avatar*. In *True Lies* Cameron used the articulation of American foreign policy as the rationale for Aziz' terrorist operations. The filmmaker extends this theme in *Avatar*. The actions of the RDA represent a perspective on American policy since 9/11. The whole enterprise is framed with post–9/11 rhetoric. One character refers to the "winning of the hearts and the minds of the natives." Another describes the RDAs preparation for the final battle as a "full mobilization. They're rigging a shuttle as a bomber ... for some kind of shock and awe campaign." Sully, the marine and RDA spy who turns native, observes, albeit simplistically, the nature of the RDAs imperial urge: "this is how it's done. When people are sitting on shit that you want, you make them your enemies. Then you're justified in taking it." Perhaps the most interesting example of Cameron's political message comes in Colonel Quaritch's speech on the eve of the final battle:

> Everyone on this base, every one of you is fighting for survival. That's a fact. There's an aboriginal horde out there massing for an attack. Now these orbital images tell me that the hostiles' numbers have gone up from a few hundred to well over two thousand in one day and more are pouring in. In a weeks' time there could be twenty thousand of them. At that point they will overrun our perimeter. That's not gonna happen. Our only security lies in pre-emptive attack. We will fight terror with terror. Now, the hostiles believe that this mountain stronghold of theirs is protected by their deity. When we destroy it we will blast a crater in their racial memory so deep that they won't come within a thousand clicks of this place ever again. And that too is a fact.

Coming, as it does, after the destruction by Quaritch and his forces, of the Na'vi Home Tree, his presentation of the humans as a group being threatened and terrorized is outrageous. The destruction of Home Tree is replete with imagery from footage taken on the day of 9/11. The resonances are too many and too specific to be coincidental, among them the sight of orange fires and billowing smoke, the projections of the images on screens, the extremely similar visualization of tree's collapse, the Na'vi running away from the debris, and their expressions of shock and grief at the scale of the atrocity. This may be the heart of Cameron's intention with the film. By manipulating the audience's perceptions and sympathies, by compelling the audience to witness the perpetration of such a horror by an American Colonel, Cameron is attempting to "open our eyes," and in doing so advocating a more measured and sophisticated approach to U.S. engagement with the world.

Conclusion

The period 1984 to 2009 was a challenging and rapidly shifting one for the United States. The old certainties of the Cold War gave way to the uncertainties that followed the collapse of the Soviet Union, the Berlin Wall and "the End of History." The trajectory of the post–Cold War years — the loss of Cold War enmity, the subsequent search for a new enemy and the horror when that enemy made itself known — underpin Cameron's narratives released in this twenty-five year period. His films deal with the repercussions of the defeat in Vietnam and the implications of the "victory" of the Cold War; they depict a period where the United States moved through feelings of anxiety to elation to relief and from ennui to fear to hope to frustration to anger; a period wherein the very concept of "American" was debated and contested.

Under such scrutiny, to suggest that *Avatar* is the beginning of Cameron's political journey is demonstrably false and does a disservice to a fascinating series of political readings of American culture and history. *Avatar* is merely the latest waypoint in a much larger intellectual and aesthetic voyage. It might be ironic that it is the Canadian, James Cameron, who so fully captures the trends of American political realities in his films — but they remain, none-the-less, political films to their respective cores.

Cameron's self-reflexive acknowledgment of *Avatar's* political dimension is not necessarily inaccurate. This is his most overt attempt at political filmmaking. It is not however his first attempt. Cameron has evinced in his work, from the outset, a steady political concern via a series of consistent and recurring themes and motifs. As the political landscape of the U.S. evolved so too have Cameron's visions. While it may be true to observe that his primary intentions lay in other directions (entertainment, technology, eco-messages),

Cameron has nevertheless been immensely successful in, passively or otherwise, capturing and offering perspectives on the contemporary tone and texture of American political culture in his films.

His reluctance to trumpet the political dimension of his work until now is perhaps understandable. There is a general understanding in Hollywood that politics and popular cinema should not mix. The old maxim that "politics is poison at the box-office" or in Sam Goldwyn's more colorful articulation "if I want to send a message, I'll call Western Union" seem to have been at some level internalized by Cameron. In that sense he plays the Hollywood game: action, spectacle, universal characters and extraordinary situations packaged for mass audiences: the very model of the late 20th century blockbuster. However, there is another Cameron. *Avatar* offers us the vantage point from which to survey this alternative iteration of the filmmaker.

Whether we fully buy into the evocative image of Cameron surfacing into a new world, recast as a consequence of 9/11, he seems genuine in his conviction that *Avatar* represents a new departure for him. Nevertheless, his oeuvre represents a series of fascinating documents of America's troubled passage through rapidly changing times, of a nation working to understand the nature of the changes consuming it and of a filmmaker of immense talents. Among these talents, perhaps his greatest is his unerring ability to precisely and unselfconsciously capture politically meaningful narratives resonant with the mood of the age.

NOTES

1. Rebecca Keegan, *The Futurist: The Life and Films of James Cameron* (New York: Crown, 2009), 216.

2. *Time Magazine*, "Help! They're Back!" July 28, 1986. Available at: http://www.time.com/time/magazine/article/0,9171,961839-1,00.html (Access date February 14, 2011).

3. John Nolte, "Cameron's Avatar is a big, dull, America-hating, PC revenge fantasy." Access date, December 1 2010. http://bighollywood.breitbart.com/jjmnolte/2009/12/11/review-camerons-avatar-is-a-big-dull-america-hating-pc-revenge-fantasy/.

4. John Podhoretz, "Avatrocious: Another Spectacle Hits an Iceberg and Sinks." *The Weekly Standard*, December 28, 2009, Access date, November 10, 2010, http://www.weeklystandard.com/Content/Public/Articles/000/000/017/350fozta.asp?page=1.

5. Tom Shone, "James Cameron Hates America: The Conservative Attack on Avatar." *Slate*, Access date, November 11, 2010, http://www.slate.com/id/2241542/.

6. "James Cameron: Yes, 'Avatar' Is Political." *The Wrap*, January 13, 2010, Access date, November 4, 2010, http://www.thewrap.com/movies/article/james-cameron-yes-avatar-political-12929.

7. Stephen Prince, *Visions of Empire: Political Imagery in Contemporary American Film* (New York: Praeger, 1992), 175.

8. Keegan, *The Futurist*, 3, 2.

9. Dwight D. Eisenhower, "Farewell Address." Access date, November 1, 2010, http://

www.eisenhower.archives.gov/research/digital_documents/Farewell_Address/1961_01_17_
Press_Release.pdf.

10. C. Wright Mills, *The Power Elite*. (New York: Oxford University Press, 2000), 28.

11. Mills, *The Power Elite*, 276.

12. Dwight D. Eisenhower, "Farewell Address." Access date, November 1, 2010, http:
//www.eisenhower.archives.gov/research/digital_documents/Farewell_Address/1961_01_17_Press
_Release.pdf.

13. Tim Blackmore, "'Is this going to be another bug-hunt?': S-F tradition versus biology-as-destiny in James Cameron's Aliens," *Journal of Popular Culture*, Vol. 29, No. 4 (Spring
1996), 211–227.

14. For a fuller discussion see Stephen McVeigh, "The Galactic Way of Warfare" in *Finding
the Force of the Star Wars Franchise: Fans, Merchandise and Critics* ed. Matthew Wilhelm Kapell
& John Shelton Lawrence (New York: Peter Lang, 2006), 35–59.

15. Evelyn Alsutany, "The Prime Time Plight of the Arab Muslim American After 9/11"
in *Race and Arab Americans Before and After 9/11: From Invisible Citizens to Visible Subjects* ed.
Amaney Jamal and Nadine Naber (New York: Syracuse University Press, 2008), 204–5.

16. George Kennan, "The Sources of Soviet Conduct" in *Foreign Affairs* 25, no. 4 (1947):
566–582.

17. Keegan, *The Futurist*, 134.

18. Samuel Huntington, *The Clash of Civilizations and the Remaking of the World Order*
(New York: Simon and Schuster, 1996), 217–8.

19. Samuel Huntington, "The Clash of Civilizations?" *Foreign Affairs*, Vol. 72, No. 3
(Summer 1993): 22.

20. Alexandra Keller, "James Cameron," in *Fifty Contemporary Film Directors*, ed. Yvonne
Tasker (New York: Routledge, 2010) 78. [77–90].

21. Ibrahim Abukhattala, "The New Bogeyman Under the Bed: Image Formation of Islam
in the Western School Curriculum and Media," in *The Miseducation of the West: How Schools
and the Media Distort Our Understanding of the Islamic World*, ed. Joe L. Kincheloe and Shirley
R. Steinberg (New York: Praeger, 2004) 157 (emphasis in the original). [153–170].

22. Francis Fukuyama, *The End of History and the Last Man* (London: Penguin, 1993).

23. Francis Fukuyama, "The End of History?" in *The National Interest* No. 16 (1989), p. 3.

24. Jacques Derrida, *Spectres of Marx* (New York: Routledge, 2006).

25. Derrida, *Spectres*, 85.

26. Katha Pollitt, "Subject to Debate: Women and Children First," *The Nation* (30 March
1998), 9.

27. Richard Corliss, "Down, Down, to a Watery Grave," *Time Magazine* (December 8,
1997), Available at: http://www.time.com/time/magazine/article/0,9171,987509,00.html (Access
date January 1, 2011).

28. James Cameron, quoted in Janet Maslin, "A Spectacle as Sweeping as the Sea," *New
York Times* (December 19, 1997), Available at: http://movies.nytimes.com/movie/review?res=
9B0DE7DB113FF93AA25751C1A961958260 (Access date January 1, 2011).

29. Maslin, Ibid.

30. Richard Rorty, "The End of Leninism, Havel, and Social Hope," in *Truth and Progress:
Philosophical Papers* (Cambridge: Cambridge University Press, 1998), 229. [228–243].

31. Richard Rorty, "The End of Leninism," 231.

32. Keller, *James Cameron*, 18.

33. Richard Rorty, "The End of Leninism," 231.

34. Richard Rorty, "The End of Leninism," 235.

35. "James Cameron Talks '*Avatar*' at Ubisoft's E3 2009 Press Con" Access date, October
10 2010, http://www.g4tv.com/videos/38674/James-Cameron-Talks-Avatar-At-Ubisofts-E3-
2009-Press-Con/.

36. Marc Pilisuk and Thomas Hayden, "Is There a Military-Industrial Complex Which
Prevents Peace?: Consensus and Countervailing Power in Pluralistic Systems," *Journal of Social
Issues*, XXI, No. 3 (July 1965), 103.

WORKS CITED

Abukhattala, Ibrahim. "The New Bogeyman Under the Bed: Image Formation of Islam in the Western School Curriculum and Media." In *The Miseducation of the West: How Schools and the Media Distort Our Understanding of the Islamic World*, eds. Joe L. Kincheloe and Shirley R. Steinberg, 153–169. New York: Praeger, 2004.

Alsutany, Evelyn. "The Prime Time Plight of the Arab Muslim American After 9/11." In *Race and Arab Americans Before and After 9/11: From Invisible Citizens to Visible Subjects* eds. Amaney Jamal and Nadine Naber, 204–228. New York: Syracuse University Press, 2008.

Belton, John, ed. *Movies and Mass Culture*. New Brunswick: Rutgers University Press, 1996.

Blackmore, Tim. "Is this going to be another bug-hunt?": S-F tradition versus biology-as-destiny in James Cameron's *Aliens, Journal of Popular Culture*, Vol. 29, No. 4 (Spring 1996), 211–226.

Block, Alex Ben, and Lucy Autrey Wilson, eds. *George Lucas's Blockbusting*. New York: Harper-Collins, 2010.

Bukatman, Scott. *Terminal Identity: The Virtual Subject in Post-Modern Science Fiction*. Durham: Duke University Press, 1998.

Cameron, James. As quoted in Janet Maslin, "A Spectacle as Sweeping as the Sea," *New York Times* (December 19, 1997), Available at: http://movies.nytimes.com/movie/review?res=9B0DE7DB113FF93AA25751C1A961958260 (Access date January 1, 2011).

Corliss, Richard. "Down, Down, to a Watery Grave," *Time Magazine* (December 8, 1997), Available at: http://www.time.com/time/magazine/article/0,9171,987509,00.html (Access date January 1, 2011).

Derrida, Jacques. *Spectres of Marx*. New York: Routledge, 2006.

Eisenhower, Dwight D. "Farewell Address." Access date, November 1, 2010, http://www.eisenhower.archives.gov/research/digital_documents/Farewell_Address/1961_01_17_Press_Release.pdf.

Fukuyama, Francis. "The End of History?" *The National Interest* No. 16 (1989), 3–18.

_____. *The End of History and the Last Man*. London: Penguin, 1993.

Hellmann, John. *American Myth and the Legacy of Vietnam*. New York: Columbia University Press, 1986.

Huntington, Samuel. "The Clash of Civilizations?" *Foreign Affairs*, Vol. 72, No. 3 (Summer 1993).

_____. *The Clash of Civilizations and the Remaking of the World Order*. New York: Simon and Schuster, 1996.

"James Cameron Talks '*Avatar*' at Ubisoft's E3 2009 Press Con." Access date, October 10, 2010, http://www.g4tv.com/videos/38674/James-Cameron-Talks-Avatar-At-Ubisofts-E3-2009-Press-Con/.

"James Cameron: Yes, '*Avatar*' Is Political." *The Wrap*, January 13, 2010. Access date, November 4, 2010, http://www.thewrap.com/movies/article/james-cameron-yes-avatar-political-12929.

Keegan, Rebecca. *The Futurist: The Life and Films of James Cameron*. New York: Crown, 2009.

Keller, Alexandra. *Routledge Film Guidebooks: James Cameron*. New York: Routledge, 2006.

Kuhn, Annette, ed. *Alien Zone: Cultural Theory and Contemporary Science Fiction Cinema*. London: Verso, 1990.

Louvre, Alf, and Jeffrey Walsh, eds. *Tell Me Lies About Vietnam*. Milton Keynes: Open University Press, 1988.

McVeigh, Stephen. "The Galactic Way of Warfare," in *Finding the Force of the Star Wars Franchise: Fans, Merchandise and Critics* eds. Matthew Wilhelm Kapell and John Shelton Lawrence, 35–58. New York: Peter Lang, 2006.

Mills, C. Wright. *The Power Elite*. New York: Oxford University Press, 2000.

Moffitt, Kimberly R., and Duncan A. Campbell, eds. *The 1980s: A Critical and Transitional Decade*. Lanham: Lexington Books, 2011.

Newman, Kim. *Apocalypse Movies: End of the World Cinema*. New York: St. Martin's Griffin, 2000.

Nolte, John. "Cameron's *Avatar* is a big, dull, America-hating, PC revenge fantasy." Access date, December 1, 2010. http://bighollywood.breitbart.com/jjmnolte/2009/12/11/review-came rons-avatar-is-a-big-dull-america-hating-pc-revenge-fantasy/.

Pilisuk, Marc, and Thomas Hayden, "Is There a Military-Industrial Complex Which Prevents Peace?: Consensus and Countervailing Power in Pluralistic Systems," *Journal of Social Issues,* XXI, No. 3 (July 1965), 67–177.

Podhoretz, John. "Avatrocious: Another Spectacle Hits an Iceberg and Sinks." *The Weekly Standard,* December 28, 2009. Access date, November 10, 2010, http://www.weeklystandard. com/Content/Public/Articles/000/000/017/350fozta.asp?page=1.

Pollitt, Katha. "Subject to Debate: Women and Children First," *The Nation* (30 March 1998).

Prince, Stephen. *Visions of Empire: Political Imagery in Contemporary American Film.* New York: Praeger, 1992.

Pursell, Carroll W., Jr., ed. *The Military Industrial Complex.* New York: Harper & Row, 1972.

Roper, Jon. *The American Presidents: Heroic Leadership from Kennedy to Clinton.* Edinburgh: Edinburgh University Press, 2000.

Rorty, Richard. "The End of Leninism, Havel, and Social Hope." In *Truth and Progress: Philosophical Papers,* 228–243. Cambridge: Cambridge University Press, 1998.

Sarkesiann Sam C., ed. *The Military Industrial Complex: A Reassessment.* Beverly Hills: Sage Publications, 1972.

Schiller, Herbert I., and Joseph D Phillips, eds. *Super State: Readings in the Military Industrial Complex.* Urbana: University of Illinois Press, 1972.

Seed, David. *American Science Fiction and the Cold War: Literature and Film.* Edinburgh: Edinburgh University Press, 1999.

Shone, Tom. "James Cameron Hates America: The Conservative Attack on *Avatar.*" *Slate.* Access date, November 11, 2010, http://www.slate.com/id/2241542/.

Time Magazine. "Help! They're Back!" July 28, 1986. Available at: http://www.time.com/time/ magazine/article/0,9171,961839-1,00.html (Access date February 14, 2011).

Films Cited

The Abyss. Directed by James Cameron. Twentieth Century–Fox, 1989.

Alien. Directed by Ridely Scott. Twentieth Century–Fox, 1979.

Aliens. Directed by James Cameron. Twentieth Century–Fox, 1986.

Avatar. Directed by James Cameron. Twentieth Century–Fox, 2009.

The Birth of a Nation. Directed by D.W. Griffith. David W. Griffith Corp., 1915.

The Day After. Directed by Nicholas Meyer. ABC Circle Films, 1983.

Invaders from Mars. Directed by William Cameron Menzies. National Pictures Corporation, 1953.

Invasion of the Body Snatchers. Directed by Don Siegal. Walter Wagner Productions, 1956.

Platoon. Directed by Oliver Stone. Hemdale Films, 1986.

Rambo: First Blood Part II. Directed by George P. Cosmatos. Tri-Star, 1986.

Star Wars. Directed by George Lucas. Twentieth Century–Fox, 1977.

Strange Days. Directed by Kathryn Bigelow. Twentieth Century–Fox, 1995.

The Terminator. Directed by James Cameron. Hemdale Films, 1984.

Terminator 2: Judgment Day. Directed by James Cameron. Carolco Pictures, 1991.

Titanic. Directed by James Cameron. Twentieth Century–Fox, 1997.

La Totale. Directed by Claude Zidi. Film par Film et al., 1991.

True Lies. Directed by James Cameron. Twentieth Century–Fox, 1994.

WarGames. Directed by John Badham. MGM, 1983.

Fighting the History Wars
on the Big Screen:
From *The Terminator* to *Avatar*

ACE G. PILKINGTON

"Cousteau is the god": Cameron's Beginnings

Orson Welles had the instinctive ability to walk onto a movie set, hold up his hand, and say, "Put the camera here." He did not use a viewfinder or look through the camera. He made no attempt to cover the scene (and his editing choices) by shooting from multiple angles. As he said, "I know instantly where it goes. There's never a moment of doubt."[1]

James Cameron seems to have a similarly uncanny ability to locate that point on the cultural and historical axis where important things meet, resonate, and echo. Often, what Cameron is doing seems risky to others or even perhaps unmarketable, but somehow the rumors of disaster are never true, and the negative predictions by critics are swept away in the waves of success, or at most remain behind underwater as artifacts of the failure — of the critics. In a comparison between the success of *Titanic* and the failure of *The Postman*, Bernard Weinraub wrote, "Several marketing executives said privately that the very concept of the film — a postman who saves the day in a post-apocalyptic world — was a turn-off to audiences. 'The concept was impossible to grasp,' Mr. Gerbrandt said."[2] Perhaps so but the notion of a costume drama where nearly everybody dies and the audience knows the ending in advance was no easy sell either,[3] and most of Cameron's films (plus his television series *Dark Angel*) have been set just before, during, or after an apocalypse of some sort. Without criticizing Kevin Costner's film (or the David Brin novel on which it was based), it is still possible to say that Cameron's placement of his stories in historical time and cultural space is far more effective. In explaining part of what went in to *Avatar*, he says, "By then [1995] we were in Iraq, so all the sort of colonial period reference points, the historical reference points were now resonating in the exact present moment."[4] David Heard argues that as early as *The Terminator*, "Cameron tried to construct a movie that would work on several levels. He wanted equally to impress twelve-year-old boys with nonstop action and high-impact special effects and to inspire fifty-year-old film professors to read all kinds of sociopolitical significance into the movie."[5]

James Cameron has indeed done something extraordinary (and especially fascinating to film professors). Even though most of his work has been science fiction, history informs and structures all of it, resonating with actual historical events outside the films. As David Simpson points out in his very clever analysis of *Titanic*, "Cameron's own previous films have been mostly futuristic, although they play upon a relation between present, past, and future within the fictional time scales of the narratives (*Aliens*, *The Terminator* and *Terminator 2: Judgment Day*, and *The Abyss*), as they also invest heavily in the more formal temporalities embodied in quotation of other films and of themselves."[6] In addition, Cameron repeatedly lengthens those "fictional time scales."

Cameron's approach to and use of history is particularly powerful because he equates it with Truth. Starting with *The Terminator*, Cameron builds one of the central conflicts of each film around the struggle to discover that Truth. And in what amounts to a kind of history war, the process of discovery can be as rigorous as that of any scientific expedition. First, the main characters must gather their data, then, they must place it in context and evaluate its validity, including the reliability of any witnesses. Next, they draw conclusions from what they now know (the truth stage), and finally, since all this is taking place inside an action film, they must do something about what they have discovered (though this phase may also include some last minute evaluation of data). In Cameron's worlds, this is almost always a larger and more violent phase than is usual for historians and scientists. In similar fashion, the proof for a particular thesis may be — instead of the discovery of an artifact or manuscript — the wiping out of the entire night shift at a police precinct office, and the disagreements between rival "historians" routinely result in assault, attempted murder, and worse.

James Cameron is clearly not the kind of historian that Edward Hallett Carr (in his seminal *What Is History?*) would call a "relativist," the kind who would say "that one interpretation is as good as another, or that every interpretation is true in its own time and place."[7] I do not mean to suggest that the many uses of, approaches to, and benefits from history in Cameron's films have a single explanation. To take just one peripheral example to the contrary, David Simpson says, "Many predicted that the movie [*Titanic*] would be a washout, a pastiche, a hopeless anachronism. But pastiche and anachronism are in fact highly marketable and theorized as such in the culture of the postmodern, and they do indeed find a place in Cameron's film, which may be an instance not just of nostalgia but of nostalgia *for* nostalgia."[8] However, Cameron's central view of history and the world comes from scientific expeditions and indeed from his experience of science itself.

Describing his childhood and youth, James Cameron says, "I was like a science geek, and I was so curious about everything... My idea of a hot Saturday was drawing at the museum."[9] As a teenager, "He would regularly hop a bus in Niagara Falls and take it into Toronto where he would spend hours walking the dimly lighted halls of the Royal Ontario Museum, sketching dinosaur bones, ancient Etruscan helmets, and other exhibits."[10] In ninth grade, "He eschewed sports and instead became president of the science club, which, he recalls, 'consisted of me and one Czechoslovakian girl.'"[11]

It was at this point in Cameron's science saturated life that history made its first big appearance, "In tenth grade, he was bitten by the history bug in a class on the ancients. 'The Egyptians, Minoans, Greeks, Romans. I can picture every class, every slide show, and almost quote the lessons,' he says."[12] Cameron's favorite history teacher was Kathryn Englund, "To this day, most recently on the set of his record-smashing epic *Titanic*, when the subject of his high-school days comes up he mentions his beloved history teacher as someone who gave him the confidence to dream and dream big."[13] For a time in college, he reports, "I studied physics, which was something that I was really interested in. I was pretty good at it, except for the math."[14] He says that at this time, "I went to the USC Library... Trying to approach the filmmaking process like it was something I could dismantle like a watch and put back together."[15] When James Lipton asked the standard Actors Studio question, "What profession other than your own would you like to attempt?" Cameron answered, "Astronaut, scientist."[16]

Cameron's fascination with science, his deep interest in ancient history, and his love for adventure found a focus and role model in the activities and films of one man — Jacques Cousteau. Discussing his sources of inspiration in the documentary *Explorers*, Cameron says, "When I was a kid in Canada ... I watched the Jacques Cousteau specials on TV, and I thought they were absolutely incredible."[17] Paula Parisi writes, "Jacques Cousteau was his hero." She goes on to quote Cameron, "'I was fascinated, watching them take those little scooters inside caves.'"[18] He learned to scuba dive at the age of sixteen even though his father had to "drive him twenty-five miles to the YMCA in Buffalo, New York."[19] It was in winter and sometimes "through blinding blizzards."[20] Cousteau's influence has stayed with him throughout his career. One of his latest projects is *Sanctum*. "Based on a true story and using technology developed by executive producer James Cameron," according to the Netflix description, "this breathtaking thriller follows the adventures of expert diver Frank McGuire ... who heads an expedition to map a network of underwater caverns."[21]

In his 2002 "wreck diving" documentary *James Cameron's Expedition: Bismarck*, he states, "I enjoy this. To me it's an alternative to making movies which is as technically challenging, as emotionally challenging, and it's something that I can use my skills as a filmmaker, but it's not just about the filmmaking — it's about creating the technology. It's about the personal challenge of actually going into the hostile environment, doing things right, doing things safely, and coming back with results. You know I find that exciting."[22] Could there be a better summary of the plots of most of Cameron's films than those last two sentences, especially if we omit (as Cameron sometimes does in his expeditions and filming) the part about "doing things safely"? No wonder Cameron's documentaries and blockbusters seem to be, not discrete entities separated by genre boundaries, but a continuum. As he says in *Explorers*, "I just took it a step further with the documentary films."[23] "Between 2001 and 2004 he spent seven months at sea and went on forty-one deep-submersible dives."[24] Charles Pellegrino calls him, "a polymathic explorer and engineer (and part-time rocket designer) who seemed to invent movie projects intended to take him into the depths of the sea, onto Antarctic ice sheets, and eventually out into space."[25] Cameron's two most successful documentaries are *Ghosts of the Abyss* (an exploration of the wreck of the *Titanic*) and, not surprisingly, *Aliens of the Deep* (a film that makes comparisons and connections between the very deep sea and what we might find in outer space).[26]

Asked if he was "attempting to assume the mantle/void left vacant by Jacques Cousteau?" Cameron responded, "'Cousteau was kind of the guy who defined the nexus of exploration and filmmaking... He's far shifted over to the explorer side, but he understood the value of sharing it with an audience to fund his explorations. First of all Cousteau is the god, right? But the other difference is that he dedicated his life to it. I'm not doing that. For me it can never go that far because I still want to make movies, you know, the way I've been doing in the past. But I'm very, very serious about trying to facilitate research and exploration in any way that I can. I think that's at least equally important as anything that I might do in Hollywood.'"[27]

Perhaps the best way to demonstrate Cousteau's influence on Cameron in his roles as filmmaker/scientist/historian is with a brief description of Cousteau's 1977 documentary "*Calypso's Search for the Britannic*." Cameron has said many times that his motivation for making *Titanic* was exploration, not movie making, "I became obsessed with the idea of actually diving to the shipwreck. The fact that I would have to make this gargantuan film after that was really ... a kind of penance."[28] In fact, the film he did make resembles in many ways Cousteau's documentary of his own diving to the wreck of *Titanic*'s sister ship.

Britannic was launched six months before World War I and then requisitioned as a hospital ship in 1915. She did not survive long in her new role. On November 21, 1916, *Britannic* "was wracked by explosions and quickly sank."[29] With their usual professionalism and skill, *Calypso*'s crew discovers the wreck, dives to it, and by the end of the film, determines what sank *Britannic*—a mine, not a torpedo. Far more important in the context of *Titanic* and Cameron, though, is the method Cousteau used to put the disaster in historical context. Cousteau has one of the survivors flown to *Calypso* by helicopter, just as the elderly Rose is flown to the *Keldysh*. "Eighty-six year old Sheila Macbeth Mitchell, a volunteer nurse aboard the *Britannic* on her last voyage ... still holds sharp, clear memories of that fateful November morning in 1916."[30] And like Rose, she has an important impact on the crew of the exploratory vessel and through them, on the audience.

"Invited by Cousteau to visit the scene of the tragedy after a lapse of sixty years, she was quick to come adventuring."[31] Cousteau asks her to tell him the story of the ship's sinking. They discuss, among more serious things, the possibility of finding one of her lost possessions — in this case a traveling clock. She says, "It'll be a nice souvenir."[32] Sheila Mitchell comments on the class distinctions on board *Britannic*, the enforced separation of doctors and nurses by the woman in charge, saying she is "surprised the old dame didn't put a notice to say doctors and sisters shouldn't drown on the same side of the ship."[33]

Cousteau and Sheila Mitchell look at old photographs of her. She comments (in words that would fit well in Rose's mouth), "I've had a very lucky life. I've been to many countries."[34] When she leaves the ship, the narrator says, "Aboard the *Calypso*, each has been touched by a bright and indestructible lady."[35]

The Terminator: *Setting the Pattern*

James Cameron's directorial debut (not counting the disastrous, debilitating, and demeaning *Piranhas II*) was not about the sea, but it was about science and history and the future of the planet,[36] and it did set the pattern in many ways for the blockbusters to come. *The Terminator* is a fiction of nuclear disaster, a science fiction subgenre that is hard to write successfully. Set in post-apocalyptic worlds, the stories become trivial sex farces, implausible character studies, or scenarios of destruction with survivors so alien that there is no understanding their actions or sympathizing with their motivations. Set in worlds on the verge of apocalypse, the stories become didactic, political, and top-heavy, weighed down with presidents, senators, generals, and KGB officials. Even the James Bond films, whose narratives have teetered repeatedly on the verge of thermonuclear war, suffer from some of these problems. From his excellent book on the subject, here is David Dowling's expression of some of the difficulties and possibilities, "We live in an age of constant threat, of potential apocalypse. The magnitude is beyond our reckoning, the technology and perhaps the politics beyond our ken, but what can be explored and dramatized is what it is like to feel in the post–1945 world ... the end towards which we drive insanely is not known, only known about."[37]

Perhaps Cameron's success came partly from the very personal nature of the story he told. For him it was both a revenge fantasy of "a sophisticated killing machine traveling back from the future to slay *Piranha II*'s producer"[38] and a nightmare. In Cameron's words, "I got sick, and in this kind of fevered state, I had a dream about this kind of a chrome skeleton emerging out of a fire, and you know it was this horrible, horrible nightmare. And I love nightmares."[39] It was also an expression of a fear that had been with him from the time he was eight years old and the Cuban Missile Crisis convinced him "that the safe and nurturing world I thought I lived in was an illusion, and that the world as we know it could end at any moment."[40] In Rebecca Keegan's words, "From that time on, he was fascinated by the idea of nuclear war, his fears fueled by the apocalyptic scenarios depicted in the science-fiction books he devoured."[41] He refers to the Cuban Missile Crisis (and in a sense recreates it) in *The Abyss* his second fiction of nuclear disaster.

At the core of *Terminator*, like the "hyper-alloy combat chassis" under the cyborg's human exterior, is the question of Truth, of scientific and historical reality. Kyle Reese tells a seemingly impossible story that Sarah Connor is understandably reluctant to believe. The police have plausible alternative explanations, involving body armor and PCP, that make sense to Sarah even though the evidence of her own observations seems to validate Reese's account. At first, she follows him blindly to escape danger, but she balks at the notion of robotic killing machines and time travelers. It is Reese's description of the Terminator's deadly nature that first shakes her skepticism, "Listen and understand. That Terminator is out there. It can't be bargained with. It can't be reasoned with. It doesn't feel pity or remorse or fear. And it absolutely will not stop. Ever. Until you are dead."

Of course, part of her response is driven by fear, a natural reaction to such a terrible picture of her future. But another part of her response is to the internal logic of Reese's account, including what he says about the Terminator. Even Dr. Silberman, the police psychiatrist, acknowledges this consistency, though it is in his usual flippant, wrongheaded fashion, "Great stuff. I could make a career out of this guy. See how clever it is? It doesn't require a shred of proof. Most paranoid delusions are intricate, but this is brilliant." Sarah is reluctant to believe Silberman's conclusion that Reese is "in technical terminology ... a loon" because Reese has additional characteristics of rationality. For instance, when Sarah asks him, "Can you stop it?" He responds with honesty and objectivity, "I don't know. With these weapons, I don't know." Delusions should be made of more positive stuff. If he were out of touch with reality, he should sound more like the police, "You'll be perfectly safe. We got thirty cops in this building."

Sarah Connor's doubts are resolved when the Terminator lives up to his promise of, "I'll be back." Certainly, the killing of the entire night shift at a police precinct must qualify as proof, but she has made up her mind before the final body count is in. Unfortunately, the police officers are not as mentally flexible as Sarah Connor, and their failure to adjust their view of the world as a result of significant new data results in their attacking the Terminator in ways that guarantee their elimination. There is nothing surprising about such obliviousness by this point in the movie, nor are the police the only ones to suffer from it. Sarah's roommate dies because her headphones keeps her from hearing the destruction of their apartment so that she walks toward instead of running away from the killing machine that has already murdered her boyfriend. The aptly, yet as it turns out, ironically named Tech Noir nightclub stylistically suggests the dark side of machines, but no one there is ready for what happens.

The Terminator is Cameron's extraordinary metaphor for the reality of nuclear war. After the explosion of the first atomic bomb, Robert Oppenheimer quoted the *Bhagavad Gita*, "I am become Death, the shatterer of worlds."[42] Cameron's version of Death may be smaller, but it is also deadly and far harder to ignore than the massive missiles slumbering in their silos. And its ultimate outcome, Cameron suggests, may be the same — the destruction of humanity. Oppenheimer himself was to be disgraced, in large part, because of his opposition to Truman's top secret development of the hydrogen bomb, which Oppenheimer thought "would be a weapon not of warfare but, quite possibly, of genocide."[43] In Cameron's story, the representative of thermonuclear war goes door to door, killing a few in the present so that all may die in the future.

Of course, the audience, unlike Sarah Connor, knows from the film's first establishing shot and voice over that there was (or will be) a nuclear war in the future, that there is an intelligent machine mind which uses robots and cyborgs to kill humans, and that time travelers are fighting each other in an attempt to change history in 1984. An element of the entertainment in watching *Terminator* is the satisfaction of knowing the Truth, of being on the right side, and sympathizing with the people who understand the nature of the world. Nor is it simply the opening of the movie that tells the audience what to think. We see the arrival of the Terminator and of Kyle Reese. We watch the Terminator's strength and ruthlessness, and we are prepared for the police to fail because we have seen Reese effortlessly steal a gun from them and the Terminator commandeer a police car.

It is not until after the destruction of the police station that Sarah Connor and the movie audience begin "reading" from the same page of Cameron's screenplay. Even then, the audience has a tremendous advantage in observing events. Cameron's vision is objective. His camera shows reality (even in a science fiction film). There are no expressionist film tricks and no distortions of viewpoint to match the physical state of the characters, only filming in slow motion so that even the action does not blur. Memory flashbacks are as sharp and clear as present experience because they all happen in the camera's "real" time. No wonder the transition from films to documentaries is so seamless for Cameron.[44]

In addition in *The Terminator*, Cameron provides the audience with a form of seeing that is at once characterization and scientific demonstration. In Alexandra Keller's words, the Terminator's "vision is the definitive articulation of his machine nature. It is an infrared screen that combines a number of different readings and readouts: a compass, a target sight centered on Sarah and Reese, and a variety of data, program directives, and codes that move so fast the spectator can't possibly read them — though, as a cyborg, of course, the Terminator can."[45] The ultimate vision of reality in this film, the final proof for Reese's assertions, and the nightmare prefiguring of nuclear holocaust are the data collection readouts in the cyborg's head that Cameron throws onto the movie screen. Although *The Terminator* does not place its heroes in hostile environments where they can easily drown or die from breathing the toxic gases of alien atmospheres as some of Cameron's other films do, the sense of a deadly environment because of the machine menace is just as strong here. The safe world where Sarah Connor's biggest problem is balancing her checkbook is revealed to be a place where, as Cameron says in his "Foreword" to *Ghosts of the Titanic*, "the harnessing of nuclear energy has brought us to the brink of a precipice from which we may yet not escape."[46]

Again, perhaps Cameron's personal and emotional involvement with this story makes his plot work so well and so resonate with many issues. He has built an action film about nuclear war in which no one is guarding or trying to steal a bomb. Instead, the doomsday device has become the movie's villain and (as *T2* demonstrates) action hero in waiting. The huge issues of mutually assured destruction and looming genocide are pushed to the periphery of the story while a drama of personal survival and romantic love takes center stage. But the big issues work more believably in the shadows, adding depth to the nearly nonstop action. And the big issues are surely there, expanded by the science fiction format beyond their usual limits. There may be no presidents or KGB spymasters, but there are two powerful manipulators attempting to control time itself, Skynet — the machine mind — and John Connor himself, guaranteeing his own birth at the cost of his father's life.

The ultimate irony in this vast struggle (available to audience members who want to think about it but easily ignored by those who accept the semi-happy ending[47]) is the irony in many time loop (or ontological paradox) stories: John Connor has created himself (though he has not gone as far as the character in Robert Heinlein's "All You Zombies" who is both his own father and mother).[48] Far worse, by saving his mother's life and ensuring the destruction of the Terminator, John Connor has created Skynet just as surely as Skynet has created John Connor by trying to kill him. Both Connor and Skynet exist in a time loop without outside causality. The Terminator's surviving arm makes Skynet possible, but it is never invented, only found and back-engineered. Kyle Reese comes across time for Sarah Connor because of a picture and because John Connor asks him to, but neither the picture nor John Connor would exist if Reese had not already gone back in time. The simplest way to save the world is to let the Terminator kill Sarah Connor. Then (in all probability), no one would find a piece of the advanced technology, and Skynet could not be built. But, Cameron's plot suggests, the "perils to come that would result from our hubris and blind faith in technology" may be inescapable, a time loop, a feedback loop, leading directly if not necessarily inevitably to destruction.[49]

The possibility of redemption in the film comes, as it almost always does with Cameron, from the actions of individual human beings in history. Kyle Reese and the Terminator share a future, a past, a culture of unending conflict, and a goal — to travel into their past and find Sarah Connor. Man and machine seemingly have more in common with each other than with any of the people in the green and comparatively peaceful world they have reached by a process which Reese describes as "rebirth." And yet there is another history, already completed and filed away in memory, that is, nevertheless, still being shaped, with a tragic love waiting in the shadows, and a savior who must still be conceived and — if his mother can survive that long — born.

Cameron presents Reese as a pure warrior, a Galahad from the future who tells Sarah, "I volunteered. It was a chance to meet the legend." It becomes clear that for Reese, Sarah Connor's history is the one that matters, her heroic image as the person who trained John Connor and made the future possible, plus the youthful photo of her that he carried with him and memorized. In his dark life filled with death and monsters, she is the only woman who has ever meant anything. Sarah asks, "Was there someone special... A girl, you know." And he replies, "No. Never." At last Reese speaks the words he has been holding back, "I came across time for you, Sarah. I love you. I always have." While John Connor's message to his mother says, "The future is not set," Kyle Reese seems to have worked out what his own destiny was and will be. He tells Sarah, "John Connor gave me a picture of you once. I didn't know why at the time." Perhaps Cameron needs the long spans of time that he almost always uses and the multiple perspectives on history he consistently creates in order to find and foreground such rare narratives and characters. What he knows now is that he has found the woman he loves, and he will die saving her. It will continue to be in Cameron's films, as it is in this first one, love and sacrifice that make a difference, that will save the world if it can possibly be saved.

Bad and Good Aliens: The Pattern Expanded

James Cameron wrote his screenplay for *Aliens* in the interval when he was waiting for production to begin on *The Terminator*, but his script was partly based on a treatment he had already written just after he had first seen *Alien*. Since that original version of the screenplay was written substantially before *The Terminator*, the common elements in the two scripts are likely to have as much or more to do with Cameron's basic mindset as with any conscious repetition of his first successful screenplay. In addition, *Aliens* was influenced by another script Cameron had been working on, the sequel to *Rambo*. Cameron says, "While I was doing research for *Rambo*, I'd read every book I could get my hands on about Vietnam. That research was still very much in my head while I was finishing *Aliens*. One day, it just hit me that the basic story I was telling here was the perfect metaphor for America's involvement in Vietnam. In both cases, you had the most technologically advanced army in the world going off to wage battle against an enemy that was working barely above the medieval level. Yet the advanced forces lose ... so the Vietnam analogy in *Aliens* was absolutely intentional."[50]

Again, Cameron has a historical context — a sort of echo chamber — for his science fiction film, and again it is the history of a disaster. But Cameron is never satisfied with one set of echoes; his films resonate in what sometimes seems to be counterpoint. *The Terminator* is about thermonuclear war, but it also contains clear references to vigilantism and home defense in a paranoid time and place. *Aliens* references an SF war novel as well as an actual war. Cameron says about *Starship Troopers* by Robert A. Heinlein, "That's a great book ... about Earth warring against a race of intelligent insects. So I included a few throwaway references to it. .. In fact, when I heard they were making a film out of Heinlein's novel ... my first thought was, "Why are they making that movie? I already did it."[51] Cameron also draws on Isaac Asimov's robot stories (and not his own Terminator) for the android Bishop's rules of behavior, "It is impossible for me to harm or, by omission of action, allow to be harmed a human being."[52] Asimov, working to counter what he called the "Frankenstein complex," set out to create a positive vision of robots, "a robot that was wisely used, that was not dangerous, and that did the job it was supposed to do." The programming instructions to Asimov's fictional machines which made all that possible came to be known as "Asimov's Three Laws of Robotics." The First Law states, "A robot may not injure a human being, or, through inaction, allow a human being to come to harm."[53]

As part of his connection to and continuation of the first *Alien* film, Cameron added details to Ripley's nearly blank background. He gave her a daughter, and typically for him, he created a historical perspective for the story by spreading the events over decades. At the end of the original screenplay for *Alien*, Ripley says, "I should reach the frontier in another five weeks. With a little luck the network will pick me up."[54] In the movie she says "six weeks," but Cameron has her drift in space for fifty-seven years, long enough for her daughter to die. Similarly, the Terminator and Reese time travel from 2029 to 1984, for an interval of forty-five years, and Rose returns to the *Titanic* an implausible eighty-four years after she lived through the shipwreck. The histories in *The Abyss* and *Avatar*, where Cameron has alien cultures, and not merely individuals to deal with, are naturally considerably longer.

Aliens continues the pattern set by *The Terminator*. Here too there is a central conflict built around the struggle to discover the truth. Ripley, like Reese (and Sarah Connor in *Terminator 2*), knows what has happened and fears what is to come, and like Reese (and again like Sarah Connor in *Terminator 2*), she is treated as psychologically unstable. There is no clear physical evidence to support her story, and the events she relates are so extraordinary as to make belief difficult even for unbiased observers. It quickly becomes clear, though, that the corporate officials who are judging Ripley and her narrative are driven to find the highest possible profit margin, not the most precise version of past events. While the police officers in *The Terminator* were stubbornly oblivious to what was happening around them, Ripley is faced with people who, even when they have made the painful discovery of the truth, will deny it if there is any possibility of profiting from the lie. At one point in her journey of anger and frustration, Ripley goes so far as to suggest that the monstrous creatures she is fighting are better than the corporate minion who stands in her way, "You know, Burke, I don't know which species is worse. You don't see them fucking each other over for a goddamn percentage." In fact, the fresh-faced, seemingly innocent Burke (played by Paul Reiser) plans to kill everyone else on the expedition so that he can successfully smuggle samples of the aliens back to corporate headquarters in the cryogenically frozen bodies of Ripley and Newt.

In this film Cameron brings into the open what was merely a shadowy suggestion in *The Terminator*: There are powerful groups in business and government whose secret agendas determine the course of history and falsify the accounts of it. There is nothing new in those notions. Revisionist histories are partly built on them, and popular skepticism concerning standard histories also grows from them. General Burgoyne's statement in Shaw's *The Devil's Disciple* that "History, sir, will tell lies, as usual," is their witty, throw away summation.[55] The danger for any popular filmmaker is that such a position can easily descend into labyrinthine conspiracy theories, leaving any hope of realism and credibility far behind. Cameron's emphasis on the facts of science and history and his focus on individual characters keeps him and his stories safe from such dangers. Burke, for instance, is a representative of corporate greed and ruthlessness, but he is a single person, not a corporation. We see the environment that spawns him and are free to conclude that it is no more human than the monsters that Ripley and the Colonial Marines fight, but the battleground in this history war remains small and self-contained.

Aliens is Cameron's first use of the military, and he employs them in a variety of effective ways. They are initially, like the police in *The Terminator*, part of the disbelieving multitude who discount Ripley's experience. They are also foolishly confident in their own ability to win. Sergeant Apone, who is one of the first Marines to die, says, "We come here, and we're going to conquer." Newt, the little girl who is the sole survivor of the civilian colony, is not impressed. When Ripley, of all people, tries to reassure her by telling her, "They're soldiers," she replies, "It won't make any difference." Unlike the police, at least some of the Colonial Marines will live long enough to share that very realistic assessment.

Although Cameron presents the Marines as idiosyncratic personalities, he does not suggest that they are anything worse than overconfident and unthinking. They (especially Hicks) begin to see Ripley's value, starting when she volunteers to run the loader and does it with great skill. After she takes the initiative of command away from the inexperienced, indecisive Lieutenant Gorman and rescues the squad's survivors, they accept her evaluation of the situation. Against Burke's strident objections and smarmy persuasions, Corporal Hicks (by then the ranking member of the military and therefore officially in charge of the expedition) repeats Ripley's solution as his orders, "I think we'll take off and nuke the site from orbit. It's the only way to be sure." Even Executive Officer Bishop, the android Ripley has treated with contempt for most of the film, passes a final, positive judgment on her, "Not bad for a human."

For the first time here Cameron is using a larger group of positive characters around the hero, what David Brin calls "a few stalwart, archetype sidekicks numbering no more than the dozen or so our ancestors knew in a tribal hunting band."[56] The result is the isolation of Burke (especially when the Marines threaten to kill him on Ripley's evidence) and the affirmation of Ripley and her position. It is a new kind of proof in Cameron's structure, almost as though his hero is going through a process of peer review, though it may simply be that the evidence is now obvious to a larger group of people. In any event, Cameron has tipped the evaluative balance in favor of Ripley to a substantially greater extent than he does in either of the *Terminator* films. He will repeat and extend this process in both *The Abyss* and *Avatar*.

Of course, the film cannot end with a safe liftoff and a neat nuking from space (though there will be a thermonuclear explosion). Cameron's love story for this narrative is the love between mother and surrogate daughter that is shared by Ripley and Newt. "Ripley and the Alien Queen battle one another to protect their respective 'children.'"[57] This is scarcely surprising given the fact that Cameron's initial screen treatment (written before anyone had asked him for one) was titled *Mother*. Again, love and the willingness to sacrifice for another person are the transcendent forces that make success and survival possible. Ripley, who inadvertently missed her own daughter's eleventh birthday and then the rest of her life as well, refuses to abandon Newt, no matter what the cost. Finally, of course, they both survive, along with Hicks and enough of Bishop for repairs to be effective. It is a substantially better outcome than the one Ripley had at the end of *Alien*, where only she and Jones, the ship's cat, made it out alive.[58]

It should now be possible to catalogue as well as describe the elements in Cameron's films, especially if we keep his beginnings plus recurring interests and motifs in mind. Not surprisingly, "*The Abyss* began as a short story Cameron wrote at age sixteen, when he was devouring Jacques Cousteau's underwater TV documentaries."[59] A science lecture on breathing liquid oxygen inspired him to write about "an underwater science lab perched on the edge of the Cayman Trough, the deepest point in the Caribbean."[60] The story changed and grew, and the group of scientists became a group of deep water oil drillers, but as usual when he had a comparatively free hand, Cameron was making a movie about science, history, and if at all possible, sea water.

He decided to film the underwater scenes underwater, a radically new choice in filmmaking that would demand the creation of helmets that left the actors' faces visible and that had microphones to record their voices underwater, making it in Cameron's words from *Explorers*, "The first recorded dialogue underwater on film for a theatrical motion picture in the history of the world."[61] It would also require, among many other things, the remodeling and re-purposing of the containment vessel of "the never-completed Cherokee Nuclear Power Plant (outside Gaffney, South Carolina)" to stand-in for the ocean.[62] The actors would be pushed to the limits of frustration and exhaustion, and Cameron, himself, who spent more time underwater than anyone else, would nearly drown. But he would also, obviously, get to do many of his favorite things, including a science experiment with liquid oxygen and five rats, one of which required resuscitation from Cameron, "rhythmically pumping the little rodent's sternum, not unlike Bud reviving Lindsey."[63]

The Abyss is another of Cameron's fictions of nuclear disaster, one that references the Cuban Missile Crisis, sets its events some eighty miles from that island, and uses as its background a similar standoff between the superpowers. This is the larger historical context, and throughout the film, we see what is happening, as the tension ramps up, on television screens. Even the aliens in the abyssal trench are watching. Though historical ships and shipwrecks are never far from Cameron's mind, he also uses (at least as a starting point) sonar echoes from movies such as *The Bedford Incident, Run Silent, Run Deep,* and *The Enemy Below,* with perhaps a ping for Jules Verne. However, while the sinking of a U.S. nuclear submarine is the beginning of the story, and the question of how it sank (and if the Soviets sank it) remains at the center of the narrative, *The Abyss* rapidly morphs into something entirely different. Lindsey's sarcastic questions mark the point where all doubts of an alien presence must be abandoned, "So, raise your hand if you think that was a Russian water tentacle. Lieutenant? No, well. A breakthrough."

Interestingly, Cameron has not really changed subgenres; he has just decided to construct two fictions of nuclear disaster instead of one. The first is a nuclear submarine at the bottom of the ocean which precipitates a nuclear crisis, complete with difficulties between the crew of the hastily impressed "salvage" ship and the military contingent they are forced to take with them. The second is an advanced alien civilization that decides to take action against the dangerous follies of humanity before things get "out of hand" and their own environment, inhabited for longer than humanity has been in existence, is harmed. They seem to agree with John Connor's pet Terminator from *Terminator 2,* "It is in your nature to destroy yourselves." And, in what is very likely a nod to *The Day the Earth Stood Still* (and "Farewell to the Master," the far more sophisticated story behind it), the aliens provide humanity with a choice, "live in harmony or face obliteration."[64]

Of course, in the light of Cameron's other films with their emphasis on history and science, the way in which he will unify these two stories is immediately clear. The question about what happened to the American submarine will lead inevitably to a question about the existence of the aliens, and the answers will be the answers for everything in the movie. One of the greatest difficulties with introducing aliens into a film (especially benevolent, advanced aliens) is to limit their contact with the other characters to a manageable portion of the plot. Evil aliens, as Cameron had already demonstrated, could simply be killed. Benevolent aliens might be expected to transform human society in countless ways, while destroying the story line in the process. Instead, they deal with only one issue — thermonuclear war — while providing the most conclusive proof for any of the questions of Truth in Cameron's films.

This is perhaps necessary because *The Abyss* has no overriding truth imposed by authoritative establishing shots or a previous movie. The aliens themselves remain for most of the film nebulous (in most senses of that word) and inexplicable. They look like sea creatures (Cameron is especially good at creating such images, for obvious reasons) and angels and "non-terrestrial intelligences." But that resounding proof isn't reached without Cameron's obligatory individual struggles. Lindsey (the strong female who sees more clearly and defends her position more firmly than the other characters) discovers the aliens. Her struggle with those who will not accept the truth about them (especially Lieutenant Coffey, who, in addition to paranoia and misogyny, is suffering from depth psychosis) is Cameron's central struggle for this film, the microcosm, of which the international crisis is the macrocosm. Turned finally from his determination to attack the Russians, Coffey seizes on the aliens as his new enemy and sends an armed nuclear bomb to destroy them.

Early on in the struggle, Lindsey is supported by her crew and her estranged husband, Bud Brigman. As in *Aliens*, the small support group is enormously powerful, in getting to a correct theory of what is happening and in fighting for survival. Finally, as we have come to expect, love and sacrifice transcend hatred and stupidity to save humanity. The non-terrestrial intelligences, as Lindsey labels them, shut down their tidal waves, leaving them as a warning and not using them as a permanent solution. The reason they give for their decision is the last message Bud sent to Lindsey during his long descent into the depths, "Knew this was one way ticket but you know I had to come. Love you wife." Perhaps the aliens appreciated Cameron's most complex love story, and the fact that Bud disarmed the bomb that was meant for them probably didn't hurt either.

Real History Imagined: Back to the Source

In the light of what James Cameron had already done, and his repeated emphasis on history and science, there is nothing surprising about him making a straightforwardly historical film. The surprise is that it had taken him so long to do it. In fact, a Cameron film set in the past that would involve a shipwreck and wreck diving seems inevitable. *Titanic* was that inevitable film, complete with a wreck diving challenge, newly available technology, and a framing device sketched out by Jacques Cousteau, himself, in his dive to *Titanic*'s sister ship. In addition, there were historical and archaeological controversies to be explored, plus layers of movies and other narratives to be echoed, referenced, and contradicted, going back to Morgan Robertson's 1898 novel *The Wreck of the Titan*. It was a strangely prophetic account of "the largest craft afloat," which, while carrying too few lifeboats, struck an iceberg in the North Atlantic and sank, losing half its passengers.[65]

The love story this time is primary and tragic. As Cameron recalls pitching the film, "I said Romeo and Juliet on the *Titanic*. That's all I said."[66] The central conflict is, as usual, a struggle to discover the Truth, but that Truth emerges gradually from the experiences of Rose and Jack, just as the danger the ship is in becomes ever clearer as the voyage continues. The framing device, with Rose's much older self and the crew of the *Keldysh*, gives Cameron a historical perspective, an emotional lodestone to bring the humans in the past to life, and an investigative structure that allows the film simultaneously to tell the story, comment on it, and conduct a scholarly examination of it. The various narratives and narrators mean that no "fact" in the film is held up as absolutely true; there is room for doubt and re-evaluation. The Truth is a scholarly Truth, complex, layered, and frequently qualified, though those who are emotionally caught up in the tragedy at the end may miss the nuances.

As usual with Cameron, individuals become the focus for societal problems, the romance of Jack and Rose links one of the people least likely to be saved in the shipwreck with one of the people most likely to survive. And Rose tells us from her first voice over that there is trouble in her particular paradise, "It was the ship of dreams ... to everyone else. To me it was a slave ship, taking me back to America in chains." The final judgment in the film, the proof of what was true and what was not, is to be found in Rose's long life. Her survival is itself an answer, and her success on her own terms in a society that has for much of her life been indifferent or hostile to her is a kind of guarantee that she was right. Her position is additionally validated by the history we see in the movie and the way the crew of the *Keldysh* responds to her.

There has been much argument over the accuracy of Cameron's history in the film. Clearly, he was fanatical about details. Historian Ken Marschall, brought in by Cameron for the "making of" feature, "knew it would be ambitious, but he had no idea of the lengths to which Cameron ... would go to achieve perfection. Up until now, the high point ... had been ... *A Night to*

Remember, which Titaniacs revere for its technical accuracy. Marschall must have seen the film a hundred times. *Titanic* made *A Night to Remember* look like a child's production..."[67] A few examples make that clear: "Cameron even had them detail the ceiling... In the farthest corners of the sizable dining room, tables are set with patterned plates and silver. The ornately carved wall paneling on the grand staircase is not typical movie land plaster of Paris but oak. Real oak. Acres and acres of it, deck after deck... Newel columns are molded from real fittings lent from Marschall's collection acquired from *Titanic*'s sister ship *Olympic*."[68] No wonder one of the rumors about Cameron's film was that "the $200 million *Titanic* cost around $50 million more than the actual ship would have taken to build in 1997."[69]

There have, of course, been reviews that criticized Cameron's emphasis on the different treatment of different social classes and even, to some extent, the different behaviors of the different social classes, with many members of the upper class appearing to be unsavory, unintelligent, or uncaring. In the words of James P. Delgado, "Such reviews do an injustice to the film and to Cameron. In a larger scale, *Titanic* succeeds in a different way. It more accurately depicts what happened to the ship, based on Cameron's integration of the years of underwater survey and research and as a result of his own dives. The film also provides an accurate depiction of the forward section of the wreck as it rests on the seabed. Cameron achieved this through dive footage, models, and full-scale recreations based on the dives."[70] As Charles Pellegrino says about Cameron, "He resembled a latter-day Da Vinci whose paintings moved and sang, so it came as no surprise when, with 'a little tweaking,' he turned a movie prop into a functional robot that penetrated deeper into the *Titanic* than anything hitherto invented by the French or American navies... His results and conclusions turned out to be, archaeologically speaking, at least as important as those obtained from other expeditions sent to the *Titanic* specifically *for* archaeology."[71]

It is not, therefore, surprising that Cameron got the physical details right. In fact, his recreation was so accurate that he helped to validate one of the theories about the structure of the Grand Stairway.[72] But his depiction of the people on board may be much closer to reality than his critics realize. The account of the way the rich treated the poor has been part of the sinking of *Titanic* from the beginning. The broadside ballad "The *Titanic*," which seems to have appeared almost immediately after the shipwreck, contains the lines, "The rich had declared they would not ride with the poor,/ So they put the poor below,/ They were the first to go."[73] The French and Italian *à la carte* staff were locked in their quarters to die. "The people in the Third Class had an easier race for the boat deck than members of the *à la carte* restaurant staff, but not by a very wide margin. As it turned out, first-class dogs were afforded a greater opportunity of reaching the lifeboats than third-class passenger Rosa Abbot's children."[74] The inquiries into the causes of the shipwreck and the high casualty rate among passengers were run by the upper class. "No one would ever ask ... any ... third-class passenger to speak at the British inquiry, where it would be denied vehemently that gates had ever been locked, or that 'any attempt ... [had been made] to keep back third-class passengers.'" But robot searchers would dive deep into the wreck, "finding those murderous gates still locked."[75]

Finally but not unexpectedly, Cameron's painstakingly accurate recreation of the *Titanic* and its passengers becomes a metaphor for all the terrible disasters to come in the twentieth century and perhaps beyond. In David Simpson's words about the original catastrophe, "The sinking of the *Titanic* was a proleptic instance of a potentially global catastrophe, but one that remained historically specific and unrepeatable."[76] Or in the words of Cameron himself, "From our current vantage point at the end of this remarkable century, we can view the *Titanic* disaster as a kind of Cassandran prophecy, a foreshadowing of the perils to come that would result from our collective hubris and blind faith in technology."[77] Perhaps by the end of the film, Rose and a few others have learned that lesson, and perhaps the crew of the *Keldysh* have realized that what they found was more valuable than what they had first sought.

"They Killed Their Mother": The Pattern Transplanted

Avatar (at least the first treatment of the script) was written in 1995, but put aside because the technology it required did not yet exist, and even Cameron didn't feel up to creating it. It was then meant to be his next project after *Titanic*, but by 1998, performance capture had not yet reached the flexibility and capacity to show emotion that Cameron demanded. In his words, "I was thinking I would do another theatrical film, but I wound up doing a number of expedition projects which were documentary films, and I wound up doing four docs and six expeditions, and then I went back and I looked at *Avatar*."[78] At last, the technology could be pushed and prodded into readiness, and the movie that Cameron describes as "nearest and dearest to my heart" could go forward.[79] In explaining the importance of this film for him, he says, "If I had one more movie to make, it would have had to have been *Avatar*."[80]

As with *The Abyss*, the themes and issues in *Avatar* go back to Cameron's early fears and enthusiasms. Talking about the beginnings of his ideas for *Avatar*, he says, "When I was in high school, one of the plays that we put on was a play that I wrote called *Extinction Syndrome*, and it was about our human proclivity to destroy ourselves and the world around us."[81] Not surprisingly, *Avatar* is another Cameron story about the end of the world, but in this science fiction film, it is a world other than Earth that faces destruction (since Earth has been largely destroyed already). Cameron's new film technology gave him believable aliens, strange and beautiful inhabitants of an Eden which never fell, a garden that is part fairyland, part Atlantis, with phosphorescent creatures and plants that mirror the denizens of the deep sea even though they shimmer and shine in the air. Cameron had been thinking of them for a long time too. He says, "The Bio-Luminescent world, I wrote a script called 'Xeno Genesis' in '76 or '77. It never got made, but it had a bio-luminescent force in it."[82]

Indeed, Cameron's vision has proved so powerful that "Movie-goers have admitted being plagued by depression and suicidal thoughts at not being able to visit the planet Pandora."[83] While some of this response can safely be ascribed to the 3-D technology, making the experience seem more like life than films, much of it comes from Cameron's usual obsessive attention to detail and his clear determination to make his world seem plausible and even scientifically explicable. He says, "When you see an indigenous group, they tend to not have the big variety that we have. We're a cultural melting pot, so we have people that have developed all over the world. Whereas indigenous populations tend to not travel much so they tend to be more physically alike. So we applied those rules. The Na'vi have a very attenuated and graceful physique which is slightly pushed beyond human, wider across the shoulders, hyper-developed lats because they're supposed to be partially arboreal. Things are really thought out in this movie to an almost ridiculous level."[84]

It is standard practice for Cameron to provide pleasant alternatives to the nightmare visions of the futures he presents — the green Earth of the past contrasted with the thermonuclear devastation of the future in *The Terminator*, human families and friendships versus the monsters in *Aliens*, the alien Atlantis compared to the human strife in *The Abyss*, the glittering life of the passengers on *Titanic* and then their frozen corpses, and the memories of pre-pulse America placed side by side with the shattered present in *Dark Angel*. Perhaps a part of the power in the comparison for *Avatar* comes from the immediacy and universality of Cameron's warning. In his words, "It's something [the feeling that we're entitled to take whatever we want] that if we don't correct, we're going to drive off a cliff at ninety miles an hour with the top down and the radio playing in about ten to twenty years."[85] As one audience member put it, "I still don't really see any reason to keep doing things at all. I live in a dying world."[86] Of course, Cameron's actual message is that you should stop before you drive off the cliff, don't just get discouraged because you're in the car. And, of course, there are plenty of people who see nothing wrong with convertibles. As Cameron tells it, "When I turned the script in to the studio,

I got a lot of pushback along the line of you know, 'Can we cut down on the New Age, hippie, tree-hugger bullshit?' (From a trusted friend and confidant of mine at the studio.) And I said, theoretically we could, but then I wouldn't want to make the film."[87]

In fact, the science fiction trappings of space ships and energy weapons aside, Cameron seemed to be making a movie that went against his personal beliefs and his past practice of filmmaking. On the surface of the plot (and the planet), *Avatar* seems to be a fantasy film, with sets that many directors of *A Midsummer Night's Dream* would sell their souls for — or at least the souls of their set designers. But while Pandora is a long way from Kansas, it is not Oz either. While there are plenty of tree huggers, there is no mysticism, New Age or otherwise. Cameron's usual pattern of building one of the central conflicts of each film around the struggle to discover the Truth is just as much a part of *Avatar* as it is of *The Terminator*, and the proof will meet equally high historical and scientific standards. Indeed, if anything, those standards are higher in *Avatar* because at last Cameron has found a way to include a group of scientists in one of his films.

As he almost always does, Cameron built a movie that resonates at many frequencies and taps into many traditions. He says "it is very much like" several films, including *Dances with Wolves, At Play in the Fields of the Lord*, and *The Emerald Forest*, though obviously he is talking more about affinities and categories than direct plot links.[88] Before its release Cameron described *Avatar* as "an old-fashioned jungle adventure with an environmental conscience. It aspires to a mythic level of storytelling."[89] He was, he said, drawing on "pulp classics like Edgar Rice Burroughs and ... even higher end classics, whether it's Rudyard Kipling or, you know, H. Rider Haggard and that sort of thing but kind of manly adventure where a hero goes to a foreign culture and has to learn their ways and see as they see."[90] That allowed Cameron to tap into Iraq and other colonial issues, and to bring in corporate and government involvement.[91] Ultimately, Cameron's manly adventure became the kind of film he almost always makes. As he puts it, "Of course, it turned into a chick flick."[92]

The history war in *Avatar*, the struggle to discover the Truth, is a three-sided exploration for the first time in Cameron's films. *The Abyss* has humans and aliens who must make correct judgments about each other, but on Pandora, there are humans, Na'vi, and Eywa. The humans, especially Jake and Grace, must correctly interpret the data on Pandora and act accordingly. They are helped by the group of scientists, who side with the Na'vi, and by some of the military. The Na'vi (especially Neytiri) have a more difficult task — to evaluate the danger of the invaders correctly but also to judge individual humans fairly. Eywa, who is herself the planet's central mystery, will draw the correct conclusions from the data she has gathered, and then take the appropriate action in this action film to destroy the invaders.

Grace, as the conscientious scientist, sets the parameters, "All right, look — I don't have the answers yet, I'm just now starting to even frame the questions. What we think we know — is that there's some kind of electrochemical communication between the roots of the trees. Like the synapses between neurons. Each tree has ten to the fourth connections to the trees around it, and there are ten to the twelfth trees on Pandora... That's more connections than the human brain. You get it? It's a network — a global network. And the Na'vi can access it — they can upload and download data — memories — at sites like the one you destroyed."

If that proves to be true (and it does), then the superiority of human culture to that of the "blue monkeys" as Selfridge calls the Na'vi, is in doubt. Eywa, whom Cameron calls "the goddess, the female, the female spirit if you will," has greater computing power than the human brain, a remarkably comprehensive set of biological connections, and, in all probability, an unimaginably long life span.[93] And, of course, on a planet and in a story created by James Cameron, none of that has to be taken on faith. Grace, the scientist, the skeptic, now supposedly joined to Eywa, tells us with her last human breath, "I'm with her Jake — (an amazed whisper) — she's real."[94]

Nor is that the end of the proofs both about and for Eywa. When he is linked to her, Jake tells her, "If Grace is there with you — look in her memories — she can show you the world we come from. There's no green there. They killed their Mother, and they're gonna do the same thing here." Arguably his most important function in the story is not his heroics in battle but the courage he displays in condemning his own people and helping to convince Eywa that the enemies she faces are evil. The war for the Truth that Jake fights is, as we expect from Cameron, more important than the actual war that will follow. Without this victory, Jake and his army would be destroyed, a fact he knows only too well. When he asks Eywa for help, he makes something very clear that at least a few of the film's critics have missed. This is not a story of a white man becoming a messiah and leading a native population to success.[95] He asks, "Look, you chose me for somethin.' And I'll stand and fight, you know I will. But I could use a little help here."

It's more than clear both from what Jake says and from what actually happens in the battle that the army he has managed to raise is no match for the high tech military they face. If the arrival of Eywa's forces feels like one of those last-minute cavalry charges from adventure films, that's exactly what it is. Left unsupported any longer, the Na'vi would have suffered extraordinary losses and then near-total defeat. Plus, of course, Eywa's rescue of Jake, Neytiri, and much of the rest of the army is the most conclusive proof for the validity of a particular position that Cameron has offered since the tidal waves and giant ship in *The Abyss*. Within the world of Pandora, there is a living presence, a planetary mind, a kind of goddess and super computer. Science and the evidence of our own observations (in 3-D) say so. There is also a love story here that suggests hope and even the possibility (hinted at, not spelled out) of something better for humans. In that sense, Jake is not a savior for the Na'vi, he is a promise of redemption for humanity.[96]

Perhaps that is ultimately what the pattern behind Cameron's movies is about — a promise of redemption for humanity, not through fantasy or mythology, though they may be found along the way, but through the asking of honest questions and the finding of accurate answers. In history, in science, in Truth, and in the telling of stories that contain them all, Cameron suggests, is the salvation of the world, which is much in need of saving, teetering as it does on the edge of many dooms. Maybe his warnings will be heard and his hard-bitten optimism will be (after a last-minute rescue or two) justified.

NOTES

1. Orson Welles and Peter Bogdanovich, *This Is Orson Welles* (New York: HarperCollins Publishers, 1992), 62.

2. Bernard Weinraub, "'Postman' Sinks; 'Titanic' Sails," *New York Times*, January 5, 1998. www.nytimes.com/1998/01/05/movies/postman-sinks-titanic-sails.html?ref=james_cameron& pagewanted=print

3. As Cameron notes in the documentary *Explorers*, "*Titanic* is just about death. That's what it's about."

4. James Cameron, interviewed by James Lipton, *Inside the Actors Studio*, Bravo TV, March 8, 2010.

5. Christopher Heard, *Dreaming Aloud: The Life and Films of James Cameron* (Toronto, Ontario: Doubleday Canada Limited, 1998), 81.

6. David Simpson, "Tourism and Titanomania," *Critical Inquiry* 25, no. 4 (1999): 683.

7. Edward Hallett Carr, *What Is History? The George Macaulay Trevelyan Lectures Delivered at the University of Cambridge January–March 1961* (New York: Vintage Books, 1961), 161.

8. Simpson, "Tourism and Titanomania," 683. As Svetlana Boym wrote in *The Future of Nostalgia*, "Nostalgic longing was defined by loss of the original object of desire ... in the West objects of the past are everywhere for sale. The past eagerly cohabits with the present. Americans are supposed to be antihistorical, yet the souvenirization of the past and obsession with roots and identity here are ubiquitous. One could speak about "inculcation of nostalgia' into merchandise as a marketing strategy that tricks consumers into missing what they haven't lost. Arjun Appadurai defines it as 'ersatz nostaligia' or armchair nostalgia, 'nostalgia without lived experience or collective historical memory'" (Svetlana Boym, *The Future of Nostalgia* [New York: Basic Books, 2001], 38).

9. Cameron interviewed by Lipton, *Inside the Actors Studio*.

10. Marc Shapiro, *James Cameron: An Unauthorized Biography of the Filmmaker* (Los Angeles: Renaissance Books, 2000), 31.

11. Rebecca Keegan, *The Futurist: The Life and Films of James Cameron* (New York: Crown Publishers, 2009), 7.

12. Ibid.

13. Heard, *Dreaming Aloud*, 6.

14. Cameron interviewed by Lipton, *Inside the Actors Studio*.

15. Ibid.

16. Ibid.

17. *Explorers: From the Titanic to the Moon*, directed by Jean-Christophe Jeauffre (2006; Sherman Oaks, CA: Go Planet, 2002), DVD.

18. Paula Parisi, *Titanic and the Making of James Cameron: The Inside Story of the Three-Year Adventure That Rewrote Motion Picture History* (New York: Newmarket Press, 1998), 47.

19. Ibid.

20. Ibid.

21. *"Sanctum." Netflix*, Access date, November 22, 2010, http://www.netflix.com/Wi Search?oq=&vl=Sanctum&search_submit=.

22. *James Cameron's Expedition: Bismarck*, directed by James Cameron and Gary Johnstone (2002; Silver Spring, MD: Discovery Channel Pictures, 2002), DVD. The nature of the underwater experience undoubtedly helped to shape Cameron's notion of personal responsibility and his belief that questions have clear, provable, and sometimes deadly answers. In *Explorers*, he says,"When you're scuba diving, you're really on your own. If you make a mistake, you'll die."

23. Jeauffre, *Explorers*.

24. Keegan, *The Futurist*, 229.

25. Charles Pellegrino, *Ghosts of the Titanic* (New York: William and Morrow, 2000), 128.

26. In one way or another, Cameron has been involved with the following documentaries: *The Alien Saga* (2001), *James Cameron's Expedition: Bismarck* (2002), *Volcanoes of the Deep Sea* (2003), *Ghosts of the Abyss* (2003), *The Cutting Edge: The Magic of Movie Editing* (2004), *Aliens of the Deep* (2005), *Tony Robinson's Titanic Adventure* (2005), *The Exodus Decoded* (2006), *Explorers: From the Titanic to the Moon* (2006), *The Lost Tomb of Jesus* (2007), and *Mars Rising* (2007). Soon to come supposedly are 3-D documentaries about a tribe in Brazil (see note 41) and the journey of the next Mars Rover (David Lane, "James Cameron is Taking 3-D to Mars! Helping to Build 3-D Camera for Next Mars Mission in 2011." *(Collider DotCom*, http://collider.com/james-cameron-is-taking-3d-to-mars-helping-to-build-3d-camera-for-next-mars-mission-in-2011/23531/ April 29, 2010).

27. Spence D., "An Interview with James Cameron," *IGN*, 10 April 2003, http://movies.ign.com/articles/393/393141p1.html.

28. Cameron interviewed by Lipton, *Inside the Actors Studio*.

29. *"Calypso's* Search for the *Britannic" Jacques Cousteau Odyssey* (1977; Los Angeles, CA: Cousteau Society, KCET, The Greek Film Centre, French Television [TF-1], Bavaria Atelier GMBH, 1977), TV.

30. Ibid.

31. Ibid.

32. Ibid.

33. Ibid.

34. Ibid.

35. Ibid.

36. Cousteau's documentaries were "Dedicated to Those Who Fight to Preserve Life on Our Planet." *"Calypso's* Search for the *Britannic" Jacques Cousteau Odyssey.*

37. David Dowling, *Fictions of Nuclear Disaster* (Iowa City: University of Iowa Press, 1987), 11.

38. Paul M. Sammon, "Mothers with Guns," in *Aliens: The Illustrated Screenplay* ed. Paul M. Sammon (London: Orion, 2001), 10.

39. Cameron interviewed by Lipton, *Inside the Actors Studio*.

40. Keegan, *The Futurist*, 1–2.

41. Ibid., 2.

42. Gerard J. DeGroot, *The Bomb: A Life* (Cambridge, MA: Harvard University Press, 2005), 64–65.

43. Priscilla J. McMillan, *The Ruin of J. Robert Oppenheimer and the Birth of the Modern Arms Race* (New York: Viking, 2005), 3.

44. Indeed, one often leads directly to another. The Documentary Blog reports on the latest example, "James Cameron has announced his next project and it's not Avatar 2 — or maybe it is, in a roundabout way. The film will be a documentary about the Xikrin-Kayapó tribe in Brazil and their fight to prevent construction of a hydroelectric dam. The tribe lives along the Xingu River, which is a tributary of the Amazon. Campaigners against the dam say that the required flooding will make the land uninhabitable for the tribe, displacing about 12,000 people and destroying the fishing industry" (Charlotte, "James Cameron to Make 3-D Documentary." *The Documentary Blog* http://www.thedocumentaryblog.com/index.php/2010/09/07/james-cameron-to-make-3d-documentary/).

45. Alexandra Keller, *James Cameron* (New York: Routledge, 2006), 105.

46. James Cameron, foreword to *Ghosts of the Titanic*, Charles Pellegrino (New York: William Morrow, 2000), vii.

47. Not everyone enjoys thinking about these complexities. In the words of one of the Sara Pezzinis from the "Periculum" episode of *Witchblade*, "Yeah, yeah, I saw *The Terminator*. It made my head hurt."

48. Robert A. Heinlein, *6xH: Six Stories by Robert A. Heinlein* (New York: Pyramid Books, 1961), 143–156.

49. James Cameron, foreword to *Ghosts of the Titanic,* vii.

50. Paul M. Sammon, "Mothers with Guns," 17, 18.

51. Ibid., 18.

52. First published in *Astounding* in March 1942 in Asimov's story "Runaround" (Isaac Asimov, *The Complete Robot* [New York: Doubleday & Company, Inc., 1982], 219).

53. Isaac Asimov, *Robot Visions* (New York: ROC, 1990), 6–8.

54. Walter Hill and David Giler, "Alien (1979) Movie Script," *Screenplays for You*. Access date, December 5, 2010, http://sfy.ru/?script=alien.

55. Bernard Shaw, *Complete Plays with Prefaces* Volume III (New York: Dodd, Mead & Company, 1963), 338.

56. David Brin, *Otherness* (New York: Bantam Books, 1994), 265.

57. Paul M. Sammon, "Mothers with Guns," 19.

58. Ripley deliberately leaves Jones behind when she sets out for what may be another encounter with the creature she met in *Alien*, which was undoubtedly a wise choice for the cat. The tagline for the first movie was "In space, no one can hear you scream." *Cats in Space*, edited by Bill Fawcett, has as the tagline on its cover an equally troubling circumstance, "In space, no one can hear you meow."

59. Keegan, *The Futurist*, 81.

60. Ibid., 82.

61. Jeauffre, *Explorers*.

62. Keegan, *The Futurist*, 88.

63. Ibid., 105.

64. Ibid., 86.

65. Morgan Robertson, *The Wreck of the Titan or, Futility* (Rahway, NJ: The Quinn and Boden Co. Press, 1912).

66. Cameron interviewed by Lipton, *Inside the Actors Studio*.

67. Paula Parisi, *Titanic and the Making of James Cameron*, 127.

68. Ibid.

69. James Inverne, *Inverne's Stage & Screen Trivia: The Greatest Entertainment Trivia Book Ever ...* (New York: MJF Books, 2004), 18.

70. James P. Delgado, "Titanic," in *Box Office Archaeology: Refining Hollywood's Portrayals of the Past*, ed. Julie M. Schablitsky (Walnut Creek, CA: Left Coast Press, 2007), 83.

71. Pellegrino, *Ghosts of the Titanic*, 127.

72. Ibid., 174.

73. Albert B. Friedman, *The Penguin Book of Folk Ballads of the English-Speaking World* (New York: Penguin Books, 1977), 323.

74. Pellegrino, *Ghosts of the Titanic*, 70.

75. Ibid., 71.

76. Simpson, "Tourism and Titanomania," 694.

77. Cameron, foreword to *Ghosts of the Titanic*, vii.

78. Cameron interviewed by Lipton, *Inside the Actors Studio*.

79. Ibid.

80. Ibid.

81. Ibid.

82. James Cameron, interview by John Landau, http://www.comicbookmovie.com/scifi_comic_book_movies/news/?a=9657 , August 29, 2009.

83. Liz Thomas, "The *Avatar* Effect: Movie-goers Feel Depressed and Even Suicidal at Not Being Able to Visit Utopian Alien Planet," *Mail Online*. January 12, 2010, http://www.dailymail.co.uk/news/article-1242409/The-Avatar-effect-Movie-goers-feel-depressed-suicidal-able-visit-utopian-alien-planet.html.printingPage=true *Two and a Half Men* provides a possible example of a sitcom imitating real life when Charlie Harper breaks up with his girlfriend (played by Jenny McCarthy) at least in part because he was fantasizing about someone else while they were making love, "I pretended you were the big blue Chick from *Avatar*" ("Chocolate Diddlers or My Puppy's Dead." Directed by James Widdoes [2010; Chuck Lorre Productions], TV).

84. Mekado Murphy, "A Few Questions for James Cameron," *Carpetbagger—The Hollywood Blog of The New York Times*. December 21, 2009, http://carpetbagger.blogs.nytimes.com/2009/12/21/a-few-questions-for-james-cameron/?pagemode=print.

85. Cameron interviewed by Lipton, *Inside the Actors Studio*.

86. Thomas, "The *Avatar* Effect."

87. Cameron interviewed by Lipton, *Inside the Actors Studio*.

88. James Cameron, interview by Geoff Boucher, *Los Angeles Times*, http://herocomplex.latimes.com/2009/08/14/james-cameron-the-new-trek-rocks-but-transformers-is-gimcrackery/, April 14, 2009.

89. "James Cameron: King of All He Surveys," *The Independent*. December 19, 2006, http://www.independent.co.uk/arts-entertainment/films/features/james-cameron-king-of-all-he-surveys-429268.html.

90. Cameron interviewed by Lipton, *Inside the Actors Studio*.

91. The entity which runs Pandora is the RDA. "The largest single nongovernmental organization in the human universe, the Resources Development Administration (RDA) has monopoly rights to all products shipped, derived, or developed from Pandora or any other off-Earth location" (Maria Wilhelm and Dirk Mathison, *James Cameron's Avatar: An Activist Survival Guide* [New York: itbooks, 2009], 147).

92. Cameron interviewed by Lipton, *Inside the Actors Studio*.

93. Ibid.

94. James Cameron, "*Avatar* Screenplay," *The Internet Movie Script Database*. Access date, December 5, 2010, http://www.imsdb.com/scripts/Avatar.html.

95. Because Jake is presumed to be the necessary savior of the Na'vi, Cameron has been accused of racism by both liberals and conservatives. Clearly, this is a misreading of the film's plot and particularly of the events in the final battle. However, in his choice of story type and literary echoes, Cameron may have contributed to the misunderstandings or at least have provided them with a congenial environment in which to grow. In the words of Brian Taves, "The mixing of seemingly incompatible liberal and conservative ideas that is typical of adventure (and of Hollywood films generally) is nowhere more apparent than in its depiction of colonialism" (Brian Taves, *Romance of Adventure: The Genre of Historical Adventure Movies* [Jackson, Mississippi: University Press of Mississippi, 1993], 172). Alas, not everyone who went to see *Avatar* left his or her expectations and prejudices behind.

96. It is not accidental that Cameron chose a Marine for that task. He says, "My younger brother was a Marine, and I happen to have a great deal of respect for Marines and how they

think and how they act, so Jake to me was the epitome of that, that Marine Corps spirit" (Cameron interviewed by Lipton, *Inside the Actors Studio*).

WORKS CITED

Asimov, Isaac. *Robot Visions*. New York: ROC, 1990.
Boym, Svetlana. *The Future of Nostalgia*. New York: Basic Books, 2001.
Brin, David. *Otherness*. New York: Bantam Books, 1994.
Cameron, James. "*Avatar* Screenplay." *The Internet Movie Script Database*. Access date, December 5, 2010, http://www.imsdb.com/scripts/Avatar.html.
_____. *Comicbookmovie.com*. By John Landau. http://www.comicbookmovie.com/scifi_comic_book_movies/news/?a=9657. August, 29, 2009.
_____. Foreword to *Ghosts of the Titanic*. Charles Pellegrino. New York: William Morrow, 2000.
_____. *Los Angeles Times. Com*. By Geoff Boucher. http://herocomplex.latimes.com/2009/08/10/james-cameron-on-avatar-like-the matrix-this-movie-is-a-doorway/. August, 10, 2009.
Carr, Edward Hallett. *What Is History? The George Macaulay Trevelyan Lectures Delivered at the University of Cambridge January–March 1961*. New York: Vintage Books, 1967.
Charlotte. "James Cameron to Make 3-D Documentary." *The Documentary Blog*. September 7, 2010.
D., Spence. "An Interview with James Cameron." *IGN*. 10 April 2003, http://movies.ign.com/articles/393/393141p1.html.
DeGroot, Gerard J. *The Bomb: A Life*. Cambridge, MA: Harvard University Press, 2005.
Delgado, James P. "Titanic." In *Box Office Archaeology: Refining Hollywood's Portrayals of the Past*. Edited by Julie M. Schablitsky, 83. Walnut Creek, CA: Left Coast Press, 2007.
Dowling, David. *Fictions of Nuclear Disaster*. Iowa City: University of Iowa Press, 1987.
Friedman, Albert B. *The Penguin Book of Folk Ballads of the English-Speaking World*. New York: Penguin Books, 1977.
Heard, Christopher. *Dreaming Aloud: The Life and Films of James Cameron*. Toronto, Ontario: Doubleday Canada, 1998.
Heinlein, Robert A. *6xH: Six Stories by Robert A. Heinlein*. New York: Pyramid Books, 1961.
Hill, Walter, and David Giler. "*Alien* (1979) Movie Script." *Screenplays for You*. Access date, December 5, 2010, http://sfy.ru/?script=alien.
Inverne, James. *Inverne's Stage & Screen Trivia: The Greatest Entertainment Trivia Book Ever...* New York: MJF Books, 2004.
"James Cameron: King of All He Surveys." *The Independent*. December 19, 2006. http://www.independent.co.uk/arts-entertainment/films/features/james-cameron-king-of-all-he-surveys-429268.html.
Keegan, Rebecca. *The Futurist: The Life and Films of James Cameron*. New York: Crown, 2009.
Keller, Alexandra. *James Cameron*. New York: Routledge, 2006.
Lane, David. "James Cameron Is Taking 3-D to Mars! Helping to Build 3-D Camera for Next Mars Mission in 2011." *Collider DotCom*. April 29, 2010. http://collider.com/james-cameron-is-taking-3d-to-mars-helping-to-build-3d-camera-for-next-mars-mission-in-2011/23531/.
McMillan, Priscilla J. *The Ruin of J. Robert Oppenheimer and the Birth of the Modern Arms Race*. New York: Viking, 2005.
Murphy, Mekado. "A Few Questions for James Cameron." *Carpetbagger—The Hollywood Blog of The New York Times*. December 21, 2009. http://carpetbagger.blogs.nytimes.com/2009/12/21/a-few-questions-for-james-cameron/?pagemode=print.
Parisi, Paula. *Titanic and the Making of James Cameron: The Inside Story of the Three-Year Adventure That Rewrote Motion Picture History*. New York: Newmarket Press, 1998.
Pellegrino, Charles. *Ghosts of the Titanic*. New York: William and Morrow, 2000.

Robertson, Morgan. *The Wreck of the Titan or, Futility*. Rahway, NJ: Quinn and Boden, 1912. http://www.gutenberg.org/cache/epub/24880/pg24880.txt.

Sammon, Paul M. "Mothers with Guns," in *Aliens: The Illustrated Screenplay* ed. Paul M. Sammon, 10. London: Orion, 2001.

"*Sanctum*." *Netflix*. Access date, November 22, 2010, http://www.netflix.com/WiSearch?oq=& vl=Sanctum&search_submit.

Shapiro, Marc. *James Cameron: An Unauthorized Biography of the Filmmaker*. Los Angeles: Renaissance Books, 2000.

Shaw, Bernard. *Complete Plays with Prefaces* Volume III. New York: Dodd, Mead, 1963.

Simpson, David. "Tourism and Titanomania." *Critical Inquiry* 25, no. 4 (1999): 683.

Taves, Brian. *Romance of Adventure: The Genre of Historical Adventure Movies*. Jackson: University Press of Mississippi, 1993.

Thomas, Liz. "The *Avatar* Effect: Movie-goers Feel Depressed and Even Suicidal at Not Being Able to Visit Utopian Alien Planet." *Mail Online*. January 12, 2010, http://www.dailymail. co.uk/news/article-1242409/The-Avatar-effect-Movie-goers-feel-depressed-suicidal-able-visit-utopian-alien-planet.html?printingPage=true.

Weinraub, Bernard. "'Postman' Sinks; 'Titanic' Sails," *New York Times*, Jan. 5, 1998. www.ny times.com/1998/01/05/movies/postman-sinks-titanic-sails.html?ref=james_cameron&page wanted=print.

Welles, Orson, and Peter Bogdanovich. *This Is Orson Welles*. New York: HarperCollins, 1992.

Wilhelm, Maria, and Dirk Mathison. *James Cameron's Avatar: An Activist Survival Guide*. New York: itbooks, 2009.

FILMS AND TELEVISION CITED

The Abyss: Special Edition. DVD. Directed by James Cameron. 1989; Beverly Hills, CA: Twentieth Century–Fox, 2002.

The Alien Saga. Directed by Brent Zacky. AMC, 2002.

Aliens: Collector's Edition. DVD. Directed by James Cameron. 1986; Los Angeles, CA:Twentieth Century–Fox, 2003.

Aliens of the Deep. Directed by James Cameron. Walt Disney Pictures, 2005.

Avatar. Directed by James Cameron. Twentieth Century–Fox, 2009.

"*Calypso*'s Search for the *Britannic*" *Jacques Cousteau Odyssey*. 1977. Los Angeles,CA: Cousteau Society, KCET, The Greek Film Centre, French Television [TF-1] Bavaria Atelier GMBH, 1977.

Cameron, James. *Inside the Actors Studio*. By James Lipton. Bravo TV, March 8, 2010.

The Cutting Edge: The Magic of Movie Editing. Directed by Wendy Apple. BBC, 2004.

The Exodus Decoded. Directed by Simcha Jacobovici. Associated Producers, 2006.

Explorers: From the Titanic to the Moon. Directed by Jean-Christophe Jeauffre. Go Planet, 2006.

Ghosts of the Abyss. DVD. Directed by James Cameron. 2003; Burbank, CA: Walt DisneyPictures, 2003.

James Cameron's Dark Angel. DVD. Created by James Cameron and Charles H. Eglee. 2000; Los Angeles, CA: Twentieth Century–Fox, 2000.

James Cameron's Expedition: Bismark. DVD. Directed by James Cameron and Gary Johnstone. 2002; Silver Spring, MD: Discovery Channel Pictures, 2002.

The Lost Tomb of Jesus. Directed by Simcha Jacobovici. Discovery Channel, 2007.

Mars Rising. DVD. Directed by Michael Jorgensen et al. 2007; Marseille, France: 13 Productions, 2007.

The Terminator. DVD. Directed by James Cameron. 1984; London, UK: Hemdale Films, 2006.

Terminator 2: Judgment Day. DVD. Directed by James Cameron. 1991; USA: Carolco Pictures, 1991.

Titanic: Special Collector's Edition. DVD. Directed by James Cameron. 1997; Los Angeles,CA: Twentieth Century–Fox, 1997.

Tony Robinson's Titanic Adventure. Directed by Mel Morpeth. Earthship Productions, 2005.

Two and a Half Men. "Chocolate Diddlers or My Puppy's Dead." Directed by James Widdoes. 2010. Chuck Lorre Productions, 13 December 2010.

Volcanoes of the Deep Sea. Directed by Stephen Low. The Stephen Low Company, 2003.

"She's a goddamn liar": Perspectives on the Truth in *Aliens* and *Titanic*

Andrew B. R. Elliott

When it comes to re-imagining our historical past through film, and the frequent accusations of revisionism involved in the process, James Cameron is perhaps understandably not the first name that springs to mind. Far more prevalent among the history and film debates are names like Oliver Stone, Ridley Scott and Steven Spielberg, reaching all the way back to Cecil B. DeMille and D.W. Griffiths in the Hollywood tradition, who stand alongside a plethora of others outside of it, ranging from Eisenstein to Ozu, Sembane to Rossellini and many, many more besides. Yet as Ace Pilkington's essay in this collection has shown, this in no way means that Cameron's oeuvre has no place among these history wars; even if he is not consciously addressing the arguments over historical accuracy, his work clearly reflects a complex relationship with history and certainly a recognition of the flawed nature of representation, truth and credibility. The obvious candidates here are of course *Titanic* and *Avatar*, which together offer intriguing alternatives to established history, proposing provocative narratives which run counter to accepted versions of events. The lived reality of the *RMS Titanic* was, Cameron proposes, "quite different" from Bodine's computer simulation of it; though Pandora belongs to the realms of fantasy, the clear parallels with Western supremacy allow the perspectives of the Na'vi to express a sinister underside both to colonial expansion and to current incursions in the Middle East, and their name ("the people") suggests a privileged perspective of history "from below."[1]

In part, such a challenge to the master narratives of History — in this case the "History with a capital H" to which Rosenstone refers — chimes neatly with the core tenets of postmodernism, which like Rose Dawson, Ellen Ripley and *Avatar*'s Neytiri assert that there *is* no single truth, only different ways of seeing.[2] *In extremis* the removal of grand narratives contains a concomitant freedom with which films like *Rashomon*, *The Usual Suspects* and *Memento* play to extraordinary effect, producing fragmented "perspectives on the truth," and which each serve to undermine the possibility of one, single truth. However, working not only within the Hollywood tradition but at the very top of the studios' A-List, Cameron is to some extent denied this narrative ambiguity, and his legendary budgets demand that he appeal to the widest possible audience base in order to recoup the initial outlay. Such a necessarily broad appeal requires him, then, to stick to what Bordwell and Thompson have defined the Classical Hollywood tradition (that is, that the film has a clear beginning, a strong middle and an unambiguous resolution) in order to attract sufficient viewers to warrant the massive financial investments.

Does this, therefore, mean that Cameron is simply a paint-by-numbers director? Not necessarily. What I intend to show here is that Cameron's ability as a director and screenwriter is such that he manages to incorporate fragmentary perspectives on the truth within the classical Hollywood narrative, yet without allowing postmodern narratives full sway. In its simplest terms, my argument is that Cameron consistently offers us a choice of perspectives which are equally valid, but which are ultimately reconciled by an underlying truth which confirms one or other of these perspectives and offers a clear narrative resolution. On the one hand, I will argue that in both *Titanic* and *Aliens* he enables — and in some cases forces — character empathy in order to frame one character's perspective, even if such a perspective runs counter to given truths. Nevertheless, in order to avoid those kinds of fragmented and inconclusive narratives which postmodernity offers, he places these against a firmly established and infrangible Real (yes, with a capital R) which is able ultimately to reconcile these seemingly incompatible perspectives into a conclusive ending through which the truth is revealed. In *Titanic*, though Rose, Brock Lovett, Lewis Bodine and the representatives of the White Star company may each have their own viewpoint on the events of 1912, the whole is underpinned by Cameron's inviolable sense of the Real — that there is a ship at the bottom of the sea, the wreck of which he has personally observed — which will ultimately provide the key to reconcile each perspective. Following this schema, then, I will first demonstrate how such perspectives on the truth function within Cameron's films, relating it to historiography, before moving on in the second section to examine how he uses what I have termed a "rhetoric of the Real" to negotiate his way through these conflicting truths.

Perspectives on the Truth

The first question which my title poses, of course, concerns the seeming paradox of the terms "perspectives on the truth." Put simply, for a society that is accustomed to a strict dialectical opposition between "pure" truth and lies, how can there be any perspective on the truth other than the true one? Surely if there *are* different versions, this is sufficient to cast doubt on the single truth of the matter?

A simple demonstration of different truths which are equally valid can be found in the world of advertising — or specifically in the world of branding. According to an experiment undertaken by the American Color Institute in the 1950s, a number of housewives were each given 3 different brands of laundry detergent to test. Among their reports were various examples of defects (one was too harsh and had ruined clothes, another too weak and left clothes gray, etc) and drawbacks discovered by the users; the punch line being of course the revelation that the three detergents differed only in package design, but in fact, contained exactly the same powder.[3]

Fast-forward to the modern day, and we can see a situation of much greater complexity in which users of detergents will tell a similar range of stories about how Brand A was too harsh, Brand B too weak, and so on, which may be contradicted by another user's experience: in this more complex environment, neither is true, yet neither is a lie. Thus, in reporting the truth of each brand, each detergent user will construct a tale and full back story according to what he or she *believes* they have seen. This belief is crucial, since by a long process of extraction we come eventually to realize that in a world with multiple truths, it is precisely our belief in the truth of a given perspective which distinguishes it from others which, by elimination, we therefore perceive to be lies. Consequently, when everything is a lie from some viewpoint or another, the truth becomes simply that which is most *credible*.

If I may be permitted a broad generalization here for the sake of brevity, this same metaphor may be extended to history itself. A great deal of work in historiography in recent years has gone to show that each writer of history plays a part in establishing a narrative formed by piecing together the facts, rather than revealing the inherent truth of the narrative. This can even be taken to extreme positions by which, as Paul Veyne, argues, even the facts themselves are subject to doubt, as is the choice of which facts to use, meaning that "history is that which we choose."[4] Just as *Titanic*'s Lewis Bodine, a relentless pragmatist, ignores the romantic elements of *RMS Titanic*'s maiden voyage in favor of the facts, Rose's inverse view of it is similarly predicated on a simple choice; to discuss the atmosphere, the smell of the paint and the emotional resonance of the ship's demise, the elements which Julian Stringer calls "the patina of perfect images."[5] It is only because she has *chosen* this perspective that she is able to say that "the reality was quite different," since as the film unfolds we learn that Bodine's perspective was just as true as Rose's — if not more so.

I have shown elsewhere, too, that these tenets of historiography in fact accord well with the basic principles of cinematography, a process which takes a series of isolated perspectives — what would normally be regarded as the facts — and combines them together to convince the viewer of their truth.[6] What I tried to show was that when viewing a film the viewer is constantly comparing these facts with their own experiences, to the extent that the greater the resonance between the on-screen facts of the film and the off-screen beliefs of the viewer, the greater the belief in the "truth" of the narrative being told. In other words, *if what we see on screen does not contradict what we believe to be the truth, we are likely to perceive it as true.* This is explicitly noticeable in the case of, say, the highly contentious Holocaust deniers, who put together a controversial perspective on a highly visible and well-known historical event which, however we might feel about that perspective, is often based on facts (though, of course *which* facts they select is the major issue here). When they put forward a theory (their own perspective on the truth) based on these isolated facts about the Holocaust, they clash violently with our own series of facts, and thus become at best ridiculous, and at worst downright offensive, ways of rewriting history.

To give an example of how this works in practice, such a position is demonstrated by the conflict between Ripley and the board of Weyland-Yutani, in which Ripley puts forward what, on the surface, seems to be a ludicrous and somewhat fanciful account of what happened on LV-426; in many ways, or in many other films (such as *Conspiracy Theory* or *K-PAX*), we might be inclined initially to share the skepticism of the executive board, because the story relies on "facts" which we do not possess, and which we must make a leap of faith to believe. However, because the viewer has either seen the original *Alien* or at least knows enough about the first film to know that Ripley's account — however preposterous — is true, the experiences recounted match our own "memories" and thus seem more credible. In this way, we the audience have been complicit in constructing the truth of the perspective in much the same way as the historian pieces together facts into a narrative of his or her own devising.

Perspectives in Cameron's Films

Perspectives on the truth, therefore, cannot necessarily be dismissed as lies, nor can the existence of multiple perspectives be taken as a de facto indication that one of them is necessarily flawed, since each is offering their own narrative based on what has or has not been seen. What we are faced with in Cameron's films, then, is a series of "true lies," in which the surface signs offer one immediate reading, but the inclusion of extra perspectives allow quite a different one altogether. Such tensions are brought to the surface in Cameron's 1994 film *True Lies,* in which the hero, Harry Tasker (Arnold Schwarzenegger), appears to friends and family as a nondescript computer salesman, whose frequent business trips are construed as matrimonial and familial neglect, leading his wife Helen to castigate his "boring life" and over-zealous attachment to his mundane work. On the contrary, we as an audience have already been privy to Tasker's "computer conference" in the opening sequence of the film: it is an archetypal Cameron scene in which Tasker's secret agent scales the side of a Swiss château, retrieves data using sophisticated technology, speaks at least 5 different languages, while finding time to tango with the beautiful and exotic Tia Carrere, blow up a guard-house and dodge machine-gun fire while escaping dramatically through the Swiss Alps. To the viewer, then, Tasker seems to be the archetypal 007, free from marital attachment and at liberty to risk his life on a daily basis. Each side of Tasker's character is thus a perspective, yet *neither is true*; the personae actually represent "the schizophrenic nature of marriage" (about which Cameron himself ought to know a thing or two).[7] In this way, we can immediately see that Helen's perspective is not wholly false, since it is a well-crafted persona which offers no evidence of falsehood. What is particularly strange is that at no point are we offered a staple trope in 1990s romantic comedies — Helen's suspicions that her husband is having an affair. We may take this as evidence *in absentia* that Harry's secret double life is sufficiently concealed; in this purely superficial sense of perspectives, it is therefore true.

Aliens

It is, however, one of Cameron's first feature films which offers some of the clearest examples of the construction of perspective. In *Aliens,* Cameron was faced from the outset with a tension familiar to many historical filmmakers: there is in existence a world (in this case the world of *Alien*) which is held up in some ways to be the original, and therefore the "true" world, and whose narrative logic must be upheld, while at the same time extending this world to allow for a commercially viable and narratively interesting drama. Despite the demise of the entire crew of the *Nostromo,* there were already a number of certain fixed characters or character-types (Ripley, the corporation, the aliens themselves, the planet LV-426, and even Jones the cat), which must somehow be dealt with in the sequel, yet whose characteristics have already been, to a greater or lesser extent, fixed. Cameron's rewriting of that world, then, merits a great deal of respect, since it provides a fresh perspective on that original world while respecting its rigid boundaries: instead of inventing new alien foes for Ripley to fight, Cameron injects a greater sense of psychological angst which provides the internal motivation to return. The success of his renegotiation of Scott's film can be measured most distinctively by measuring it against the far less successful sequels by David Fincher and Jean-Pierre Jeunet, to say nothing of the various franchise efforts such as *Alien vs Predator*.

One of the most powerful ways in which Cameron negotiates this constructed history is by eliding the events of the first film into a perspective on the truth which is explicitly connected to the second. This is constructed as essentially a conflict between Ripley and every new character; Burke, the corporate board, the marine units (especially Hicks and Vasquez) and the aliens themselves — those who have not lived through the original film, and are therefore not privy to her supposed insight, or are even hostile to it. None of these antagonists makes any attempt to hide their skepticism concerning Ripley's version of the story, dismissing her unique perspective as mental illness (the board), naivety or a lack of understanding (the marines), grief (Burke) and ignorance/cowardice (Hicks and Vasquez). Taking the original "facts" from the first film, Ripley has woven her own narrative describing what happened; consequently, her perspective relies on a met textual authority (we, the audience, have also shared her perspective) which is undermined the moment her sanity is called into question. Thus, because the events of the first film cannot be ratified, rather than being an accepted historical account, it is treated as an unreliable eyewitness account, which is deeply implausible and dismissed as psychological trauma.

Nevertheless, despite our solidarity with Ripley, the polarization of these character perspectives provides *Aliens* with a number of equally credible perspectives on the truth. Burke (Paul Reiser) is initially depicted as a sympathetic character (especially in the director's cut); from the outset he is set apart from the board by visiting her in her sick bed and private quarters, and his youth and urban "chic" (light suits, turned-up collar) are reinforced by his star-status (as a stand-up comic and similarly anti–Establishment figure in *Beverley Hills Cop*). This is reinforced cinematographically, too, by framing him in medium close-ups with Ripley, by offering tight close-ups which are denied to any other representative of the company, and by Cameron's lighting which singles him out with strong key lighting against light backgrounds, which individuates him from the rest of the homogeneous, gray-suited board members.

In a similar vein, Cameron is careful to elaborate a number of differing perspectives on the truth throughout the film. The board are unabashedly more interested in the "dollar value" of the human colony on the planet, and as such are seen to weave the details of Ripley's account into a perspective which renders her emotionally unstable; her frustration in front of them leads to a revealing insight into the plurality of the truth, when she resignedly demands to know "how many different ways do you want me to tell the same story?" The hubristic military unit equally pay scant attention to what "Sleeping Beauty" has to say, treating their mission as just "another bug-hunt," and nor do they show any empathy for the human colonizers of the planet. As Vasquez arrogantly claims, they only need to know one thing: "where ... they ... are." Most important among these perspectives, however, is of course the increased emphasis which Cameron places on the aliens themselves, and most especially with the alien queen and her brood. The (notably singular) alien was dramatically absent from Scott's original film, in keeping with its adherence to the horror/thriller genre; its perspective was shown rather from a voyeuristic tracking shot reminiscent of any number of Mario Bava and Dario Argento horror films, with an occasional strobe-lit shock appearance to signal the end of another character's life. In Cameron's world, however, they are given a much more active and visible role to play; the chase scene in the ventilator shaft follows a strict shot/reverse-shot sequence, centering the aliens in the frame and lighting them fully instead of relegating them to the shadows as liminal bogeymen. By their plurality, as well as by this carefully-edited balance of screen presence, there is little to differentiate them from the majority of the dispensable foot soldiers from the military corps, whose armor buries their humanity beneath an institutionalized, industrialized, cyborgian exterior — with the notable exceptions of Vasquez, Hicks and Hudson, who will each play much more narratively significant roles in the film.

The main exception to this is the alien queen, who is exposed to more screen time than the whole of her offspring combined, and whose motivation of saving her brood elicits a far greater degree of audience empathy than the alien of the original film. Far from being a simple, one-dimensional monster who lurks in the shadows awaiting her next victim, the alien queen is seen to be protecting her offspring from the company, a plot point which places her in direct opposition to (and sympathetic parallel with) Ripley herself, who in turn defends Newt as a surrogate mother figure. In Cameron's version of the film, the queen is significantly more *visible* than her brood, a strategy which can risk encouraging a certain degree of audience identification. Such a construction offers, then, an alternative perspective whose aversion to the will of the corporation mirrors that of Ripley and Newt, a perspective which is so effective that it risks derailing the plot altogether. In fact, without Ripley it might even be possible to imagine rooting for the queen, such is the aversion we feel towards the corporation and its "grunts,"[8] to use Cameron's own term. We continue to root for Ripley, however, on the grounds of her humanity, which forces us to choose a side. It is interesting to reflect here that a deliberate attempt was made to render to aliens more like insects in the sequel, a strategy which — whether intentional or not — functions to negate any potential anthropomorphism, which means that as a non-human threat she *must* be destroyed. We overlook the fact "that 'the queen fights with equal bravery to ensure that her children not yet born will be spared the fate of those Ripley has just incinerated.' Not only do we overlook it, we *do not care*. And we do not care because Cameron has constructed a film where, ideologically, it is *her* or *us*."[9]

The question thus arises, why might Cameron include such well-defined and fully-formed perspectives and motivations for each character — especially when such an explicit back-story risks derailing the plot in the case of the alien queen? Perhaps the answer to this lies less in the concept of narrative fairness, but rather in this notion of "taking sides," or favoring a perspective. In a clear-cut story like *Alien*, in which the survival of the human is dependent on the destruction of the invisible alien, there is no need for the audience to be involved in consciously evaluating the different points of view. In the absence of any explicit alternative perspectives, there are no difficult choices to be made about who exactly the enemy is. Like a great deal of horror films among which Scott's film takes its place, the invisibility of the foe is precisely the factor which precludes audience sympathy and thus simplifies the plot: audiences are placed at a distance by not seeing the enemy, or by the dehumanization of the villain. Cameron's insistence on the back-story, however, increases the urgency of the narrative, and involves the audience to a much greater extent in the plot. When we have lived through Ripley's experiences, we are much more inclined to side with her perspective (which demands the preservation of human life and the destruction of the aliens) than, say, the company (who wish to preserve them and care little for human life), the android Ash (who wishes to study them) and the marines (whose antipathy, and indeed outright hostility to Ridley's expertise lead them to rely on exclusively military power, aligning them with the institutional power of the company).

Titanic

As a hallmark of Cameron's directorial style, such a reliance on developing perspectives was to have much deeper repercussions in future films, and was to insinuate itself much more into the very grain of the film, informing not only plot development but also the use of the star-system (Cameron's re-use of the same actors is an oft-cited hallmark) and even the *mise-en-scène*, using POV camera angles, tight close-ups of the protagonists, and tracking shots to place the audience alongside the heroes and ensure that when we do take sides, we choose the correct perspective. In *Titanic*, Cameron takes on one of the most documented historical events of our time: the sinking of the White Star line's *RMS Titanic* on its maiden voyage (and its male arrogance, mud-slinging and mystery). Here, the drowning of well over half of the passengers, coupled with its distance in time means that we are necessarily, like Lovett and Bodine, trying to recreate the historical "truth" of the Titanic's voyage from a distance. Here, we are offered — both in the film and in reality — a series of conflicting perspectives, in which we must rely only on their plausibility; what is interesting is that here the actual history is less important than the various individual experiences of the event, multiple testimonies which include that of the ship itself. Aylish Wood, for example, contends that:

> The parallel editing not only allows different human stories to emerge, but also that of R.M.S. Titanic. Parallelism is, of course, nothing new, but the distinctiveness of its use in Titanic lies in how the visual spaces of the parallel narratives finally converge on-screen. In Titanic there are moments when the parallel stories of technology and human co-exist on the screen, especially in the final section where the images of human and technological destruction come together in an expanded narrative space.[10]

This suggests that "*Titanic* is a text of multiple narratives," which does not purport to tell *the* story of *RMS Titanic*, but frames it within a series of parallel histories which "cohere around a central core that controls the overall organisation of the meanings of those elements."[11]

Consequently, not only does there emerge an essential parallel between *RMS Titanic* (the ship) and *Titanic* (the film), which Studlar neatly codifies as a Titanic/*Titanic* polarity,[12] but between the multiple, parallel and sometimes contradictory perspectives which place the character sets at diametric opposites. For example, one of the clearest themes of the film is the different experiences of the classes traveling on the ship, proposed as a simple dialectic between first-class and steerage and spatially determined as a distinction between the upper and lower decks. Few attempts are made to explore the gray areas here, such as the place of the crew, musicians, and serving staff, or the spatial role of the engine room crew. Similarly ignored is the complex hierarchy which exists even among the first-class passengers, such as Molly Brown's nouveau-riche status as against the dynastic respectability of Cal Hockley, or the dignity of the supremely wealthy passengers embodied by Benjamin Guggenheim. Such oversights are partially explained as narrative and time-constraints, as well as the centrality of Rose and Jack's love affair, which is constructed as a metonymic infusion of such gray areas in its cross-class romance, the "Romeo and Juliet on a ship" which formed the conceit of the film when pitched to the producers.[13]

The absence of such gray areas, however, becomes even clearer when we consider that these different experiences either side of the class divide offer two clear perspectives on the sinking of the Titanic, wherein the social divisions take on a much more important significance. According to the film's simplified subdivision of the passengers, each grouping relates to a specific outcome: the saving of first-class passengers at the expense of the third-class "underbelly" means that the class divisions come to mean not only rich/poor but survival/death. The tradition of saving women and children first similarly polarizes genders and age groups in the same terms, as does the division between crew and passengers, with the former being sacrificed to save the latter. The rashness of the mob which breaks into in-fighting, jeopardizing everybody's chances of survival, means that the impetuous die at the expense of the rational; everywhere order quickly gives way to chaos, meaning that those needing extra help (children, the infirm) are quickly abandoned, and so on. Thus, we can prioritize the likelihood of survival into orders of probability, among which the highest would be an adult, rational, able-bodied, first-class female passenger — which might perhaps go some way to explaining the choice of Rose DuWitt Bukater as the privileged voice-over for the film.[14]

It is precisely this privileged position, then, that provides the elderly Rose the narrative authority to contradict the "scientific" representation of the *Titanic*'s demise, in her suggestion that "the reality was somewhat different." By separating her lived experience into a conflicting perspective on the same truth, Cameron essentially challenges the view of history "from above" (to reprise Ferro's terminology), both metaphorically and quite literally, since we and the archaeological team are looking at the wreck from the surface of the ocean. This contrast (between Rose's view from below and within vs. Bodine's view from above and outside) proposes a series of further divisions, between past and present, between archaeology and memory, between lived experience and its subsequent recreation, exposing the weakness of the scientific perspective as much as the fallacy of memory. Such a division also recalls Cameron's fascination with female figures discussed elsewhere in this collection, which he interprets here as an irreconcilable dichotomy between male arrogance (the scientists and shipbuilders are all male) and female intuition (the sea, Titanic as "she"). Thus the proud boasts of the men with their unsinkable ship are aligned with Bodine's unshakable belief in the infallibility of scientific exploration, constructing him as a character who "plays a crucial role in *Titanic*, for he is the representative figure of technological modernity that it is the burden of the film to soften and humanize."[15] It is significant then that both past and present claims to truth are countered by the same person, as it serves to unite potentially contradictory perspectives; it is the young Rose who remonstrates with the men's preoccupation with size, just as the old Rose counters the simulation of the Titanic with what she terms "the reality" of the Titanic experience. Such conflicting perspectives, however, ultimately come to a head with Bodine's total refusal to accept Rose's narrative, dividing the two characters into two camps, and forcing him "to play antagonist to the frame story's protagonist, the 1990s Rose. He is the one who is least prepared to accept her claim that she is the same Rose Bukater who is thought to have died in the sinking."[16] Equally, by branding both male groups as technocratic skeptics, Cameron repeats *Aliens*' strategy of offsetting male arrogance against female intuition, which was to foreshadow *Avatar*'s gender divisions, and the ignorance of male (Western) imperialism which overlooks the subtlety of female (Natural) "ways of knowing."

This strategy is established as a question and answer routine, in which the doubts of the men are posed first, and subsequently rebutted by what I suggested above exists as a rhetoric of the Real: Bodine calls her a liar, we later discover that she changed her name; Bodine's simulation is first shown on a small computer monitor, Rose's version is shown in full widescreen detail, immersing us in her narrative; the Heart of the Ocean is first reflected in a drawing, while we are treated to a real-life, full-screen, color version later on in the film. By undermining the traditional authority of the voice-off narrator in constructed history, we arrive at the same narrative situation of *Aliens*, in which each parallel narrative is equally plausible, and the only decisions about what is true and what is false can be made on the basis of the credibility of each perspective. Just as Bodine dismisses Rose as "a goddamn liar," both the corporation and the marines repudiate the truth of Ripley's perspective; "Their overly confident comments and disrespectful behavior confirm that the soldier's [sic] believe that Ripley is a hysterical woman with an overblown story."[17] In *Aliens*, we side with Ripley because we know from the outset that her narrative is true; the power of Cameron's ability to provide plausible perspectives is demonstrated by the fact that without the first film we would be considerably less sure of the credibility of Ripley's claims. Schematically, Ripley's boardroom confrontation echoes Reese's difficulty in explaining our future history to the police psychologist in *The Terminator*, and Weaver's reprisal of an anti–Establishment figure offering a different perspective on "alien" creatures in *Avatar*'s Dr Augustine.

It is when these conflicting perspectives come to such a head, however, that Cameron frequently delivers his coup-de-grace as a filmmaker fully attuned to — and driven by — what Thompson has identified as Classical Hollywood narratives. Rather than allowing each perspective to hold true, creating a *Rashomon*-esque multiplicity of truths, Cameron ultimately resolves these conflicts by falling back on a powerful mechanism which he uses to discredit a given perspective, and support another: it is this mechanism which I have termed a rhetoric of the Real.

The Rhetoric of the Real

The Rhetoric of the Real, then, emerges at the point at which we have not only one truth, but *many* possible truths, each supported by an appropriate cinematographic and narrative structure. Such a position flags up a crucial aspect of cinematography which has gained increasing significance towards the end of the twentieth century; beginning with Benjamin's work on representation, and carried on by Bazin's observations on the myth of total cinema, the history of film theory has consistently struggled with precisely such notions of truth and representation. One claim which has been comprehensively disputed, however, is that the function of the camera is to slavishly record reality; instead, critics recognize the partial, fractured and ultimately subjective way in which film tries to represent reality. If the truth is no longer identified as a simple dialectic between truth and lies, but is rather the most credible of a range of perspectives, then we can see more clearly the problems facing a filmmaker like James Cameron when he chooses a historical subject. If there is no single truth, but a range of perspectives, he must first reconcile these disparate viewpoints; yet, crucially, in order to make a film which converges to form a single, relatively unambiguous ending, his film must hold onto a belief in a given reality. It is this reality which comes to form the Real which Cameron tries to represent by a rhetorical attempt to persuade the viewer of a faultless Real, underpinning one perspective in particular. The rhetoric of the Real consequently comes to describe all of the techniques which Cameron uses to try to persuade the viewer of the truth of one single perspective.

Thus the Real becomes reflected by the rhetorical and strategic devices which Cameron employs to convince the viewer that what they are seeing is true, even if it relates to a perspective which they themselves have not experienced. Few, I imagine, have actually gone down to explore the wreck of the Titanic; nor have many encountered Alien creatures, or visited the planet Pandora, yet Cameron uses a range of techniques to create a verisimilar representation of these worlds. As his mentor Roger Corman observes, "it is difficult enough for a filmmaker to create the illusion of reality, but it is even tougher to create that same illusion in the genres of science fiction, fantasy and apocalyptic adventure... The convincing creation of new worlds, imaginary but plausible science, and the psychology and movement of the inhabitants of futuristic or unfamiliar worlds is possibly the most challenging of all tasks that a filmmaker can undertake."[18]

The difficulty of this challenge of authenticity/credibility goes some way to explaining Cameron's insistence on providing support for his versions of reality. Over the course of his oeuvre, in fact, we can see an increasing reliance on devices, both rhetorical and technical, which are designed to reassure the viewer of the reliability of the representation with which they are faced. For instance, in *Titanic*, during the pre-production stage Cameron's team was to go to great lengths and depths (quite literally) in order to establish an archaeological credibility, even chartering a Russian research vessel to explore the wreck itself and devising an elaborate camera system which could record at great pressure on the ocean bed.[19] These strategies, redolent of both archaeology and Cameron's earlier work in *The Abyss* was to establish a credibility which would survive in the film itself; "by incorporating footage of the actual wreck into the film, Cameron wanted to push documentary realism to the limit."[20] In the same vein, the special effects units were driven by Cameron's relentless perfectionism to create better — and more realistic — depictions of the shipwreck. Where "synthespians," CGI-generated actors, might have been used to recreate the passengers' despairing leaps into the sea, as indeed they had been in other roughly contemporary epics like *Lord of the Rings*, Actors' Guild representatives were shocked when they arrived on set to discover stunt men lashed to the railings of the giant model ship floating in the Mexican location shoot.[21]

Within the film, too, Cameron makes use of a number of touches in order to provide narrative credibility. The inclusion of various prominent — and identifiable — Historical figures (such as Captain Edward Smith, Margaret "Molly" Brown, Benjamin Guggenheim) is combined with the inclusion of documented events (such as Brown's survival and the return of Lifeboat 6) to provide a Historical skeleton, which is then fleshed out by the inclusion of narrative (and fictional) elements. This insistence on viewing the past through imaginary "eyewitness" accounts reflects oral and social history, which aims to view history as the accounts of real people, and not the annals of great deeds undertaken by aristocratic white men (in itself a dialectic simplification of perspectives). This approach, often privileging eyewitness accounts over politico-ideological treatises, comes to present the view from below as a privileged, and therefore more reliable, historical testimony. In turn, "*Titanic* relies on the rhetorical modes and conventions of oral and social history as they have filtered through to the general public over the past two to three decades. It wraps itself in this populist discourse of authenticity in order to heighten its audience's willingness, indeed eagerness, to suspend disbelief."[22]

The Oral History approach employed (whether consciously or not) by Cameron was thus to lend a strong rhetorical force to his film as a whole, which sought to root its authenticity in an identification with the characters; by using Rose's point of view, audiences are invited to identify with her and are thereby more inclined to side with her perspective. This is also achieved by a manipulation of the cinematography, too, from the very outset of the film; "The movie opens with a yellowed and slightly out-of-focus 'old-time' footage of the *Titanic harbored* in Southampton... *What we see is not actual historical footage but an expertly crafted fabrication of such.* A shot of a man operating an old-time, hand-cranked movie camera suggests that the footage we are viewing was filmed on-site by cameras of a similar vintage."[23] The beginning of the film thereby seeks its authenticity in a visual replication of documentary footage, which has as its aim the establishment of an incontestable truth. Thus, when it comes to the moment examined above in which Rose's perspective contrasts sharply with Bodine's computer reconstruction, we the audience are much more inclined to believe Rose's claim that "the reality was quite different," since it too begins by returning to the newsreel images, which then segue into bright, sharp images, suggesting that her recollection not only accords with the historical "reality" of the stock footage, but in fact enhances it, implying that we are privy to an eyewitness account of the Real.[24]

We may conclude by examining how these strategies are recombined to produce an overall sense of credibility lending support to one such perspective on the truth. In the same way as we have seen that *Titanic* appeals to a sense of the Real, a similar tactic is deployed in *Aliens*; having a distinct perspective which drew its authority from the experiences of the first film, Cameron (as both screenwriter and director) was obliged to conform to the pre-existent facts of the first film, but also to invent entire character aspects which would flesh out the character of Ripley and lead us to believe her version of events. He achieves this by looking at the "gaps" of the first film's characterization (which painted her as something of a Final Girl, to use Clover's famous term), and then filling in the interstices of the Real.[25] For instance, Cameron claims that "Ripley didn't have a prior life in the first movie... You knew she was a junior officer and an independent thinker capable of courageous acts, but that was about it. Ripley didn't even have a first name in *Alien*. So I made one up for her..."[26] Thus he creates a much more rounded character — Lt. Ellen Ripley, the soldier, the worker, the failed mother — for his film, which will concentrate on proving the various contradictory perspectives wrong, or at least making them seem less plausible.

One of the most potent ways in which Cameron achieves this is by using the cinematography to underscore her version of events. In the director's cut, for example, immediately prior to the board meeting Ripley is told of the fate of her daughter during her 57 years in space; beginning with a long tracking shot of Ellen against a synthesized natural background, each cut moves the camera steadily forward to isolate her from Burke (who breaks the news to her). Eventually, just before cutting to the next scene (Ripley vs. the board), the camera tightly frames the grieving Ripley in an extreme close up. The net effect of this scene, then, is that the camera replicates (or, more cynically, forces) audience sympathy with Ripley in precisely the moment of her greatest vulnerability. The softer, more natural lighting thus brings the space saga back to earth temporarily — and artificially — in order to break through the tough exterior of her character (a legacy of the first film), and to establish a "moment of truth," to paraphrase Jack's opening words in *Titanic*. This truth (though not, in fact, true, as the artificial background suggests) becomes a rhetorically-constructed Real which is then carried into the meeting, deftly causing us to side naturally with Ripley — after all, having just learnt that she has sacrificed her family for the benefit of the company, their talk of "the dollar value" seems not only brash but unfathomably insensitive.

By providing the spectator with such a back-story to his character (and by denying it to the board members), Cameron ensures that in a battle of perspectives we have already fixed a sense of the underlying reality firmly in our minds, though perhaps without necessarily knowing why or how. Though each "perspective" might be supported by an internal logical consistency within the film, the Real reaches out into the audience to ensure that we ally ourselves with the correct perspective, by ensuring that the new information presented conforms to our pre-existent experience of her. So just as *Titanic's* Rose finds her tale bolstered by its assimilation with the seemingly Real historical footage, so too do we find that by filling in the gaps of Ripley's life we can accept her perspective to a far greater extent: it simply *seems* more credible.

Conclusions

We can see here, then, that in the face of multiple perspectives on the truth, as I claimed in my introduction, truth is no longer a question of veracity or historicity, but is instead predicated on credibility. It is a credibility which has been stealthily constructed by appealing to audiences' memories of events, which comes to constitute the Real which underpins Cameron's approach to multiple perspectives. Just as the real wreck of the Titanic lies under the boat in which Rose's narrative takes place, so too do his films contain their own Reality which will eventually overpower the conflicting perspectives. *The Terminator's* protagonists split hairs between their different perspectives while the Real edges closer, waiting to burst its way into the police station; the Taskers of *True Lies* argue about their interpretations of marriage while the very Real warheads are waiting to offer their own form of resolution. The Real, single truth sustains its credibility by launching itself on the narrative like so many aliens waiting at the door of the colony, and supporting the perspective of his protagonists. And perhaps it is precisely this inviolable sense of the Real which explains the continued appeal of Cameron's films, for each contains a conflict of perspectives, a fiery clash of opinion akin to Cameron's own legendary temperament which is ultimately smoothed over by a fixed belief that the truth will out. Amid the multiplicity and confusion of postmodern life, it is perhaps reassuring to audiences to find that there are still moments in which we can separate out the truth from the lies.

NOTES

1. The Expression "history from below" makes reference to Marc Ferro's seminal contribution to the history/film debate, *Cinema et histoire*, in which he proposes that "statements about society come from four impulses": from below, from above, from inside and from outside. Quotation taken from Naomi Greene's translation *Cinema and History* (Detroit: Wayne State University Press, 1988), 163–4.

2. Robert Rosenstone introduced the concept of "History with a capital H" to history on film in order to designate a "serious kind of history" and one which is based on academic Historical enquiry. His intention here was largely to distinguish this kind of history from the historiographic model, which latter acknowledges precisely the plurality of perspectives with which this essay is engaged. See Robert A. Rosenstone, *History on Film/Film on History* (Harlow: Longman/Pearson, 2006), 2.

3. The experiment is reported in Vance Packard, *The Hidden Persuaders* (Harmondsworth: Penguin, 1962), pp. 19–20. A later version of this experiment equally demonstrated the myth of the correlation between price and quality, see P. Charlton and A. S. C. Ehrenberg, "An Experiment in Brand Choice," *Journal of Marketing Research*, 13 (1976), 152–160.

4. "...l'histoire sera ce que nous choisirons" (my translation). Paul Veyne, *Comment on écrit l'histoire* (Paris: Éditions du Seuil, 1971), 42.

5. Julian Stringer, ""The China Had Never Been Used!": On the Patina of Perfect Images in *Titanic*," in *Titanic: Anatomy of a Blockbuster*, ed. by Kevin S. Sandler and Gaylyn Studlar (New Brunswick, NJ: Rutgers, 1999), 205–19.

6. Andrew B.R. Elliott, *Remaking the Middle Ages: The Methods of Cinema and History in Portraying the Medieval World* (Jefferson, NC: McFarland, 2010), Chapter One.

7. Cameron's own reading of *True Lies*, in Heard, *Dreaming Aloud: The Life and Films of James Cameron* (Toronto: Doubleday Canada, 1997), 188.

8. Heard, *Dreaming Aloud*, 86.

9. Ximena Gallardo C. and C. Jason Smith, *Alien Woman: The Making of Lt. Ellen Ripley* (NY& London: Continuum, 2004), 114.

10. Wood, "Expanded Narrative Space: *Titanic* and CGI Technology," *Titanic in Myth and Memory: Representation in Visual and Literary Culture*, ed. by Tim Bergfelder, Sarah Street (London: I.B. Tauris & Co, 2004), 226.

11. Wood, "Expanded Narrative Space," 226.

12. Gaylyn Studlar, "Titanic/*Titanic*: Thoughts on Cinematic Presence and Hollywood History," in *Titanic in Myth and Memory*, 155–62.

13. Tom Shone, *Blockbuster: How Hollywood Learned to Stop Worrying and Love the Summer* (London: Simon and Schuster, 2004), 250.

14. Though, of course, I am scarcely suggesting that Rose's escape from Titanic was easy; my point is rather that these characteristics place her among those with the highest probability of survival, which has a compelling effect on her subsequent credibility. Had she led with her near-death and leap from the ship, for example, we would be considerably more inclined to agree with Bodine's opinion that she is a liar.

15. David M. Lubin, *Titanic* (London: BFI, 1999), 19.

16. Lubin, *Titanic*, 19.

17. Gallardo and Smith, *Alien Woman*, 90.

18. Heard, *Dreaming Aloud*, ix.

19. For more on the extensive preparations and the *Titanic* pre-production, see Paula Parisi, *Titanic and the Making of James Cameron: The Inside Story of the Three-Year Adventure that Rewrote Motion Picture History* (NY: Newmarket Press, 1998).

20. Peter Krämer, "Far Across the Distance: Historical Films, Film History and *Titanic,*" in *Titanic in Myth and Memory*, 164–5.

21. See Heard's final chapter on the making of *Titanic*, in *Dreaming Aloud*. For more on synthespians, see Dan North's excellent study *Performing Illusions: Cinema, Special Effects and the Virtual Actor* (London & NY: Wallflower Press, 2008), especially Chapter 5).

22. Lubin, *Titanic*, 17.

23. Lubin, *Titanic*, 15, my emphasis.

24. Lubin, *Titanic*, 24.

25. Carol Clover, *Men, Women, and Chainsaws: Gender in the Modern Horror Film* (Princeton: Princeton University Press, 1993).

26. "Mothers with Guns," Paul M. Sammon, in *Aliens: The Illustrated Screenplay* (London: Orion Books, 2001).

Works Cited

Bergfelder, Tim, and Sarah Street, eds. *The Titanic in Myth and Memory: Representations in Visual and Literary Culture*. London: I.B.Tauris, 2004.

Cameron, James, and Paul Sammon. *Aliens: The Complete Illustrated Screenplay*. London: Orion, 2001.

Charlton, P., and A. S. C. Ehrenberg. "An Experiment in Brand Choice." *Journal of Marketing Research* 13, no. 2 (May 1976): 152–160.

Clover, Carol J. *Men, Women, and Chain Saws: Gender in the Modern Horror Film*. Princeton, NJ: Princeton University Press, 1993.

Elliott, Andrew B. R. *Remaking the Middle Ages: The Methods of Cinema and History in Portraying the Medieval World*. Jefferson, NC: McFarland, 2010.

Ferro, Marc. *Cinema and History*. Detroit: Wayne State University Press, 1988.

Gallardo C., Ximena, and C. Jason Smith. *Alien Woman: The Making of Lt. Ellen Ripley*. London: Continuum, 2006.

Heard, Christopher. *Dreaming Aloud: The Life and Films of James Cameron*. Toronto: Doubleday Canada, 1997.

Krämer, Peter. "Far Across the Distance: Historical Films, Film History and Titanic." In *The Titanic in Myth and Memory: Representations in Visual and Literary Culture*, edited by Tim Bergfelder and Sarah Street, 163–172. London: I.B. Tauris, 2004.

Lubin, David M. *Titanic*. London: BFI Publishing, 1999.

North, Dan. *Performing Illusions: Cinema, Special Effects and the Virtual Actor*. London: Wallflower Press, 2008.

Packard, Vance. *The Hidden Persuaders*. Harmondsworth: Penguin, 1962.

Parisi, Paula. *Titanic and the Making of James Cameron: The Inside Story of the Three-year Adventure That Rewrote Motion Picture History*. New York: Newmarket Press, 1998.

Rosenstone, Robert A. *History on Film/Film on History*. Harlow: Longman/Pearson, 2006.

Sandler, Kevin S., and Gaylyn Studlar, eds. *Titanic: Anatomy of a Blockbuster*. New Brunswick: Rutgers University Press, 1999.

Shone, Tom. *Blockbuster: How Hollywood Learned to Stop Worrying and Love the Summer*. New York: Simon & Schuster, 2004.

Stringer, Julian. ""The China Had Never Been Used!": On the Patina of Perfect Images in Titanic." In *Titanic: Anatomy of a Blockbuster*, edited by Kevin S. Sandler and Gaylyn Studlar, 205–219. New Brunswick: Rutgers University Press, 1999.

Studlar, Gaylyn. "Titanic/Titanic: Thoughts on Cinematic Presence and Hollywood History." In *The Titanic in Myth and Memory: Representations in Visual and Literary Culture*, edited by Tim Bergfelder and Sarah Street, 155–162. London: I.B.Tauris, 2004.

Veyne, Paul. *Comment on écrit l'histoire: texte intégral.* Paris: Seuil, 1996.

Wood, Aylish. "Expanded Narrative Space: Titanic and CGI Technology." In *The Titanic in Myth and Memory: Representations in Visual and Literary Culture*, edited by Tim Bergfelder and Sarah Street. London: I.B. Tauris, 2004.

Art, Image and Spectacle in High Concept Cinema

BRUCE ISAACS

Vision and Visuality

> Just as John Ford made his mark in the Western, and Alfred Hitchcock spoke through the thriller, so Cameron, once called Cecil B. DeMille of his generation, seems to have gravitated toward the blockbuster as his format, and in so doing he has helped re-define radically what that means.[1]

In spite of the waning of "authorship" as an analytical trajectory in recent film studies scholarship, the auteur remains ever-present in the landscape of American cinema, and most indelibly inscribed in the industrial and aesthetic histories of Hollywood. Just as the Old Hollywood cherished the individual brushstroke of a Hitchcock or Ford, or the iconoclastic vision of a Sam Fuller, so the New Hollywood reverberates with the spectacle aesthetic of James Cameron, upon which Christopher Nolan's *The Dark Knight* and *Inception*, The Wachowskis' *The Matrix* franchise, Michael Bay's *Transformers* and Roland Emmerich's *2012* have forged new spectacle modalities and new aesthetic experiences. Keller's suggestion that James Cameron speaks through a form of cinema, described pejoratively as blockbuster, reaches into a broad and discursive lineage of the auteur filmmaker. This is the conception of the filmmaker (Truffaut's scriptwriter/director) as a visionary of cinematic spectacle in spite of the vicissitudes of a collaborative medium. More profoundly, it is the conception of an individual artist bearing the heart, mind and soul of the dominant entertainment form of the 20th and 21st centuries.

While Thomas Schatz, in turning to genre, and Laura Mulvey, in turning to psychoanalysis and patriarchy, championed a waning of auteurship theory and an opening up of the alternative (and ideologically inscribed) practices of the medium,[2] the vision of the Hollywood filmmaker, through Ford, Hawks and Hitchcock, coheres. Auteurs create hermetic, internally coherent texts, and potentially construct a vision that maintains form and trajectory in an industry that craves the clarity of vision. As Schatz argues, there is something

90

profoundly romantic about cinema as classical artwork,[3] maintaining its hold on Benjamin's failing aura of modernity. Cameron's proclamation on Oscars night, 1998, that he had become the "King of the World," was an overstatement in a narrow sense. In a broader sense, *Titanic's* acceptance by the Academy of Motion Picture Arts and Sciences into its Best Picture pantheon signified Cameron's assumption to the throne of High Concept Hollywood (that he would not again relinquish) and acknowledged the clarity of the vision of a contemporary blockbuster auteur. The spectacle filmmaker had been recognized by an artistic *enclave*, as Spielberg and Lucas had not.[4] For Cameron, the artist in the machine had been legitimated.

This chapter attempts to make some headway toward synthesizing two of the prevailing analytical approaches to Hollywood cinema: its aesthetic orientation toward spectacle and vision, and its industrial (and post-industrial) orientation toward commercialism and what has been broadly described by Justin Wyatt as "High Concept Cinema."[5] In the wake of similar investigations, the essay can but offer a step forward in advancing a thesis concerning the current use of spectacle in the work of the spectacle filmmaker *par excellence*, James Cameron. I locate Cameron's aesthetic orientation at the intersection of the two competing interests of the High Concept film. The auteurist vision subsists in the attempt to "invent cinema," to make cinema new through the exponentially advancing technologies of the spectacle.[6] As Keller argues,

> Cameron is obsessed with vision itself, and in ways that far exceed the preoccupation with vision any film director has. Every film he has ever made has spent a significant amount of time, aesthetic and narrative energy conveying to the viewer not only the requisite thrills and emotional and visceral intensity of Hollywood blockbuster entertainment, but also complex and quite serious meditations on what it means to see.[7]

For Cameron, vision is more than a medium for the conveyance of "reality." The special effect is never purely mimetic, but transformative. There is a vicarious thrill to be had from viewing the world through the eyes of a cyborg–Being in *The Terminator* and *Terminator 2: Judgment Day*; this is not unlike the thrill one experiences through the new visuality of the One, born anew in the simulated Matrix — the One's binary code and ours are, magically, synchronized. Jake Sully's (Sam Worthington's) "birth" in Pandora is surely a birth into the newness of vision, an ontological space where he not only has new legs with which to run, but new eyes with which to survey the digitally rendered world. These are new modes of experience attained through *visuality*. The spectacle is never built exclusively of the fabric of reality but is a technological creation that offers an expansion of the capacities of vision. Much as Kubrick attempted to reinvent the spectacle of cinema with *2001: A Space Odyssey* (a film that obsessed the young Cameron,[8] and a film ostensibly about the nature of cinematic vision), so Cameron has proffered ever increasing depths and technological subtleties in image-making, culminating in the experiment of 3-D cinematography in the production and exhibition of *Terminator 2: 3-D* (1996) and *Avatar* (2009).

There is for Cameron something elemental in cinema that engages with the first principle of the medium itself, the technological formulation of the image. It is perhaps why Cameron begins his auteurist romance with cinema via the medium of the science fiction genre, which, he appreciates, inscribes into its generic criteria a fascination with and promethean desire to makeover the visual (and aural) image. As Bukatman suggests, this quality of the science fiction film has located its generic tendency as spectacle-oriented: "The precise function of science fiction, in many ways, is to *create,* the boundless and infinite stuff of sublime experience."[9] This sublimity, for Bukatman, is that moment which exceeds the spectator's capacity for rational contemplation: "The phenomenal world is transcended as the mind moves to encompass what cannot be contained."[10] The sublimity of the image subsists in Kubrick's space journey to Strauss's "Blue Danube," iterating a performance of "pure spectacle," imaging (and enabling the spectator to visualize) that which exceeds the bounds of contemplation, and has heretofore not existed. The rupture of classical shot-reverse shot in the final sequence of *2001,* effectively conflating subject and object point of view, is, for Kubrick, an evolution of *vision as being.*[11]

Cameron's High Concept auteurism is similarly founded upon the technology of cinematic spectacle. Each new Cameron film is a landmark in technological spectacle advancement, re-imagining a prior existing materiality. Each new technological spectacle presents a new way of seeing. The low-fi spectacle of the T-800 in *The Terminator* functions as a creative re-imagining of the body, the alien-cyborg frame visualized and differentiated from the human-organic form. The image of the Terminator — Schwarzenegger's half man-half machine — is one of the most viscerally charged images of the body in High Concept cinema. The rupturing of skin to reveal an endoskeleton is a spectacle of astonishment in High Concept cinema in 1984. *Terminator 2: Judgment Day* reprises the spectacle fascination with the body, but here the tactility of the endoskeleton of the T-800 is replaced with the fluidity of the liquid-metal T-1000, infinitely malleable and formless. The "birth" of the T-1000 from the floor of a hospital foyer is also Cameron's investment in the birth of a new technological spectacle, a scene remarkable for the unprecedented duration of the digitally expanding image. This is Cameron's (and the spectator's) astonished contemplation of the capacities of the technological spectacle in early 1990s cinema; it is the impossible image, composited digitally, rendered on film.

Cameron's *Titanic,* which is perhaps turgid romantic melodrama on a narrative level, leaves its spectacular ship for the epiphanic spectacle reveal: the ship that exists only in the past, lost to the visual acuity of the present, is reborn technologically through the effects apparatus company Digital Domain.[12] One of Cameron's deft narrative strategies is to show the spectator *Titanic* as a relic in the opening sequence of the film, testifying to its presence in the distant past, only to reanimate it through a technological spectacle. I would argue that *Titanic*'s first significant plot point is inscribed not through character or action (the conventional practice of High Concept cinema), but through the revelation of the spectacle of the recreated ship. The spectator is brought into a visual contemplation[13] of the ship (in a sense, boarding with the passengers, who are themselves fragments of the past), a spectacle that is at once awesome and frightening in its impossibility. Much like the Kubrick or Lucas vision of the cinematic spectacle of outer space, Cameron's vision of *RMS Titanic* is forged out of the technological building blocks of the medium. This is cinematic spectacle — a world of sound and vision that exists only when filtered through a camera lens — or the digitized space of a computer simulation.

Unlike the auteurist impulse attributed by Truffaut and his *Cahiers* colleagues to the classical Hollywood filmmakers, Cameron's auteurism must be analyzed against the technological (and commercially inscribed) constraints imposed on the filmmaker. Cameron's auteurism is not modernist in sensibility, and thus not classically auteuristic. The classical auteur is a figure of independence, striving for artistic distinction within (and separation from) the prevailing machinery of the system.[14] The contemporary blockbuster auteurist vision coheres *only within* the commercial structure of High Concept cinema. Cameron's blockbuster auteurism is *systemic*, equally the formative material and commodity output of a commercially oriented system. As Keller rightly points out, we cannot address Cameron's *oeuvre* without acknowledging that each of his works is in turn the "most expensive film ever made."[15] Each film is projected thus as a new form, a new manifestation of cinematic art, and a new manifestation of the cinematic commodity. I argue that High Concept cinema reveals the intersection of two competing impulses: the impulse toward the exponential advancement of the technological spectacle (as evidenced in the work of Christopher Nolan, Michael Bay, Roland Emmerich, but more overtly in the production and global reception of Cameron's *Avatar*), and the impulse toward the exponential increase in box-office returns. The concept of an auteur within the commercial domain supports Keller's notion of the redefinition of blockbuster cinema, revealing the vision of the spectacle filmmaker as a function of the commoditization of High Concept cinema itself.

Rombes astutely reads this tension at the heart of Hollywood High Concept, to my mind the most illuminating analysis of current cinematic practices.[16] Much of film theory continues to read High Concept as a revelation of the ideology of a controlling capitalist construct. In Beller's enormously ambitious work on the cinematic image, he introduces the notion that the image *is* labor and that spectators are inscribed into the material and non-material processes of the commodity.[17] This is possibly the case. But the image is not merely a function of a material reality, inscribed by and inscribing capitalist ideology. Disappointing in such work is a failure to appreciate High Concept aesthetics as art (possessed of the remnants of an aura), as well as, commodity. Consumers of Cameron's *Avatar* or Nolan's *Inception* (the intricacy of the story distracts the spectator briefly from the realization that the film is indeed High Concept spectacle) are astonished by *moments* of visuality and viscerality — the spectacle of the image in movement — Paris enfolding itself in an Escheresque rendition of the possibilities of the digital image in *Inception*; Bay's spectacle of the machine-body in *Transformers*, or the slow-motion rhythmic movements of the Transformers on a freeway. These are moments in cinema in which technology manifests as aesthetic inscription, at which point we might say that the commodity of effects technology becomes the individual brush-stroke of the spectacle auteur, pioneering, visionary and highly individualized.

The Dialectic of Spectacle in High Concept Cinema

There are moments in cinematic history that galvanize the spectator with a virtuosity of spectacle. I was sitting in a cinema recently anticipating the next evolution of High Concept spectacle in Christopher Nolan's *Inception*; these are event films not least because they instantiate an event horizon in cinema history. As Dudley Andrew suggests, new cinema practice reminds us to ask not only what cinema is, but also what cinema was. The High Concept spectacle event brings into sharp relief the past, present and future of cinema.[18]

There is perhaps a single moment in *Inception* that contributes to what I would consider an evolutionary progression of spectacle cinema. Ariadne (Ellen Page), the Architect (more a symbolic designation in the film; how dreamscapes are built is left frustratingly vague) builds the interior physicality of the dream through a cognitive process. As she walks the streets of Paris, contemplating the composition of the physical space, the environment is reconfigured by the Architect of the dream. At this point in the film, there is a moment of the virtuosity of the image (what Bukatman calls sublimity), in which the spectator is abruptly ejected from the narrative and borne into contemplation of the image in itself; the astonished contemplation of the spectacle image is, as Tom Gunning reminds us, a primal initiation.[19] Seated in a darkened theatre nearer in size to a stadium, a Parisian streetscape reconfigured itself before me on a gargantuan Imax screen, and I let the arresting narrative go, so to speak, brought into confrontation with the virtuosity of the spectacle as an object of my own astonishment. I turned to my partner and found myself murmuring, "that's magical." The moment called to mind a similar experience of the impossibility of the image upon seeing *The Matrix* in 1999 and Trinity inaugurating bullet-time in the first action sequence of that film; seeing time and space so cavalierly dislocated on screen, I was astonished.

This is a virtuosity that Ndalianis argues underscores the new aesthetics of contemporary cinema, a neo-baroque impulse toward spectacle and ocular thrill.[20] Seeking to undo a legacy of film theory privileging narrative (story, character, theme) over spectacle, Tom Gunning presents an analysis of the inherent *attractive* potential of the image.[21] For Gunning, the origins of cinema are less interesting as a narrative complex than as a technologized image spectacle. Early spectators reacted to the image not purely as an information cell but as a spectacle in itself, a mode of visuality (without sound) that gave rise to new modes of seeing and experiencing the world. Thus, says Gunning, when Lumiére's locomotive entered a train station on a Parisian screen in 1895, "according to a variety of historians, spectators reared back in their seats, or screamed, or got up and ran from the auditorium (or all three in succession)."[22] The primal experience of seeing a train enter a station on a screen is for the early spectator the image of the impossible, and the impossibility brings the spectator into contemplation of the spectacle in itself, rather than as the object of an encompassing narrative. Lumiére's *L'Arrivée d'un Train à La Ciotat* is a section of film of 45 seconds' duration, hardly the stuff of classical narrative form. But this early encounter with spectacle reveals an initial and yet abiding fascinating for the spectator with a *technology* of the image and screen, untheorized and non-reflexive for the casual spectator in 1895,[23] but increasingly a part of spectacle cinema in the High Concept tradition.

Wyatt's invaluable research into High Concept cinema, while detailed in its analysis of the processes of production and distribution, unfortunately privileges a reading of the film text as a product of industry, acted upon or inscribed by commercial interests rather than self-creating: "All mainstream Hollywood filmmaking is economically oriented, through the minimization of production cost and maximization of potential box office revenue. However, the connection between economics and high concept is particularly strong, since high concept appears to be the most market-driven type of film being produced."[24] The book focuses on the production and reception contexts of cinema, yet there is little treatment of the aesthetic rendering of the image. Implicit in much consideration of High Concept aesthetics (often conflated with popular or mainstream cinema aesthetics) is a pejorative reading of the "market," an amorphous mass of spectators who privilege cinema as entertainment.[25] This formulation of a mass-market spectatorship (which Wyatt rightly argues is projected by the industry itself) recuperates various culture industry models in which mass culture is always already inculcated into the ideology of a controlling capitalist structure. Beller reads this phenomenon most directly: "Cinema and its succeeding (if still simultaneous), formations, particularly television, video, computers, and the internet, are deterritorialized factories in which spectators work, that is, in which we perform value-productive labor."[26] Cubitt not only accepts the function of image as labor but attributes the abjection of a tradition within contemporary cinema to this ontological state: "Cinema's failure arises from its slavery to the commodity."[27] Yet equally, we must accept that *cinema* (I'm less interested in an evaluation of its success or failure — indeed, I'm not quite sure what this would entail for a contemporary mass cultural spectator) *is commodity*. The itinerary of the image as commodity is not a tangential relation but a matter of the composition of the image itself. High Concept spectacle makes sense *only* as commodity-oriented. This is surely a position we must integrate into our analyses of cinema's "being," and certainly if we are to ascribe some meaningful ontology of the "new" or "post" cinema milieu.[28] Why must the theorist privilege the image as labor? Rather than taking issue with such a notion (which is developed in Beller's work in intriguing fashion), an analysis of a contemporary cinematic spectacle must address various *modalities* of the image and image-making, which surely have some investment in the creative vision of a "blockbuster auteur" and a mode of spectatorship fashioned on an engagement with spectacle.

To this end, Rombes offers a dialectical reading of the spectacle image of High Concept cinema:

> Surely you have felt, even in the most terrible CGI movie, that there is something radical and beautiful lurking there in the images, beneath the surface, some image worth dwelling on, some moment of beauty undermined by the mundane dialogue, something flapping by, like silly pages and you want to say: wait, go back, show me that again. Yes, the movie comes up a little short on the "please respect my intelligence" scale, but the sequence itself is beautiful, artistic, visually stunning. Despite the fact that the film is little more than *visual highlights* with *no particular interest in coherence* you find yourself wondering what would happen if you no longer judged the film by the usual, tired standards of the usual, tired critics, but rather by a new standard, one that took into account the crazy, incoherent tradition of innovation and experimentation that characterized early cinema.[29]

I quote Rombes at length here because his articulation of a visionary aesthetics within the formula of High Concept narrative illuminates a path to a consideration of popular cinema as a meaningful engagement with an aesthetics and experience of spectacle. Is it possible for an image ensconced in a High Concept narrative structure to *break free*, to attain a status and stature as an autonomous image, and thus to engage the senses in astonishment? Might High Concept aesthetics evolve further toward a performance of "pure spectacle," in which cinema attends to its status as a visual/aural production rather than narrative cell?

Hollywood High Concept is fashioned on narrative. The industry, classical and post-classical, cut its teeth on genre, on an assemblage of readily accessible, packageable and re-packageable, narrative structures. Yet as Rombes argues, the High Concept image maintains a dialectical relationship to the narrative frame, opening up the possibilities of a cinema of the spectacle even as tired old stories become ever more formulaic, generic, conservative and reactionary.[30] This is auteurist cinema built of the technologies of the image rather than the technologies of story. A mid–Act One point in Spielberg's *Jurassic Park*, like Cameron's narrative turning point of the revelation of the *RMS Titanic* as impossible spectacle, comes in the digitized shape of a Brachiosaurus.[31] Indeed, Spielberg initially captures our astonishment (a conflation of fascination and awe, and fear of the unknown) with a reaction shot of Dr. Grant (Sam Neill) without the prior revelation of the object of fascination. As Dr. Grant must steer Dr. Sattler (Laura Dern) toward a contemplation of the impossible image of the dinosaur (literally a turning of Dern's head) so Spielberg alters the experiential mode of the spectator, previously immersed in the narrative exposition, to a contemplation of the dinosaur. It is a liminal moment in cinema's history at which point an image materializes on screen (much like Lumiére's arrival of a train) in dialectical relation to a past cinema, evolving the potentiality of High Concept spectacle imaging.

The sequence cuts to a wide shot to visually composite the image — Grant and Sattler comprise only peripheral figures and the image in itself is revealed against the open backdrop. The camera now pans with the dinosaur, panning not with the personification of the animal as character, but with the *animation* of the image as a spectacle of vision and movement.[32] The shot compositing Grant and Sattler into the wide frame encapsulated by the dinosaur has less to do with establishing the astonishment of the characters (this is now redundant as the spectator is adequately astonished) than with establishing the technological parameters of the image — size, clarity, rhythmic cadence, indexicality. Grant and Sattler are never granted a close-up that functions separately from the reaction to the image. Much as Nolan shoots the reconfiguration of a Paris street from the ground, a veritable worshipping of the image by Cobb, Ariadne and the spectator, Spielberg brings us into contemplation of the image of the dinosaur from the ground, emphasizing the impossible size of the object. The cut to an extreme wide/long shot to conclude Spielberg's spectacle performance holds momentarily as the dinosaur rises onto two legs, screaming at the moment of its cinematic birth: and the digital image poses for the contemplative gaze of the astonished spectator.

John William's soaring score accompanies the immersion in spectacle aesthetics, which is multi-sensory experience. Here Williams' score draws on a lexicon of spectacle images that resonate quite apart from a classical narrative structure, images cut to music rather than character action — the strings that incrementally build the "image" of a shark in *Jaws* (1975), the grandeur of the entry of a space cruiser in *Star Wars: A New Hope* (1977), a bicycle circumventing the stars in *ET* (1982), surely the metonymic spectacle-image of High Concept cinema itself.[33]

The performance of this spectacle — inaugurating an evolution in visuality — is *rhythmic*, integrated into the spectator's experience (and memory) of spectacle cinema. Bukatman's reading of the science fiction genre is entirely appropriate here: "the effect is designed to be seen, and frequently the narrative will pause to permit the audience to appreciate the technologies on display."[34] The final cut in the *Jurassic Park* sequence is to the capitalist Gennaro (Martin Ferrero). Equally astonished at the presence of a new mode of spectacle, he murmurs: "We're going to make a fortune with this place." The dialectic at the heart of High Concept aesthetics is revealed here in the dual impulses of the auteur's vision. Spielberg materializes as the artist of a digital age, a pioneer of the evolving cinematic image, yet a plier of old stories and old mythologies, inscribed by familiar narrative structures. This is Spielberg as the capitalist-auteur, who will indeed make a fortune through a rendition of a revolutionary digitally composited image, establishing yet again the inter-relatedness of art and commodity in High Concept cinema.

The Paradox of the 3-D Spectacle Image

Eventually, 3-D will make its way into mainstream cinema the way color and sound did: it will be considered useless until it's available with a reasonable price tag. And then, all of a sudden, it will be unavoidable and ubiquitous, to the point that the very mention of "3-D" will disappear from posters.[35]

The irony with Avatar is that people think of it as a 3-D film and that's what the discussion is. But I think that, when they see it, the whole 3-D discussion is going to go away... That's because, ideally, the technology is advanced enough to make itself go away. That's how it should work. All of the technology should wave its own wand and make itself disappear.[36]

Hollywood appears to wage a perpetual war against its own obsolescence. The rhetoric of newness is couched also in terms of the rhetoric of survival. The fragmentation of the studio system in the late 1950s presaged the "newness" of independence, a spirit of innovation that would enrich the studio aesthetic during its decades of transformation. Robert C. Allen has declared the end of the Hollywood era, arguing convincingly that audiences engage with cinema (which is now perhaps an object of nostalgia) in the intimate and highly individualized spaces of their homes.[37] What becomes of "cinema" when the theatre is outmoded as a social and aesthetic space, as film gives over to digital technology, or the multiplex gives over to 3-D TV?

Now digital aesthetics in the High Concept mold is not enough. Now Spielberg's dinosaur seems a relic of a bygone era as new green-screen, blue-screen and digital artistry bring us closer to realizing the fantasies of the imagined Real. Now the spectator craves ever expanding psychological and visceral experience. The once sublime and impossible "reality" of the digital image (anyone who has seen Scott's *Blade Runner: Final Cut*, exhibited on a multiplex screen in 4k projection, appreciates the hyper-real potential of digitization) gives over to the pursuit of new experiential modalities. The Real in image-technology is not enough; we now desire the realism of immersive experience; we desire the conflation of the imagined space in the screen with the real space of the theatre. Hollywood projects this as a cinematic evolutionary moment — an event horizon in High Concept aesthetics, pioneered by corporation and filmmaker (notably, Cameron) alike.

Cameron's 3-D experiment with *Avatar* is a curiously paradoxical intrusion into the evolution of the spectacle image. On the one hand, the rhetoric surrounding the production of the film projected the experiment as the next evolutionary moment in cinematic history: the perfection of the cinematic spectacle, and perhaps more explicitly (and hyperbolically), the idealization of the cinematic experience.[38] Harkins' position on *Avatar's* experiential potential is exemplary here: "What is different about *Avatar* in 3-D as compared to more recent 3-D movies is its immersive effect. Rather than using the technology as a visual gimmick, Cameron worked to create a cinematic experience. The aesthetics of three-dimensional depth perception utilized and the visuals *required by the storyline* work in concert, lending particularly well to a real-world experience."[39] Note here that Harkins falls back on the primacy of narrative as cinematic experience. *Avatar's* 3-D works because it works in concert with story, a story that of course maintains in 2-D projection.

Reading much of what came out in the months after the film's release, I could not help but reflect on the project of André Bazin, who wished to articulate for cinema its abiding myth of the moving image and spectatorial experience. For Bazin, cinema was no less than a confrontation with the purity of image, a myth of total cinema as a guiding myth also of total experience. Bazin privileged the capacity of cinema to reveal the Real, to bring the spectator into contemplation with the presence of reality in the image.[40] There is something transcendental in Bazin's mythology of the cinematic image, evidenced in the work of Jean Renoir or Orson Welles. Of Welles' use of depth of field and focus (the optimum term here being "depth," to which I'll presently return), Bazin writes: "That is why depth of field is not just a stock in trade of the cameraman like the use of a series of filters or of such-and-such a style of lighting, it is a capital gain in the field of direction — a dialectical step forward in the history of film language."[41] Bazin acknowledges and champions the experiential potential of the image itself in depth, pioneering a reading of depth of field and focus as dialectically constituted in opposition to "flatness" (usually contrived through invisible strategies of montage). The deep focus image (of Welles in *Citizen Kane* or *The Magnificent Ambersons*; or of Renoir in *Le Regle du Jeu*) is a transformation of a cinema of "plastics" to a cinema of the Real, in which the *depth* of the shot provides the space for the Real to materialize within the image.

It is the question of "depth" and visibility that is most problematic in Cameron's conception of the newness of 3-D as a spectacle image. I argued that the autonomous spectacle images of the body in *The Terminator* and *Terminator 2: Judgment Day* constitute dialectical advancements in the image as spectacle. This is a performance of spectacle integral to the High Concept aesthetic: the image is always already a technologized object; the image is always already a commoditized object. The image has been built by the High Concept filmmaker and, born technologically, must demonstrate the virtuosity of itself and its creator.

Jurassic Park's Brachiosaurus presents a veritable birth of the digital High Concept image. Yet whereas Spielberg unveils the "otherness" of the digitized form, surely a transformation in image as profound as Bazin's depth spectacle in the late 1930s and early 1940s, *Avatar* renders *invisible* the attraction of the image, reinstating the image as narrative cell, immersed not in the performance of spectacle (as the spectator is strategically immersed in the performance of the image spectacle in the birth of the T-1000 in *Terminator 2: Judgment Day*), but in the wholeness of the narrative space. Upon seeing *Avatar* in 3-D, I had great difficulty recalling the experience *in 3-D*; it seemed my initial point of experiential contact with the film was in *2-D,* privileging the flatness of narrative. Depth had been rendered so naturally, so familiarly, for the greater part of the film it ceased to have significance beyond the first Act (Jake Sully's entry into his Avatar-body).[42] Bazin's depth/flatness dialectic, so visible in Renoir and Welles, had been erased. And thus, my recollection of the experience was primarily of *narrative* progression. The greater significance of

Avatar's technological achievement, it seemed to me, was in the articulation of a seamless virtual world as a realm of astonishment (an entirety of spatial orientation encompassing the narrative frame of the film), rather than the novelty of 3-D depth perception.

Yet one could not turn away from the bald fact that *Avatar* had re-energized the High Concept event, illuminating a path for the technological and commercial evolution of the image. Cameron projected (and projects) *Avatar* as an evolution of cinema, an evolution of experience, and a vehicle for mass culture engagement. This is a cinema conceptualized as at once interactive, *and* immersive. Yet his claim that the final evolutionary phase of image technology (the teleology of Cameron's reading of the image is also misguided) is to enable the technology to disappear runs counter to the performative and self-aware characteristics of the spectacle image. Image as spectacle arrests the spectator's contemplative astonishment as an *image in itself.* The spectacle image is *visible.* As Rombes and Ndalianis argue, High Concept cinema must be accorded the status of the individual brushstroke of the artist, a virtuoso of the technologized/commoditized image. Such virtuosity is manifest in the composition of the image — the High Concept auteur (Keller's "blockbuster auteur") is rendered as visible, if not more visible, than the auteur of Hollywood's classical period (Ford, Hawks, Hitchcock), or the auteur of Hollywood's modernist renaissance period (Coppola, Scorsese, Altman). What strikes one about Spielberg, Lucas and Cameron (more recently Nolan and Bay) is their aesthetic *visibility* as creators of the High Concept image. Their technique (visual, aural, technological, commercial) is demonstrated through the performative spectacles of their work. One can recognize a Spielberg High Concept image (inscribed spatially rather than temporally) just as one can recognize a Scorsese modernist image (inscribed spatially and temporally).[43]

Cameron's "invisibility of style" of his 3-D technology (which runs diametrically against the visibility of 3-D of the 1950s and onward) is thus a recuperation of a classical ideal rather than a radical departure from current spectacle aesthetics. Cameron wishes to assert the purity of the image dislocated from the technology that builds it. Yet we know this is an ideal that cannot be achieved. We know that as Bazin championed the Real within the image, he appreciated the artificial rendering of cinema itself. We know that cinema is a function of its technology, and of that technology's capacity to perpetually make the image anew. I argue that the wish to efface the artist and art of the High Concept spectacle image is a dialectical step *backward* in the evolution of the "language" of High Concept cinema.

There is a single moment in *Avatar* that presents a demonstration of the purity of the spectacle image, an image that resounds with the magic of attraction only new cinema can afford.[44] In the film's opening, Jake Sully awakes from hibernation in a chamber, one of William Gibson's "coffins" of the cyber-punk tradition. Cameron employs a familiar spatial setting — the hibernation chamber resembles the chamber of *Aliens*, in which Ripley (Sigourney Weaver) is first discovered and later in which the Marines will awaken to their mission. The sequence awaking from hibernation presents a fascination for Cameron — in *Aliens*, his camera moves slowly over the chambers, not only as an intro-duction to the occupants but as a visualization of a fantastical setting. The sequence in *Avatar* is thus quotation — surely of Kubrick's *2001*, but more explicitly, of Cameron's own *Aliens*. Hibernation is a sci-fi trope, and no less a trope of the Cameron *oeuvre*. Rendered now in 3-D in *Avatar*, the sequence is Cameron's self-conscious demonstration of a technological advancement of a prior cinematic rendering.

The sequence in *Avatar* comprises only 45 seconds (a "long shot" by High Concept standards, interrupted by a single flashback of 15 seconds). In 2-D we see the spectacle of the Bazinian Real, materialized in the striking depth of the shot. Cameron holds on the hibernation chamber, the camera moving almost imperceptibly, permitting the uninterrupted contemplation of the space. We are reminded perhaps here of Renoir's depth of field that pioneered for Bazin the materialization of the Real. Bodies float in zero gravity space at various depths of field, collapsing the classical composition of separate frames of the shot: foreground, middle-ground, background.

In this sequence, Cameron has orchestrated the *mise-en-scène* for 3-D. Depth is *tangible*. Bodies in depth are rendered "visible," aware of their pres-ence in relation to the extreme depth of the shot and strikingly interposed against the openness of the chamber. Much as Renoir used vertical lines to accentuate depth in complex sequence shots,[45] Cameron provides a grid struc-ture by which to measure depth. I thus read Cameron's shot in depth as a reflection on a classical depth shot, augmented here by the technology of 3-D. The autonomous 3-D image is held for a fleeting moment (45 seconds in the context of a 150 minute film). But whereas Harkins suggests that the 3-D cinematography constructs an immersive field for the spectator (previously unrealized in cinema), my astonishment in reaction to the image in itself con-strued the experience as anything but immersive. My spectatorial gaze was attuned to the composition of the image in depth, the crystalline features of the shot, the clarity of the space. Neither Renoir nor Welles were this self-conscious, this *visible*, with depth cinematography.

What does this visibility of depth construe as spectatorial *experience*? Cer-tainly not immersion nor, I'd argue, interactivity in the fashion of that term in relation to new media art.[46] Rather, I argue that Cameron's High Concept 3-D contrives a level of *materialization* of depth. It is a technological augmen-tation of the depth-image, but it is not a purveyor of depth in spectatorship.

This is a distinction that Harkins (and more significantly, Cameron), fail to appreciate. The prevailing experiential engagement with *Avatar* is not through contemplation of its depth-image in 3-D. Depth as a mode of experiencing the image was accorded the status of "new" by Bazin in the 1950s — and Bazin suggests that the depth-image as "reality" is inscribed in the very origins of cinematic imaging in various strategies of montage. This is the fundamental paradox at the heart of Cameron's 3-D cinema. The nearer it approaches the ideal of the Real (Mendiburu's conflation of 3-D depth with reality), the further it retreats from the spectacle of contemporary attractive cinema, or what I have called High Concept spectacle. Spielberg's Brachiosaurus and Cameron's T-1000 reverberate as moments of astonishment in the evolution of a language of cinema not because they are Real but because they present the sublimity of the impossible.

This sequence in *Avatar* presents the wonder of a momentary spectacle, perhaps more exhibition than evolution of form — the novelty of depth materialized on screen, if only fleeting. Striking depth shots (far more virtuosic in construction and articulation — Bogdanovich's small-town America rendered in depth in black and white in *The Last Picture Show* (1971); Cuaron's mobile cinematography in *Children of Men* [2006]) accompany cinema's evolution for the better part of a century preceding Cameron's experiment with "immersive" 3-D in 2009.

And so what becomes of *Avatar's* 3-D? What becomes of the next projection of the High Concept image? Perhaps it fixes in the spectator's experience as a memory of the materiality of depth on screen, for the first time fused seamlessly into the narrative space of High Concept cinema, striking but no doubt soon forgotten. The abiding experiential memory of Hollywood 3-D in the wake of Cameron's *Avatar* is the supplementation and augmentation of *vision*, not as a function of *visuality*, but of the function of the technology of the glasses we gleefully wear in the multiplex and collect for future 3-D events.[47] It seems to me the current (and, I'd venture to say, short-lived) fascination with 3-D (as technological/commercial image) is not to see the world anew but to see the world through new eyes.[48]

NOTES

1. Alexandra Keller, *James Cameron* (London and New York: Routledge, 2006), 4–5.

2. See, for example, Thomas Schatz, "The Whole Equation of Pictures," in *Film and Authorship*, ed. Virginia Wright Wexman (New Brunswick, NJ: Rutgers University Press, 2003), 89–95; exemplary of film theory's departure from an auteur-centered film analysis is Laura Mulvey, "Visual Pleasure and Narrative Cinema," in *The Sexual Subject: A Screen Reader in Sexuality*, ed. Screen (London: Routledge, 1992), 22–34.

3. Schatz, 91.

4. *Schindler's List* (1993) represents Spielberg's departure from the spectacle aesthetic of High Concept Hollywood while *Saving Private Ryan* (1998) represents an awkward and unwieldy negotiation of spectacle and "serious" melodrama.

5. Justin Wyatt, *High Concept: Movies and Marketing in Hollywood* (Austin: University of Texas Press, 1994).

6. Cameron articulates this position in a keynote address in 1991: "Only through mastery of all the tools for image-making can the mind and the imagination truly soar free." See James Cameron, "Effects Scene: Technology and Magic," *Cinefex* 51 (1992), 5.

7. Keller, 4.

8. See David M. Lubin, *Titanic* (London: BFI, 1999), 84.

9. Scott Bukatman, "The Artificial Infinite: On Special Effects and the Sublime," in *Alien Zone II: The Spaces of Science-Fiction Cinema*, ed. Annette Kuhn (London and New York: Verso, 1999), 256. Emphasis in the original.

10. Bukatman, 255.

11. For a more comprehensive analysis of the conflation of object and subject in *2001: A Space Odyssey*, see Bruce Isaacs, *Toward a New Film Aesthetic* (New York and London: Continuum Press, 2008), 23–24.

12. Digital Domain formed in 1993 with its James Cameron project, *True Lies*. For an analysis of the contribution of Digital Domain to effects cinema, see Piers Bizony, *Digital Domain: The Leading Edge of Visual Effects* (New York: Billboard Books, 2001).

13. In this essay, I distinguish between two modes of contemplation in the analysis of spectacle. Bukatman's sublimity is "contemplated'" in an attempt to contain the "uncontainable" world. I distinguish this mode of contemplation of the spectacle image from the more conventional reading of contemplation as a rationally inscribed activity.

14. See Schatz, 92–93.

15. Keller, *James Cameron*, 6.

16. See Nicholas Rombes, *Cinema in the Digital Age* (London: Wallflower Press, 2009), 148–153.

17. See Jonathan Beller, *The Cinematic Mode of Production: Attention Economy and the Society of the Spectacle* (Lebanon, NE: Dartmouth College Press, 2006), 19–29. Beller concludes that "the cinematic organization of society has led to the restructuring of perception, consciousness, and therefore of production. Furthermore, this production vis-á-vis the cinematicization of society has become increasingly dematerialized, increasingly sensual and abstract, to the point that it occupies the activities of perception and thought itself" (296).

18. See Dudley Andrew, *What Cinema Is: Bazin's Quest and Its Charge* (Chichester, UK: Wiley-Blackwell, 2010).

19. Tom Gunning, "An Aesthetic of Astonishment," *Art and Text* 34 (1989): 31–32.

20. Angela Ndalianis, *Neo-Baroque Aesthetics and Contemporary Entertainment* (Cambridge, MA: MIT Press, 2004), 23–29.

21. Gunning, 36–38.

22. Gunning, 31.

23. See Gunning, 34. Gunning quotes Maxim Gorky's account of a screening of the Lumiére film *L'Arrivée d'un train à La Ciotat* (Arrival of a Train at La Ciotat) (1895): "It speeds right at you — watch out! It seems as though it will plunge into the darkness in which you sit, turning you into a ripped sack full of lacerated flesh and splintered bones...."

24. Wyatt, 15.

25. See David Thompson, "Who Killed the Movies," *Esquire* 126/6 (2009).

26. Beller, 1.

27. Sean Cubitt, *The Cinema Effect* (Cambridge, MA: MIT Press, 2004), 364. See also, 361: "The void in the heart of the commodity spectacle drives it into movement, the hollowness of its perpetual deferral and displacement gives to stillness the glamour of the profound." It isn't quite clear where Cubitt locates the commodity image in the fullness or "transparency" of its form, but no doubt High Concept aesthetics offers such an expressive configuration. At base here is a reading of the "abject" image of cinema: "The film world is a windowless monad, a

simple structure unafflicted by connections to the rest of the world, entirely inward" (Cubitt, 242).

28. For a recent account of the transformational (and non-transformational) aesthetics of "new cinema," see David Rodowick, *The Virtual Life of Film* (Cambridge, MA: Harvard University Press, 2007).

29. Rombes, 149–150. Original emphasis.

30. For a comprehensive reading of the High Concept narrative tradition as "monomythic," see John Shelton Lawrence and Robert Jewett, *The Myth of the American Superhero* (Grand Rapids, MI: W. B. Eerdmans, 2002).

31. *Jurassic Park* Collector's Edition DVD (Universal, 2000), chapter 5: 21:00–22:45.

32. For a fascinating reading of the "effect" as object-animating, see Alan Cholodenko, "Objects in Mirror Are Closer Than They Appear: The Virtual Reality of *Jurassic Park* and Jean Baudrillard," in *Jean Baudrillard: Art and Artefact*, ed. Nicholas Zurbrugg (London: Sage, 1998), 68: "The history of special effects, of which the dinosaur genre has been a privileged testing ground, is the history of animation as the mechanism for the incorporation of the special effect in the cinema."

33. Spielberg appropriated the image for the logo of Amblin Entertainment, formed in 1981, a co-owned production company that funded films such as *ET* (1982) and *The Goonies* (1985).

34. Bukatman, 259. See also Cubitt, 236–238 for a discussion of the "modular events" in the Hollywood neobaroque tradition.

35. Bernard Mendiburu, *3-D Movie-Making: Stereoscopic Digital Cinema from Script to Screen* (Burlington, MA: Elsevier, 2009), 2.

36. Cited in Michael E. Harkins, "The Spectacle in 3-D: Is *Avatar* Really Something New?" *Depth of Field*, February 19, 2010, Access date, May 6, 2010, http://myportfolio.usc.edu/meharkin/2010/02/is_avatar_really_something_new_the_spectacle_in_3-D.html.

37. Robert C. Allen, "Going to the Movies" (guest lecture presented in the Department of Art History and Film Studies/Department of English, August 26, 2010).

38. See, for example, William Langley, "Is James Cameron's *Avatar* the Future of Movies?" *Telegraph,* 12 December, 2009, Access date, May 12, 2010, http://www.telegraph.co.uk/culture/film/6797862/Is-James-Camerons-Avatar-the-future-of-movies.html.

39. Harkins. My emphasis.

40. André Bazin, "The Myth of Total Cinema," in *What Is Cinema, Volume 1,* trans. Hugh Gray (Berkeley and Los Angeles: University of California Press, 1967).

41. André Bazin, "The Evolution of the Language of Film," in *What Is Cinema, Volume 1,* trans. Hugh Gray (Berkeley and Los Angeles: University of California Press, 1967), 35.

42. I'm pleased to note a congruity in perception with Terry Gilliam's comments on an early viewing of segments of *Avatar*: "I've seen great chunks of Avatar in 3-D, but I don't know if the experience is any better. And perhaps what they have to do with Avatar is make the same experience, the same film we've seen before only that it is 3-D and more glorious. I mean, it is very beautiful looking ... but is it a new experience?" An interview conducted by César Alberto Albarran with Terry Gilliam, November 4, 2009 (Cine-Premiere Magazine). I gratefully acknowledge Mr César Albarran in providing this source.

43. For a very detailed and comprehensive analysis of the unique visionary traits of Spielberg's direction, see Warren Buckland, *Directed By Steven Spielberg* (New York: Continuum Press, 2006).

44. *Avatar* DVD (20th Century–Fox, 2010), chapter 1: 1:18–2:04.

45. See, for example, *Le Regle Du Jeu* (*The Rules of the Game*) (Criterion 2-Disc Special Edition DVD), chapter 26.

46. See, for example, Sabine Himmelsbach, "The Interactive Potential of Distributive Networks. Immersion and Participation in Films and Computer Games," in *Future Cinema: The Cinematic Imaginary After Film*, ed. Jeffrey Shaw and Peter Weibel (Cambridge, MA: MIT Press, 2003).

47. Benjamin writes, upon opening his "library": "Ownership is the most intimate relationship that one can have to objects. Not that they come alive in him; it is he who lives in

them." See Walter Benjamin, "Unpacking my Library: A Talk About Book Collecting," in *Illuminations: Walter Benjamin: Essays and Reflections*, ed. Hannah Arendt (New York: Shocken Books, 1988), 67.

48. For an analysis of Cameron's auteur aesthetic founded upon "prosthetic vision," see Keller, 15–16. While the prosthetic vision is not overtly incorporated into the narrative of *Avatar*, Cameron's fascination with sight here transposes seamlessly to the "prosthetic" sight of cinematic spectatorship in 3-D.

WORKS CITED

Allen, Robert C. "Going to the Movies." Guest lecture presented in the Department of Art History and Film Studies, Department of English, University of Sydney, August 25, 2010.

Andrew, Dudley. *What Cinema Is: Bazin's Quest and Its Charge*. Chichester, UK: Wiley-Blackwell, 2010.

L'Arrivée d'un Train à La Ciotat (*Arrival of a Train at La Ciotat*). Dir. Auguste and Louis Lumiére. 1895. Access date, July 16, 2010. http://www.youtube.com/watch?v=1dgLEDdFddk.

Bazin, André." The Evolution of the Language of Film." In *What Is Cinema, Volume 1*, trans. Hugh Gray, 23–40. Berkeley and Los Angeles: University of California Press, 1967.

_____. "The Myth of Total Cinema." In *What Is Cinema, Volume 1*, trans. Hugh Gray, 17–22. Berkeley and Los Angeles: University of California Press, 1967.

Beller, Jonathan. *The Cinematic Mode of Production: Attention Economy and the Society of the Spectacle*. Lebanon, NE: Dartmouth College Press, 2006.

Benjamin, Walter. "Unpacking My Library: A Talk About Book Collecting." In *Illuminations: Walter Benjamin: Essays and Reflections*, edited by Hannah Arendt. New York: Shocken Books, 1988.

Bizony, Piers. *Digital Domain: The Leading Edge of Visual Effects*. New York: Billboard Books, 2001.

Buckland, Warren. *Directed by Steven Spielberg*. New York: Continuum Press, 2006.

Bukatman, Scott. "The Artificial Infinite: On Special Effects and the Sublime." In *Alien Zone II: The Spaces of Science-Fiction Cinema*, edited by Annette Kuhn, 249–275. London and New York: Verso, 1999.

Cameron, James. "Effects Scene: Technology and Magic." *Cinefex* 51 (1992): 5–7.

Cholodenko, Alan. "Objects in Mirror Are Closer Than They Appear: The Virtual Reality of *Jurassic Park* and Jean Baudrillard." In *Jean Baudrillard: Art and Artefact*, edited by Nicholas Zurbrugg, 64–90. London: Sage, 1998.

Cubitt, Sean. *The Cinema Effect*. Cambridge, MA: MIT Press, 2004.

Gilliam, Terry. An Interview Conducted by César Alberto Albarran for Cine-Premiere Magazine. November 4, 2009.

Gunning, Tom. "An Aesthetic of Astonishment: Early Film and the (In)Credulous Spectator." *Art and Text* 34 (Spring, 1989): 31–45.

_____ "An Aesthetic of Astonishment." In *Art and Text* 34 (1989): 31–45.

Harkins, Michael E. "The Spectacle in 3-D: Is *Avatar* Really Something New?" *Depth of Field*, February 19, 2010. Access date, May 6, 2010. http://myportfolio.usc.edu/meharkin/2010/02/is_avatar_really_something_new_the_spectacle_in_3-D.html.

Himmelsbach, Sabine. "The Interactive Potential of Distributive Networks. Immersion and Participation in Films and Computer Games." In *Future Cinema: The Cinematic Imaginary After Film*, edited by Jeffrey Shaw and Peter Weibel, 530–535. Cambridge, MA: MIT Press, 2003.

Isaacs, Bruce. *Toward a New Film Aesthetic*. New York and London: Continuum, 2008.

Keller, Alexandra. *James Cameron*. London and New York: Routledge, 2006.

Langley, William. "Is James Cameron's *Avatar* the Future of Movies?" *Telegraph*, 12 December, 2009. Access date, May 12, 2010. http://www.telegraph.co.uk/culture/film/6797862/Is-James-Camerons-Avatar-the-future-of-movies.html.

Lawrence, John Shelton, and Robert Jewett. *The Myth of the American Superhero.* Grand Rapids, MI: W. B. Eerdmans, 2002.

Lubin, David M. *Titanic.* London: BFI, 1999.

Mendiburu, Bernard. *3-D Movie-Making: Stereoscopic Digital Cinema from Script to Screen.* Burlington, MA: Elsevier, 2009.

Mulvey, Laura. "Visual Pleasure and Narrative Cinema." In *The Sexual Subject: A Screen Reader in Sexuality,* edited by Screen, 22–34. London: Routledge, 1992.

Ndalianis, Angela. *Neo-Baroque Aesthetics and Contemporary Entertainment.* Cambridge, MA: MIT Press, 2004.

Rodowick, David. *The Virtual Life of Film.* Cambridge, MA: Harvard University Press, 2007.

Rombes, Nicholas. *Cinema in the Digital Age.* London: Wallflower Press, 2009.

Schatz, Thomas. "The Whole Equation of Pictures." In *Film and Authorship,* edited by Virginia Wright Wexman, 89–95. New Brunswick, NJ: Rutgers University Press, 2003.

Thompson, David. "Who Killed the Movies." *Esquire* 126/6 (2009).

Wyatt, Justin. *High Concept: Movies and Marketing in Hollywood.* Austin: University of Texas Press, 1994.

FILMS CITED

Aliens. Directed by James Cameron. Twentieth Century–Fox, 1986.

Avatar. Directed by James Cameron. Twentieth Century–Fox, 2009.

Avatar. DVD. Directed by James Cameron. 2009; Los Angeles, CA: Twentieth Century–Fox, 2010.

Blade Runner: The Final Cut. DVD. Directed by Ridley Scott. 1982; Beverly Hills, CA: Warner Bros., 2007.

Children of Men. Directed by Alfonso Cuarón. Universal Pictures, 2006.

Citizen Kane. Directed by Orson Welles. RKO Radio Pictures, 1941.

The Dark Knight. Directed by Christopher Nolan. Warner Bros., 2008.

E.T.: The Extra-Terrestrial. Directed by Steven Spielberg. Universal Pictures, 1982.

Inception. Directed by Christopher Nolan. Warner Bros., 2010.

Jaws. Directed by Steven Spielberg. Universal Pictures, 1975.

Jurassic Park. Directed by Steven Spielberg. Universal Pictures, 1993.

Jurassic Park, Collector's Edition. DVD. Directed by Steven Spielberg. 1993; Universal City, CA: Universal Pictures, 2000.

The Last Picture Show. Directed by Peter Bogdanovich. Columbia Pictures, 1971.

The Magnificent Ambersons. Directed by Orson Welles. RKO Radio Pictures, 1942.

The Matrix. Directed by Andy Wachowski and Lana Wachowski. Warner Bros., 1999.

The Passenger. Directed by Michelangelo Antonioni. MGM, 1966.

Le Regle du Jeu (The Rules of the Game). Directed by Jean Renoir. Nouvelles Éditions de Films (NEF), 1939.

Le Regle du Jeu (The Rules of the Game) 2–Disc Edition. DVD. Directed by Jean Renoir. 1939; France: Criterion, 2004.

Saving Private Ryan. Directed by Steven Spielberg. DreamWorks, 1998.

Schindler's List. Directed by Steven Spielberg. Universal Pictures, 1993.

Star Wars Episode IV: A New Hope. Directed by George Lucas. Twentieth Century–Fox, 1977.

The Terminator. Directed by James Cameron. Hemdale Films, 1984.

Terminator 2: Judgment Day. Directed by James Cameron. Carolco Pictures, 1991.

Titanic. Directed by James Cameron. Twentieth Century–Fox, 1997.

Transformers. Directed by Michael Bay. Paramount Pictures, 2007.

Transformers: Revenge of the Fallen. Directed by Michael Bay. Paramount Pictures, 2009.

True Lies. Directed by James Cameron. Twentieth Century–Fox, 1994.

2001: A Space Odyssey. Directed by Stanley Kubrick. Warner Bros., 1968.
2012. Directed by Roland Emmerich. Columbia Pictures, 2009.

OTHER TEXTS

T2 (Terminator 2): 3-D. Dir. James Cameron. 1996. (Attraction, Universal Studios).

"You have to look with better eyes than that": A Filmmaker's Ambivalence to Technology

Elizabeth Rosen

"I don't like myself when I work. I'm like a machine."—James Cameron[1]

Jon Landau, one of the producers of James Cameron's *Avatar* (2009), wrote of the technological innovation involved in making the film that "When we chose to embark on this film in 2005, I felt like a NASA engineer in 1961 when it was announced they were headed for the moon... We began with various existing technologies, such as Giant Studios performance capture system, AutoDesks MotionBuilder software, and Glenn Derry's hardware, and combined them to make them work together in ways they never have before..."[2]

Landau's choice of words and analogy are illuminating. Not only was the mission to the moon one of the greatest technological achievements of humankind, one which created and spun off technologies from which we still benefit today, but Landau's choice of the word "embark" additionally suggests a journey or adventure. It is a word which evokes discovery and the unknown, even difficulty or danger. Hyperbolic and self-promotional though it may be, such an evocation seems an apt way to describe Cameron's on-going examination of technology in human civilization. Indeed, this intellectual journey — the exploration of the place of technology in human society — has, like all good adventures and adventure stories, been marked by contradictions, presuppositions, discoveries, innovations, and learning to think in new ways. *Avatar* is only the latest in his series of reflections on technology, yet it seems to mark a new moment in Cameron's thinking about technology.

For the majority of his career, Cameron has created films that, while at first appearing technophobic, are actually more complicated portrayals of technology than he has been credited for. In these films, technology is ambivalently depicted, a potential source of both horror *and* wonder. Paradoxically, the films themselves may also be taken as signs of the director's ambivalence since their superficial techno phobic stories could not have been created without state-of-the-art technologies. *Avatar* is emblematic of this ambivalence; it is simultaneously a jeremiad against technologically-based civilizations, and a warning which was only possible to deliver because of the cutting-edge technologies of 3-D cameras, performance-capture systems, and CGI effects.

But with *Avatar,* for the first time in his career, Cameron has made an unambiguous movie about technology. If Cameron has been on an intellectual journey exploring the human-technology connection, he seems to have finally arrived at a destination. *Avatar* has a clear position: technology is a curse, not a boon. The irony, of course, is that *Avatar* owes its existence to technology.

Loving the Machine in Real Life

While Cameron may be ambivalent about technology in the worlds of his movies, he does not seem to be in his real life. Other than George Lucas, perhaps no other director besides James Cameron has been so fully enthralled by the possibilities that technology promises filmmakers. *Esquire*'s Nancy Griffin recalls visiting Cameron when he was in the process of editing *Titanic* in 1997, and writes that he was:

> ... massaging *Titanic* to life. His Avid digital-editing system is an extension of his imagination, allowing him to orchestrate his vision like a conductor, marrying live action with special effects and a score by James Horner. The movie's 250-plus digital shots are being produced a few miles south in Venice at Digital Domain, the special-effects emporium Cameron co founded and co-owns. He communicates face-to-face with the staff there on his Vitel, a computer-based image phone that also transfers files. On the Vitel, he can view an effects shot and tell the animator exactly how to improve it.[3]

Cameron is not only a user of new technologies, but a creator of them. He is responsible for creating some groundbreaking film technology. "When *Titanic* (1997) called for underwater camera movement impossible with existing equipment, he simply invented what he needed (as he had done before with *The Abyss*, resulting in five patents...)."[4] *T2–Judgment Day*'s morphing T-1000 model of Terminator was created through what was then state of the art digital computer imaging.[5] In order to reach and explore the deep ocean wrecks of the *Titanic* and the *Bismarck* for his documentaries *Ghosts of the Abyss* and *Expedition: Bismarck*, Cameron and his brother, Mike, ended up designing and building two seventy-pound submersible robots. Mike Cameron, an aerospace engineer, and his team "created vehicles operable to more than 20,000 feet (enough to reach as much as 85 percent of the ocean floor)..."[6] Recalls the director, "Everything was created from scratch. The thruster motors, the printed circuit boards, the particular type of fiber-optic cables. We thought we were building something that might cost a couple hundred thousand dollars and it wound up costing almost two million."[7]

Cameron also co-developed new cameras to record this underwater experience in 3-D, systems which eventually got employed in the production of *Avatar*. Recalling how he "convinced Sony in Japan to reconfigure their high-def cameras so they'd fit in a small space side by side because we needed to get the two lens centres as close together as human eyes in order to duplicate human vision," the new camera is called the Reality Camera System and employs both 3-D and high-definition technologies.[8]

As with his previous films, *Avatar* is a showcase for groundbreaking filmmaking technologies. In addition to the 3-D camera technology used, Cameron also created a "virtual camera" system, which allowed him "interface with a CG world so that [he] could view [his] actors as their characters when [they] were doing performance capture."[9]

Yet *Avatar* seems to signal a new step in Cameron's thinking about technology. If the previous films have had a love/hate, or at least pro/con, view of technology, *Avatar* definitely takes sides in the debate. And it comes down exactly where you would not expect a real-life technophiliac like Cameron to land: steadfastly against technological civilization. If it seems that *Avatar* seems particularly strident in its tone that may be because, for Cameron, the stakes of technological progress are very high. And what is at stake is everything.

Machines at the End of the World

Almost every film or television project which James Cameron has worked on is implicitly or explicitly concerned with the consequences of technological progress. Even projects such as Kathryn Bigelow's techno phobic *Strange Days* or the television series *Dark Angel*, (for which he is credited only as an executive producer and series creator), are distinctly interested in the dystopian results of a technologically-driven civilization. His two directorial efforts which appear not to fit this description, *True Lies* and *Titanic*, still have at their core machines around which the action revolves: the nuclear bomb and the *R.M.S. Titanic*, respectively.

Even these two films indicate the high stakes with which Cameron regards the question of technology-usage, for both films are about the potential or real "end of the world." That phrase is in quotations for reasons which will become clear in a moment. In almost all of Cameron's work, the consequence of technology going bad is the destruction of everything. This is especially apparent in Cameron's overtly techno phobic *Terminator* films (*The Terminator* and *T2–Judgment Day*), *Aliens*, *The Abyss*, and *Avatar*, in which the world's fate hangs in the balance of the first and last minutes of film time. And while *True Lies* is more concerned with its domestically-located gender scuffle, its "macguffin" is the world-ending nuclear threat of the terrorists in the story. As for the film *Titanic*, Cameron is deliberate in presenting the ship as a world, complete with social, ethnic, and class structures. We should be in no doubt: when the ship goes down, so too goes the "world."[10] As one scholar has pointed out, the spectator is invited to interpret the sinking of the *R.M.S. Titanic* as God's judgment on "the brutality of class society," as well as on man's hubris about his technological advances.[11]

But here is where we must stop to clarify some terminology, for it is common practice to refer to Cameron's technology films as "apocalyptic," and, strictly, this is not so. "Apocalypse" is a Christian concept in which a deity exercises judgment on a sinful world, cleansing it through devastating means, and creating a New Jerusalem for the righteous to inherit.[12] Common usage has modified the word "apocalyptic" to refer to the merely catastrophic or overwhelmingly disastrous, and as a result of this new definition has come a whole host of secularized versions of apocalypse in which the world is at stake, but no God or New Jerusalem is involved. As Walter Benjamin noted many decades ago, mankind's "self-alienation has reached the point where it can experience its own annihilation as a supreme aesthetic pleasure of the first order,"[13] and so, many of the novels and films currently called "apocalyptic" are largely spectacles of devastation, the punishment part of the original paradigm, minus the reward of New Jerusalem which is largely the point of the original story.[14]

This destruction is directly due to human failures; no sign of God's hand is apparent. In his book *Secular Steeples: Popular Culture and the Religious Imagination*, Conrad Ostwalt has written extensively about this new breed of secular apocalyptic stories and rightfully notes how in this version of the apocalyptic story, mankind is not just the author of the End — usually through a scientific gaffe or hubris — but also plays the "Savior" role of the original paradigm and saves the world, as well. Thus, in this separate strain of apocalyptic tales, the End does not truly materialize (though the requisite havoc surely suggests it), and the Messiah does not create a new world for the good to inherit.[15] Yet, as Diane Negra has noted, Hollywood disaster films still "use elements of [the] millennialist mind-set to cultivate an expectant relationship toward disaster that infuses it with additional meanings."[16]

Cameron is working in the secular tradition of apocalyptic stories, stories in which men act in God-like ways, bringing punishment on themselves for their "sins," and the best that can be hoped for is not a New Heaven on Earth, but a saved Earth where the only "new" thing is the hope that an understanding of our own arrogance or stupidity can prevent it all from happening again. One sign that Cameron is working in this secular human-based apocalyptic genre, rather than a traditional deity-based one, is that his new worlds are utopian in nature, rather than divine.

People often interchange the ideas of Eden, Heaven, and utopia, but they, too, are very different concepts. Heaven and Eden issue from God, but utopia is a human political idea. Eden is the world before knowledge of sin entered it; utopia is a human-created vision of how people might live together peacefully in a "perfect State," rather than in a "state of perfection." Negra wrongly conflates these concepts when she writes that in American disaster films, and in Cameron's *Titanic* particularly, "a spirit of technological over-confidence hints at decadence, while apocalypse prefigures the installation of utopia. According to such narrative paradigms, cultural exhaustion gives way to a triumphant new era marked by the imagery of paradise regained."[17] Nonetheless, she is correct in noting how in at least these American catastrophe films, "many films depict the social disruption caused by disaster as essentially positive ... [concluding] with the image of a purified United States undergoing reconstruction."[18] So it would be more correct to observe that most of Cameron's technology films exhibit an ambivalence about technology that vacillates between the possibility that technology holds out to help humankind form either the ultimate dystopian world, or the ultimate utopian one.

It is an ambivalence perfectly captured by the character Lindsey in the film *The Abyss*. Trying to convince her husband, Bud that she has seen a peaceful alien life form, and not, as the Cold Warrior and pressure-sick naval officer Coffey insists, a new form of Russian war technology, Lindsey tells Bud, "We all see what we want to see. Coffey looks and sees Russians. He sees hate and fear. You have to look with better eyes than that."[19] Film critics have written of Cameron that his fetish with guns reflects an immature and over-indulged kid playing at blowing things up every chance he gets, but I would argue that his gun fetish is part of a larger, more complex intellectual position about technologies and war, and the role that such technology has in creating utopian or dystopian societies.[20] His inclusion of scenes such as the one in which the gung-ho marine Hudson euphorically lists the various weapons he has to destroy the aliens of the eponymous film is more likely meant to expose our hubris with regards to technology, not to glorify it.[21]

It's not phase-plasma pulse-rifles that kill people...

While Cameron's position may appear to be techno phobic in many of his earlier films, it is actually more complicated than that. The problem is not that technology is bad. The problem is that technology is employed in bad ways. Like his character Lindsey, Cameron sees that most of our technology seems to be in service to troubling aims. Indeed, though perhaps invented for other reasons, what Cameron seems to suggest is that technology is almost always deployed in the service of financial gain or warfare. *T2: Judgment Day*'s well-meaning, but short-sighted computer scientist Dyson is a point in fact. Boyishly excited, Dyson tells his wife that the work he is doing on the futuristic computer chip could provide amazing and world changing technologies, if only he can unscramble it. Imagine, he says, an automated "pilot" who never shows up hung over, or late, who never makes a mistake. Yet when Sarah and John Connor inform him the result of his research will be exactly this autonomous machine, Skynet, which will launch a nuclear war to annihilate the human race, Dyson is not just distraught, he seems not even to have considered this possibility. "How were we supposed to know?" he pleads with the unforgiving Sarah.[22]

The Abyss is largely built on this trope of military co-opting of technology. The experimental deep-water drilling rig is first co-opted for a "rescue" operation that turns out only to be a military salvage operation. The aim of the real operation is not to recover people, but to recover the nuclear warheads which have gone down with the submarine. Later, the mini-roving camera submersible which the crew has built is co-opted by Coffey, who attaches a nuclear warhead to it with the aim of using it to guide a bomb to the aliens he believes are his enemies. Indeed, Coffey and his marines repeatedly take over various civilian technologies–the submersibles, the cameras, the ships waiting in the ocean above–and turn them to war-like purposes.

Such re-purposing of technology is a continuing theme in Cameron films, but even non-war technologies often seem to constrict or limit our ability to achieve utopian ideals. For example, technology in Cameron films often malfunctions. *Aliens'* marine, Drake, has a malfunctioning helmet camera he gets back online by slamming his head against the wall, and there are frequent gun jams at pivotal moments.[23] Too often, technology actually fails the humans it is supposed to serve. The *Terminator* films are rife with this object lesson. There are answering machines or pagers that do not deliver messages in time to help, or worse, actually help the Terminators find their prey. There is the Walkman that not only keeps the roommate Ginger in the dark about the fatal attack taking place in the next room, but even prevents her from engaging in ordinary human communication with her boyfriend as they have sex. There are police radios, or the computer systems in the police cruisers, which paradoxically help, not hinder, the Terminators find their quarry. There are semi-trailers, helicopters, motorcycles, and factory robots that, instead of being helpful machines for the humans, are turned against them as weapons by the

Terminators. These are examples of the "Tech Noir" which Cameron playfully hints at with the dance club's name in *The Terminator*. Our technology, he seems to say wryly, is literally killing us.

Becoming Technology

One critic has argued that in Cameron's films "[t]echnology is good as long as it remains within human control and can serve human interests; it is bad when it achieves autonomy. In other words, the human cannot be replaced by the machine."[24] But this seems to misunderstand how Cameron largely depicts technology. Technology is bad when humans use it for bad ends, good when they use it for good ends. And as for humans being replaced by machines, this is exactly where Cameron's ambivalence to technology becomes most apparent, because one of the things which Cameron seems most clear on is that this line between human and technology has already been crossed: we *are* our technology.

No scene makes this clearer than the one in *Aliens* in which the marines Vasquez and Drake suit up with their enormous swivel guns and vests. Like the steadicam suits which filmmakers use, these huge machine guns attach to a vest on their wearer's torso, and have two pivot points so the marine can swivel the gun as needed. Yet Cameron inserts a moment in which both marines fetishistically and lovingly swing their guns in the same series of beautiful and balletically choreographed movements, as though rehearsing the precision gun maneuvers of the dress marine corps. It is clear: these marines *are* their technology, and vice versa.

And this is hardly the only example. In *Aliens*, Ripley is only able to defeat the alien queen because she effectually turns herself into a cyborg, encasing herself in the metal technology of the loader.[25] In both *Terminator* films, the machines are not merely "passing" as humans; they represent a more complex melding of human and machine than their cyborg exteriors suggest. In *The Terminator*, the machine imitates the voices of humans, but by *T2: Judgment Day*, the T-1000 has no machine interior to speak of. Instead, it takes on the forms of humans it comes into contact with, and when it "dies," Cameron makes explicit the connection between man and machine: as the T-1000 goes through its death-throes, it morphs repeatedly from one human form to another.[26] More than this, the T-800 which in *T2* is sent to protect John Connor "transcends" its machine origins; it learns the human qualities of emotion, improvisation, and humor. This is an uncomfortable and ironic point which Sarah Connor does not miss. Watching John with the predator-turned-protector, Sarah comments:

Watching John with the machine, it was suddenly so clear. The terminator would never stop. It would never leave him and it would never hurt him, never shout at him or get drunk and hit him, or say it was too busy to spend time with him. It would always be there and it would die to protect him. Of all the would-be fathers who came and went over the years, this thing, this machine, was the only one who measured up.[27]

Mark Jancovich makes a further observation, writing that "While the Terminator is a robot hidden beneath "living human tissue," the humans have become living human tissue encased within mechanical constructions. The film ... [shows] the extent to which human activity has been reduced to forms of mechanical behavior. People are continually presented as being caught up in patterns of repetitive and compulsive behavior."[28]

Jancovich makes a distinction between "friendly" and "unfriendly" technologies in his argument, but Cameron, at least in his early films, is not really that reductionist. As on any journey, Cameron's views on technology have been evolving as he goes. By the time he makes *Aliens* and *T2*, Cameron has come to the uncomfortable conclusion that we cannot live without our technology. If technology presents the threat to utopian ambitions, indeed to human existence, it is also technology which allows us to defeat and control that threat, and it is also technology through which this utopia can be achieved. In a 2003 interview, Cameron spoke to this potential when he said, "I see our potential destruction and the potential salvation as human beings coming from technology and how we use it, how we master it and how we prevent it from mastering us."[29] In other words, technology itself is neutral. It is the user who cannot be trusted. Or perhaps, the consequences of new technologies can never be anticipated. As the editors of the collection *Living with the Genie: Essays on Technology and the Quest for Human Mastery* write in their introduction:

Our tools have a way of taking on what seem to be lives of their own, and we quickly end up having to adjust them... Contradiction is the name of the game: the past century was history's deadliest, in terms of humanity's technological capacity for organized violence. And yet life expectancies in the industrialized world rose to approach eighty years. But a balance sheet of the good and the bad would be pointless, if for no other reason than that what is "good" depends in part on whether you get a piece of the action ... technology often seems driven by forces beyond human intent, but we do not mean to suggest that our cohabitation with this great power is something new... In the face of such capabilities, it may be easy to neglect the following fact: science and technology are not forces of nature. They are the products of human endeavor and human choice. This is not the same as saying that we can engineer the future in precise ways — the social consequences of new technological systems will always be largely unforeseen and unintended. But we can be less or more inclusive, less or more open, less or more conscious, in deciding what avenues of scientific and technological advance we should pursue, how aggressively we should push, how enthusiastically we should adopt, how stringently we should control.[30]

Cameron's shifting feelings about technology can be seen in the depiction of the cyborg Bishop of *Aliens.* In the first film, with which Cameron had no involvement, the cyborg is hidden among the humans and is a villainous figure precisely because it cannot exhibit human values (which here include empathy and valuing human life above any other life form). The human crew of the *Nostromo* dies because of this machine amongst them.[31] But when Cameron comes to create his own cyborg for the sequel, his evolving views of technology are evident. Bishop prefers to be called an "artificial person," a description which hints at the melding of man and machine which is the aim of the cyborg figure. But more importantly, Ripley's justifiable hatred of and paranoia about the cyborg simply cannot withstand her experience with this second, more advanced technology. She must revise her view of these technologies because she directly owes her life and Newt's to the cyborg. But tellingly, Cameron cannot make himself fully love the machine, either. While Bishop is "human" to the extent that he values human life, by film's end, Bishop himself is reduced back to his machine state. Ripped in half and with only his upper torso still operating, Bishop's machine nature is now exposed for all to observe; he cannot hide what he is.

Cameron swings between technophilia and technophobia here. And he continues to throughout his film career. That is, until *Avatar.*

Turning on the (Mechanical) Dime

In a twenty year career of film-making, Cameron's films, though appearing to be anti-technology in attitude, do not really hold up under that criticism. And it is not just because it has taken a tremendous amount of cutting-edge technology to make these seemingly anti-technology films. Indeed, as early as *The Terminator* film, Kevin Pask noted, "Hollywood's reliance on its own technological innovations to bring audiences to the cinema thus ensures that the simplistic technophobic message of the movie never succeeds in overcoming its equally powerful technophilia, which is thematized in the relationship between the represented technology and that of the film apparatus itself."[32] Within the movie worlds Cameron creates, technology is source of both horror *and* wonder, potential devastation *and* potential miraculous progress.

This potential wonder and progress is best exemplified by the alien technology in *The Abyss,* a water technology rendered in beautifully glowing halos, streaking water–comets, malleable jets of water, and floating carnivals of color. It is a technology, as Lindsey notes, as beautiful and graceful as it is obviously advanced. But even in Cameron films where the technology is more familiar to us, we get a sense of the wonderful possibilities of technology.

In *Aliens*, this wonder at technology is partially and paradoxically expressed through the balletic and graceful way that the marines use their weapons, but there are other moments of technological wonder that Cameron gives the film-goer: the "terra-forming technology" that allows humans to turn hostile environments into hospitable ones; the graceful, looming specter of huge spacecraft hovering on the edges of space; the peaceful Snow White–like repose of Ripley in hyper-sleep.

In *Titanic*, the grace and the luxury of the doomed ship is rendered in sumptuous detail, but the technological marvel of the great ocean liner is not lost on the viewer, who is treated to tours of the working bowels of the marvelous ship, views from the stern that emphasize the ship's grandeur and size, and an on-going narrative from a surviving passenger, Rose, that insists on seeing the *R.M.S. Titanic* as a "ship of dreams," and not as a piece of failed technology, as the expedition leader, Brock, does.

Even in *T2: Judgment Day*, where the potential horror of technology is most fully realized in the figures of the Terminators themselves (and more particularly for us, in the repeated dreams of nuclear annihilation that Sarah has), Cameron has insisted on rendering the T-1000 morphing technology as so graceful, pliable, and utterly cool that a viewer experiences a Romantic moment of Sublimity: an awe that simultaneously incorporates terror and wonder.

But *Avatar* rarely, if ever, has these mixed feelings about technology. There is certainly a moment when it first appears that Cameron's former ambivalence is coming out, and this is in the utopian possibility of the avatars themselves. The euphoria Jake feels when his crippled body is made physically whole and powerful again as he projects into his avatar is gorgeously, poignantly depicted as the avatar has its first run. But the utopian possibilities of a paraplegic feeling the strength in his legs and the dirt between his toes again are quickly and almost completely undone in *Avatar*, as we learn that the technology has once again been usurped by military and corporate entities whose vicious, unethical, and greedy behavior tramples on any utopian possibilities attached to a technology-based civilization. It is almost as if Cameron has finally decided that, with technological progress, come the accompanying sins, and that, as there is no way to separate the two, technology itself must be held accountable and avoided at all costs. The natural ways of the Na'vi people, their physical and spiritual bond with their mother planet are more than just Cameron's plea for some environmental sanity; they are a none-too-subtle reprimand to a technological civilization. As the unbearable destruction of Home Tree signals, technologically-based society has not just lost its way; it has a scorched-earth policy toward that way.

Nearly all of the technology on offer in this most recent film is war technology or used in its service. And unlike Cameron's other films, there is no "other side" to technology presented here. The choice is technology or Nature. The Na'vi have rejected Grace's education program, and they have their own very powerful medicine. As one character says, the technologically progressive society has nothing the Na'vi want. Since the viewer never sees the Na'vi become prey or predators within their natural world, he/she is forced to adopt Cameron's rather simplistic view that nature is never "bad," only technology is. Since technology is associated with the "bad guys" and Nature with the "good guys," Cameron has created a simplistic and false choice in this film.

And yet, this most recent depiction of the evils of technology only exists because of the thing it most abhors. As a philosophical stand, this Luddite position Cameron has adopted is a weak one, and not merely because the means by which he creates his jeremiad undercuts his message. What the paradox of his film-making technologies suggests is that we can never go back; we can only go forward in a more intelligent manner.

If Cameron's *Avatar* is meant as a warning about clashes between indigenous, primitive cultures and our own technologically-based society, it more than adequately illustrates the perils of such encounters. But as a warning for the viewer, a member of an already technologically-based civilization, the film is too cartoonishly one-sided to be convincing. As futurist Ray Kurzweil has written in response to technophobes who fear that the technologies of our future will be uncontrollable and lead to terrible, perhaps species-ending dangers, such people:

> [paint] a picture of future dangers as if they were released on today's unprepared world. The reality is that the sophistication and power of our defensive technologies and knowledge will grow along with the dangers. When we have "gray goo" (unrestrained nanobot replication), we will also have "blue goo" ("police" nanobots that combat the "bad" nanobots).[33]

This latest destination in Cameron's intellectual journey may be right-hearted, but it is wrong-headed. His earlier films depict the possibilities as well as the dangers of technology, and are ultimately the more thoughtful, even-handed examinations of the perils, and promises, of living with technology. These earlier films show that for every mini-rover humans can arm to deliver deep-sea missiles, they can also invent a miraculous diving suit that lets them breathe oxygenated liquid so they can travel to the ocean floor. For every technological advance that is weaponized to use against humanity, technology will be harnessed as a means to protect it.

If James Cameron wishes to compel us to regard our technological progression with more suspicion and caution, then he should return to making the more sophisticated narratives about technology that mark his earlier films, and stay away from parables. Utopia and dystopia are choices, after all. If technology is the means of achieving either, then the way to convince people to choose utopia is to show them what technology is capable of when it is adopted by "good" users for "good" purposes.

NOTES

1. Griffin, "James Cameron is the scariest man in Hollywood."
2. Fitzpatrick, *The Art of Avatar: James Cameron's Epic Adventure.* Forward.
3. Griffin, "James Cameron is the scariest man in Hollywood."
4. Keller, *James Cameron*, 3.
5. In a technical discussion of the digital effects of the film, Patrick Crogan notes that the scene in which the T-1000 morphs from a checkerboard floor to the shape of the security guard who walks over it is "a quiet in-joke amongst specialist CGI practitioners. The checkerboard pattern is a standard surface rendering option in 3-D computer imaging software packages. It is a "procedural texture"—generated mathematically as a dynamic simulation covering the moving 3-D model- often used in order to test the success of surface rendering effects on animated 3-D models (that is, to check for tears or faults in the application of the surface to the model)." Crogan, "Things Analog and Digital."
6. In a nice bit of irony, Mike Cameron is a former missile designer and in the case of this invention "took inspiration from the wire-guided torpedoes used by the military that can travel for many miles." "The Abyss Transit System." Cameron recently offered those deep-diving submersibles to BP to help in the clean-up of the disastrous Deepwater Horizon oil spill in the Gulf of Mexico. BP declined. See Quinn, "Gulf of Mexico Oil Spill: James Cameron offers private submarines to help BP clean up." and "James Cameron joins the fight against the Gulf of Mexico oil spill."
7. Eagan, "Back to the Abyss: James Cameron Returns to *Titanic* for Large-Format 3-D Spectacle."
8. Felperin, "That's Entertainment," 10.
9. "Interview with James Cameron," *Fresh Air.*
10. This variation of "world" is typical of postmodern creators who are using the religious apocalyptic paradigm in secular ways. These secularized interpretations of the idea of a "world" include time periods, worldviews, even individual consciences. For more on this and how postmodern authors and filmmakers have adjusted the traditional story of Apocalypse, see Elizabeth Rosen, *Apocalyptic Transformations: Apocalypse and the Postmodern Imagination.*
11. McGee, "Terrible Beauties: Messianic Time and the Image of Social Redemption in James Cameron's *Titanic.*"
12. End of world scenarios are part of many ancient religions other than Christianity, but Apocalypse with its ideas of a New Jerusalem and a returning Messiah are unique to Christianity.
13. Benjamin, "The Work of Art in the Age of Its Technological Reproducibility," 42.
14. I separate these punishing "end of the world" spectacles into a new category of apocalyptic story which I call "neo-apocalyptic." See Rosen, *Apocalyptic Transformation: Apocalypse and the Postmodern Imagination.*
15. David E. Aune writes that this is the difference between "restorative messianisam" which "anticipates the restoration of the Davidic kingdom," versus the "utopian messianism" which "expects the creation of a new and perfect world after the destruction of the present world." Qtd in Garrett, "'I Saw One Like a Son of Man,'" 146.

16. Negra, "Titanic, Survivalism, and the Millennial Myth," 221.

17. Negra,"Titanic, Survialism, and the Millennial Myth," 234–5.

18. She goes on to note how this reconstruction is tied to American values. Negra, 233.

19. *The Abyss.* Dir. James Cameron.

20. Of course, one might easily claim that in the process, Cameron's delight in providing the viewer with bigger, more spectacular violence in his fight scenes certainly causes a paradox which is difficult to reconcile.

21. "I am ready, man. Ready to get it on. Check-it-out. I am the ultimate badass ... state of the badass art. You do not want to fuck with me. Hey, Ripley, don't worry. Me and my squad of ultimate badasses will protect you. Check-it-out... (He slaps the SERVO-CANNON controls in the GUN BAY above them.) Independently targeting particle-beam phalanx. VWAP! Fry half a city with this puppy. We got tactical smart-missles, phased-plasma pulse-rifles, RPG's. We got sonic eeelectronic ball breakers, we got nukes, we got knives ... sharp sticks —." *Aliens.* Dir. James Cameron.

22. *The Terminator.* Dir. James Cameron. Such short-sightedness is par for the course in Cameron's films, though it is usually a corporation which allows its greed to short-circuit its sense. For a detailed discussion about the conflict between capitalism and technology, see Robert F. Arnold, "Termination or Transformation? The "Terminator" Films and Recent Changes in the U.S. Auto Industry."

23. *The Terminator*, especially, inspired many scholars to look at the role of technology within the story. See Pask, "Cyborg Economies: Desire and Labor in the *Terminator* films," Jancovich, "Modernity or Subjectivity in *The Terminator*: the Machine as Monster in Contemporary American Culture," or a particularly observant chapter in Alexandra Keller's hagiography James Cameron.

24. Arnold, "Termination or Transformation?" 25.

25. Cf. Tim Blackmore, who argues the opposite: that it is only when Ripley abandons the machine that she is able to defeat the Alien queen. "'Is this going to be another bug hunt?': S-F tradition versus biology-as-destiny in James Cameron's *Aliens.*"

26. See Kimball, "Conceptions and Contraceptions of the Future: Terminator 2, The Matrix, and Alien Resurrection."

27. *T2: Judgment Day.* Dir. James Cameron.

28. Jancovich, "Modernity and Subjectivity in *The Terminator*," 9–10.

29. Wootton, "James Cameron."

30. Introduction, *Living with the Genie: Essays on Technology and the Quest for Human Mastery*, 1–3.

31. Though it should be noted that the cyborg is acting on the instructions of other humans.

32. Pask, "Cyborg Economies: Desire and Labor in the *Terminator* films," 193.

33. Kurzweil, "Promise and Peril," 56.

WORKS CITED

"The Abyss Transit System." *Scientific American* 288, no. 6 (June 2003): 32–33.

Arnold, Robert F. "Termination or Transformation? The "Terminator" Films and Recent Changes in the U.S. Auto Industry." *Film Quarterly* 52, no. 1 (Autumn, 1998): 20-30.

Benjamin, Walter. "The Work of Art in the Age of Its Technological Reproducibility." In *The Work of Art in the Age of Its Technological Reproducibility, and Other Writings on Media*, edited by Michael W. Jennings, Brigid Doherty, and Thomas Y. Levin. Translated by Edmund Jephocott., et al. Cambridge, MA: Belknap Press of Harvard, 2008.

Blackmore, Tim. "Is this going to be another bug-hunt?": S-F tradition versus biology-as-destiny in James Cameron's Aliens, *Journal of Popular Culture*, Vol. 29, N0. 4 (Spring 1996), 211–226.

Crogan, Patrick. "Things Analog and Digital." *Senses of Cinema: An Online Film Journal Devoted*

to the Serious and Eclectic Discussion of Cinema 5 (April 2000). http://archive.sensesofcin
ema.com/contents/00/5/digital.html (Access date, May 28, 2010).

Eagan, Daniel. "Back to the Abyss: James Cameron Returns to *Titanic* for Large-Format 3-D
Spectacle." *Film Journal International* 106, no. 5 (May 2003): 30, 51.

Felperin, Leslie. "That's Entertainment." *Sight and Sound* 13, no. 6 (2003): 10.

Fitzpatrick, Lisa. *The Art of* Avatar: *James Cameron's Epic Adventure.* Preface by Peter Jackson.
Foreword by Jon Landau. Epilogue by James Cameron. New York: Abrams, 2009.

Garrett, Greg. "'I saw one like a son of man' The Eschatological Savior in Contemporary Film."
In *Reel Revelations,* edited by John Walliss and Lee Quinby. Sheffield, England: Sheffield
Phoenix Press, forthcoming 2010.

Gill, Pat. "Technostalgia: Making the Future Past Perfect." *Camera Obscura: A Journal of Feminism, Culture, and Media Studies* 40-41 (May 1997): 163–179.

Griffin, Nancy. "James Cameron is the scariest man in Hollywood." *Esquire* 128, no. 6 (Dec.
1997): 98(7).

"Interview with James Cameron." By Terry Gross, *Fresh Air,* National Public Radio, February
18, 2010.

"James Cameron joins the fight against the Gulf of Mexico oil spill." *The Telegraph* (London),
June 2, 2010.

Jancovich, Mark. "Modernity and Subjectivity in *The Terminator*: The Machine as Monster in
Contemporary American Culture." *The Velvet Light Trap* 30 (Fall 1992): 3–17.

Keller, Alexandra. *James Cameron.* London: Routledge, 2006.

Kimball, A. Samuel. "Conceptions and Contraceptions of the Future: *Terminator 2, The Matrix,*
and *Alien Resurrection.*" *Camera Obscura: A Journal of Feminism, Culture, and Media Studies*
17, no. 50[2] (2002): 69–108.

Kurzweil, Ray. "Promise and Peril." In *Living with the Genie: Essays on Technology and the Quest
for Human Mastery,* edited by Alan Lightman, Daniel Sarewitz and Christina Desser. Washington: Island Press, 2003.

Living with the Genie: Essays on Technology and the Quest for Human Mastery. Eds. Alan Lightman,
Daniel Sarewitz and Christina Desser. Washington: Island Press, 2003.

McGee, Patrick. "Terrible Beauties: Messianic Time and the Image of Social Redemption in
James Cameron's *Titanic.*" *Postmodern Culture: An Electronic Journal of Interdisciplinary
Criticism* 10, no. 1 (Sept. 1999). 45 paragraphs.

Negra, Diane. "Titanic, Survivalism, and the Millennial Myth." In *Titanic: Anatomy of a Blockbuster,* edited by Kevin S. Sandler and Gaylyn Studlar. New Brunswick: Rutgers University
Press, 1999.

Ostwalt, Conran. *Secular Steeples: Popular Culture and the Religious Imagination.* Harrisburg,
PA: Trinity Press International, 2003.

Pask, Kevin. "Cyborg Economies: Desire and Labor in the *Terminator* Films." In *Postmodern
Apcoalypse: Theory and Cultural Practice at the End,* edited by Richard Dellamora. Philadelphia: University of Pennsylvania Press, 1995.

Quinn, James. "Gulf of Mexico Oil Spill: James Cameron Offers Private Submarines to Help
BP Clean-up." *The Telegraph* (London), May 10, 2010.

Rosen, Elizabeth. *Apocalyptic Transformation: Apocalypse and the Postmodern Imagination.* Lanham, MD: Lexington, 2008.

Wootton, Adrian. "James Cameron." *The Guardian* (London), April 13, 2003. http://www.guar
dian.co.uk/film/2003/apr/13/guardianinterviewsatbfisouthbank (Access date, September
22, 2010).

Films and Television Cited

The Abyss. Directed by James Cameron. Twentieth Century–Fox, 1989.
Aliens. Directed by James Cameron. Twentieth Century–Fox, 1986.

Avatar. Directed by James Cameron. Twentieth Century–Fox, 2009.

Dark Angel. Twentieth Century–Fox Television, 2000-2002.

"So, what's your story?": Morphing Myths and Feminizing Archetypes, from *The Terminator* to *Avatar*

Strange Days. Directed by Kathryn Bigelow. Lightstorm Entertainment, 1995.

The Terminator. Directed by James Cameron. Hemdale Films, 1984.

Terminator 2: Judgment Day. Directed by James Cameron. Carolco Pictures, 1991.

Titanic. Directed by James Cameron. Twentieth Century–Fox, 1997.

True Lies. Directed by James Cameron. Twentieth Century–Fox, 1994.

"So, what's your story?": Morphing Myths and Feminizing Archetypes from *The Terminator* to *Avatar*

DEAN CONRAD

Male Narrator (V.O.)

> *They made him a machine, trained to deliver humanity from the final cataclysm. They built him a machine, the most awesome ship ever constructed, and with a mind of its own. She was raised by a machine that alone knew the power of love. Together they searched the wilderness of stars for a place where the cycle of creation could begin again. Xenogenesis: Man's ultimate adventure...*[1]

Thus begins a film career.

It is never made clear how the woman and the machine are going to rekindle the human race together, but this is unimportant. As the voice intones its hyperbole and the camera pans and fades through still images reminiscent of *Astounding Science-Fiction* magazine covers of the 1930s, students of science fiction cinema may already discern the style, scope and ambition that would come to typify the work of James Cameron. This is *Xenogenesis*, a 12-minute short, written and directed with Randall Frakes in 1978. It features William Wisher, who would go on to share the writing credits on the first two *Terminator* films (1984, 1991) and Margaret Undiel — in her first and, to date, only screen role.

Xenogenesis has little plot to speak of, the characterizations are minimal and the dialogue is basic. The majority of the effort and budget appear to have been spent on the effects and action shots. Whilst it may be unfair to look for a fully-rounded narrative and characters in what is essentially a calling-card project for the fledgling filmmaker, similar searches have regularly been made in reviews of James Cameron's subsequent feature efforts — a result, according to Laura Miller, of the director's "...limited powers of dramatic invention."[2] This criticism, directed here at *Titanic* (1997), may seem harsh, but it is indicative of a general notion that Cameron's characters and plots continue to be secondary to his ambition to create what Miller goes on to call little more than "...the most impressive movie money can buy."[3] By *Terminator 2: Judgment Day* this ambition was clear to Tony Rayns: "James Cameron's sense of his own mission seems to be growing as fast as his budgets."[4] Wider ambition and mission have ultimately affected Cameron's female (and male) characters. By his next film, *True Lies* (1994), it is clear to Leslie Felperin Sharman that developing a female lead is not a priority: "Helen's ineptitude is consistent with the demands of the action genre..."[5]

It is fair to say that James Cameron has not generally been regarded as Hollywood's most subtle or skilled writer, a perception that has been sustained by *Avatar* (2009), a film which, according to Andrew Osmond, contains "some ghastly dialogue and info-dumps..."[6] Cameron's skill as a technically-astute director is another matter; his persistence as a writer reflects the needs of a filmmaker who will brook no compromise in his expanding screen vision. The resultant, largely-undisputed, control that Cameron has had over his films is useful to the commentator, as it affords the luxury of being able safely to pin apparent preoccupations and priorities to the man himself. The foundations are already apparent in that first screen effort, *Xenogenesis*, which serves a test-bed for a number of techniques and images which will re-emerge in later projects — most notably, the *Terminator* films.

Particularly germane to this essay, however, is Margaret Undiel's character, Lori. Whilst it is difficult to discern much from her scant dialogue, her fight with an alien robot is more telling. Lori pilots her own spider-legged machine using hand-held, mimic controls, a concept re-used by Cameron for Ripley's iconic power-loader fight with the alien queen towards the end of *Aliens* (1986).[7] In *Xenogenesis*, Lori is fighting to save the android, Raj, and whilst she never quite says "Get away from him, you bitch!," this celebrated *Aliens* sentiment is close to the surface. During the fight, Lori can be seen through the transparent, hemispherical cockpit windshield, as she struggles with the controls. This distinctive image is developed for number of shots of Mary Elizabeth Mastrantonio and Kimberly Scott, piloting submarines through *The Abyss* (1989).

Such is the pervasiveness of the early Cameron woman that she is still discernable in films written but not directed by him. She is there as Julia Nickson's jungle fighter Co Bao in *Rambo: First Blood, Part II* (1985); she appears again as Juliette Lewis' character Faith Justin in the Kathryn Bigelow directed *Strange Days* (1995), a film co-written with Cameron some years after their divorce.[8]

It is not enough, however, merely to say that themes can be seen in the work of James Cameron with respect to his screen women. Critics and reviewers began to note this as soon as sufficient films had passed for a pattern to emerge and reveal what Tony Rayns calls "...Cameron's gallery of strong and resourcefully maternal women."[9] Cameron's personal investment in his female characters has also tempted critics and reviewers to draw parallels with elements of his own life: his strong, resourceful mother, a penchant for capable, independent women, and four failed marriages — including those to director Kathryn Bigelow, actor Linda Hamilton and producer Gale Anne Hurd.

Less analysis has been directed towards the evolving function of Cameron's female screen characters as his career has progressed. Closer attention reveals that they are not all hewn from the same stone. Or if they are, subtle, and not so subtle, differences chart ongoing shifts in Cameron's priorities as a filmmaker. Whether changes are the result of personal experiences is, of course, impossible to know for certain. They may betray the maturing mind of the creator; they may reflect shifting cultural and political climates; they may be a symptom of ballooning budgets. Whatever the reasons, a clear development can be seen in James Cameron's leading ladies — from the female hero, Sarah Connor to the feminine heroine, Neytiri.

Sarah Connor

Come on. Do I look like the mother of the future?[10]

Cameron was 23 years old in 1977, the year that George Lucas' film *Star Wars* kick-started a science fiction revolution whose (special) effects are still being felt. The phenomenal popular success of *Star Wars* brought the genre's commercial potential to the attention of the Hollywood studios, and resulted in a profusion of hopeful investors — such as the group of dentists who funded *Xenogenesis*— as well as ambitious young filmmakers, like Cameron, attempting to surf the new genre wave.[11]

Xenogenesis never matured into a feature project, but it did prove useful in securing Cameron's first professional feature work, on Roger Corman's *Battle Beyond the Stars* (1980). This invaluable practical film-making experience, coupled with what he had learned on *Xenogenesis*, would form the backbone of Cameron's own first feature project. However, for a plot, he would lean heavily on lessons learned from *Star Wars*.

Lucas himself had turned to the work of Joseph Campbell, the American writer and academic who explores the traditions and conventions of storytelling in his seminal text, *The Hero with a Thousand Faces*. Campbell references psychologist Gustav Jung's work on archetypes in his examination of the development of hero myths down the centuries and across cultures. The result is the identification of a unifying archetype: the universal Hero's Journey: the narrative path followed by heroes from Theseus, in his adventures with the Cretan minotaur, to Prince Siddhārtha Gautama on his quest to become the Buddha. It is part of the monomyth that lends familiarity to the character of Luke Skywalker.[12]

Cameron would have been familiar with the basic tenets of this journey through the plot of his own favorite film, *The Wizard of Oz*.[13] It is one of the movies cited by Christopher Vogler, along with *Star Wars*, as a classic example of Campbell's work, as reflected in Hollywood. Vogler's 1992 study, *The Writer's Journey*, is now required reading for would-be screenwriters, but back in the 1980s, Cameron wanted to be different. As he says himself in Rebecca Keegan's celebration of his life and work, *The Futurist*, "In writing I like to be fresh, and at the time of *Terminator*, that kind of female character hadn't really been done."[14] "Fresh" may not be the best description for a plot structure that can be traced back thousands of years; however, Cameron's claim for his female lead does carry weight. Vogler's study of Campbell's plot structure contains a preface-note that triggers some insight into Sarah Connor's central contribution to a development in the representation of women in film:

> The Hero's Journey is sometimes critiqued as a masculine theory, cooked up by men to enforce their dominance, and with little relevance to the unique and quite different journey of womanhood.[15]

Rather than offering a traditional woman's journey, akin to that of Princess Leia in *Star Wars* or Ann Darrow in *King Kong* (1933), Cameron takes his lead from Dorothy's trip to Oz. Ripley had emerged from *Alien* (1979) as the lone survivor and heroine of Ridley Scott's ensemble piece; In *The Terminator*, Cameron takes this a step further, by presenting Connor as the survivor and hero of *her own journey* through an action picture. This action is central to Cameron's re-shaping of Campbell's hero myth, as he reflects the masculine through his female lead's perspective.

According to Campbell, the traditional hero completes three stages of enlightenment: *separation*, *initiation* and *return*. Each stage is dissected into phases, which Vogler later plots across the standard three act, 120-minute screenplay structure.[16] Following the basic arc of the first stage, Sarah Connor is separated from her old world and is catapulted into a new, larger one. Her trajectory through *The Terminator* can be summarized simply using Campbell's own description of what he terms "the nuclear unit of the monomyth":

> A hero ventures forth from the world of common day into a region of supernatural wonder: fabulous forces are there encountered and a decisive victory is won: the hero comes back from this mysterious adventure with the power to bestow boons on his fellow man.[17]

Connor duly experiences *The Call to Adventure* and the *Refusal of the Call*; she meets her *Supernatural Aid* in the form of Kyle Reese, which triggers *The Crossing of the First Threshold*; finally she enters *The Belly of the Whale*. By cheating death, the protagonist demonstrates worthiness, taking one step closer to becoming a real hero. The journey continues. Sarah's speech to the tape recorder and her unborn baby at the end of the film further echo Campbell's words: "...It may be that he here discovers for the first time that there is a benign power everywhere supporting him and his superhuman passage."[18] Luke has Obi-Wan; Dorothy has the Good Witch of the North; Connor has Reese.

Added weight is brought to this spiritual force by the time-travel element of this science fiction film. Connor knows that the son she is carrying will one day send his own father, Reese, back to her in the past. The logic of this bears scant scrutiny, as Connor herself points out: "God, a person could go crazy thinking about this." But Cameron's contribution to the development of the female in science fiction cinema is reflected in the weight of destiny invested in Connor: simply by placing a woman into the Hero's Journey of an action film, he feminizes the male archetype, ushering in a new era of female action heroes. In many ways, Sarah Connor really is the "mother of the future."

The Terminator was the surprise financial and critical hit of 1984, what Julian Petley called "...an exemplary piece of virtuoso, high-tech exploitation movie-making."[19] "Exploitation" is key here, for Cameron's success was calculated on a winning formula: a classic plot, simple characters and as much of the budget as possible up on the screen. It is a model that that he would go on to employ for all of his own creations. In the meantime, his next film would bring him up against a new challenge: someone else's female lead.

Ellen Ripley

I can handle myself.[20]

Writing and directing a sequel to any film is a gamble. They rarely repeat the impact or box office success of the original and, as had been seen recently with the 5–film *Planet of the Apes* series (1968 to 1973), they can drag a franchise towards farce.[21] Attempting to reproduce the lightning strike that had been Scott and screenwriter Dan O'Bannon's 1979 hit, *Alien*, then was a risk for Cameron, but evidently also an irresistible opportunity. In any case, Sigourney Weaver's iconic Ripley character bore resemblance to Lori in *Xenogenesis*; her significance to *Alien* must have gone some way towards encouraging

Cameron to risk feminizing the archetypal hero, as Sarah Connor, in *The Terminator*.

Despite Connor's narrative importance, her character arc in this first film had been basic, relying on a simple pendulum-swing transformation from waitress-to-warrior. Cameron could not repeat this formula for *Aliens*, because Ripley had come loaded with considerable baggage. *Aliens*, then, would appear to offer Cameron an opportunity to develop his "fresh," new female hero character. The result is Ripley's considerable contribution to what Jason Smith and Ximena Gallardo-c call, in their chapter "Ripley Gets Her Gun," "By far the most popular film of the *Alien* franchise."[22] Ripley becomes, and arguably remains, Cameron's most rounded female character.

Conscious of the weight of expectation (and predictions of failure), Cameron makes a pre-emptive strike early in *Aliens*: Ripley is tortured by nightmares which end with her as the imminent victim of an alien stomach-burst. This brave, and clever, nod to the iconic sequence in Scott's original film gives Ripley a psychological depth which remains throughout the remaining narrative. Her own Hero's Journey is tinged with Freudian familial fears, a resonance, perhaps, of Luke Skywalker's development from idealistic farm-boy in *Star Wars* to the damaged hero of its sequel, *The Empire Strikes Back* (1980).

Now the subject of her own story, Ripley receives *The Call to Adventure* on LV-426, the alien-infested planet from the first film. Her experience is required on a military mission to discover the whereabouts of the humans who colonized the planet during the 57 years that Ripley was in cryo-sleep. Perhaps seeing this as the film's Macguffin, Ripley refuses the call — twice — before accepting the mission for no apparent reason, other than to set up a formula plot that John Pym describes as "efficient," "busier," "less quirky" and "essentially unchanged" from *Alien*.[23]

But Cameron's approach to his female character has changed, most notably in her development. In his work on narrative characterization, British screenwriter Jim Hawkins notes that "characters do not develop; it is an audience's understanding and perception of a character that develops."[24] Following this line, Connor's transformative pendulum-swing from waitress to warrior in *The Terminator* reveals character traits which must have been present, but hidden; she does not *become* a warrior, but rather releases the warrior within. However her trajectory allows no return to that inept waitress. She has gone for good. Ripley had reached the end of her own pendulum swing by the climax of *Alien*, so for the more rounded Ripley of *Aliens*, there is no pendulum swing; instead, Cameron mixes traits together in a crucible, encouraging more nuanced expressions of character through the introduction of elements which may be drawn upon at any point in the narrative. It is a fundamental approach to screenwriting, forced onto Cameron by Ripley's *Alien* back-story.

Much has been written about the sequence towards the end of *Alien* in which Ripley strips to her underwear and steps into a pressure suit in order to fight the alien. Harvey Greenberg describes this as "...highly arousing, in the context of the film's previous sexual neutrality."[25] And Gallardo-c and Smith describe the scene as "...highly voyeuristic, highly sexual, and obviously written for an actress...."[26] Others, however, have noted positive elements. Linking the strip to the rescue of the cat, Jonesey, James Kavanagh sees Ripley's vulnerabilities as important, "...for ideological humanism is preserved — a tough gal, rather than a tough guy, but still with that soft spot in the heart."[27] Ripley must rescue the cat in *Alien*, because it is part of her fully-rounded human (female) nature; this nature is then magnified in *Aliens* through Ripley's role as surrogate mother to the orphaned Newt. In order to balance this, she must also become a soldier.

To ease this mother/soldier conjunction, Cameron co-opts motherhood as a tool in his process that uses traditions and conventions — the universal constants of audience expectation — as shortcuts into his stock in trade: action sequences. But perhaps this is unfair; for whilst Ripley's return to rescue Newt towards the end of *Aliens* does indeed set up the iconic fight scene with the alien queen, it also broadens the psychological themes introduced earlier, as Ripley struggles to find meaning for her life. That meaning is made clearer in the *Aliens* Special Edition, released on home video in 1992, which restores scenes deleted from the theatrical version. The new edition gives Newt a flash-back sequence with her all–American, nuclear family — later killed by aliens. It also includes a scene in which Ripley learns of the death of her own daughter, during her 57 years in cryo-sleep.

The stage is now set for the bonding that forces Ripley to become a soldier in order to answer the maternal call. "Get away from her, you bitch!"; Ripley's rabid mother cry to the alien queen, who is protecting her own brood, carries the hopes of post-modernist feminism. With none of the restrictions that confine the more militant, second-wave feminist, Ripley embodies all that a woman *can* be — taking a path that she chooses for herself. It is here that Cameron appears to predict the third-wave ushered in by the more inclusive, self-reflective feminism of the 1990s. It is difficult to say to what extent this nod to feminist ideology is intentional. These extra character-rounding scenes were, after all, removed from the theatrical release. In addition, the lessons learned from developing Scott and O'Bannon's character have not been carried into the rest of *Aliens*. With perhaps the exception of Hicks, the film is populated by stock characters, including a bluff sergeant, a feckless company man and a spunky female helicopter pilot — all of whom will reappear in *Avatar*.

Of course, the gun-toting Ripley would herself inspire a plethora of stock characters in science fiction films produced in the wake of her success. But many of these miss the point, choosing to emphasis the psuedo-lesbian, militarized and militant, radical feminist of popular stereotype, rather than the subtleties of Ripley's (proto)post-modern feminist. Cameron himself trades on the masculinized feminist stereotype with Jenette Goldstein's female marine character Vasquez, most notably with her exchange with the male marine, Hudson: "Hey Vasquez. Have you ever been mistaken for a man?"; her response: "No. Have you?" The abrasive and brazen female dialogue is written for a quick laugh, but its sentiment clearly reverberates into Cameron's next film and female lead.

Lindsey Brigman

> *It's not easy being a cast-iron bitch. It takes discipline and years of training.*[28]

The Abyss marks an important point in James Cameron's film career. His ongoing mission to make a splash by pushing film technology forwards begins to take shape here with the most ambitious underwater feature production ever attempted. Prompting the invention of many new underwater innovations, *The Abyss* is the first of a number of manifestations of Cameron's passion for deep-sea diving. However, it also highlights the price paid for his relentless drive for technological innovation: everything else is secondary.

In order to concentrate energy on his machinery and his *mise en scène*, Cameron simplifies the plot of *The Abyss*, moving it towards what Julian Petley calls its "...unsatisfying ... 'Close Encounters Beneath the Sea' aspect."[29] *The Virgin Film Guide* goes further, observing that it "...recycles elements of the stellar block-busters it tries so hard to emulate."[30] This includes Scott's *Alien*, which appears to be where Cameron has returned to gather his characters — the motley crew of the deep-water mining rig, Deepcore. It is this reversion to type which informs the development of the film's female lead, Mary Elizabeth Mastrantonio's Dr Lindsey Brigman.

Rather than build upon the success of the rounded Ripley in *Aliens*, Cameron moves back towards the lateral pendulum-swing from one type to another that had carried Sarah Connor through *The Terminator*, but in *The Abyss*, this formula plays in reverse. It seems that Cameron still has his head in *Aliens* when he sets Lindsey Brigman's character up, with a male character's response to her first appearance: "Oh no, look who's with them: queen bitch of the universe." As if to prove the point, Lindsey is abrasive from the start, opening her dialogue account with a verbal attack on the company man overseeing

Deepcore from the support ship anchored a mile above the rig: "...Kirkhill, you're pathetic." Cameron soon presses his point home by setting up animosity between Lindsey and her estranged husband, Bud, who skippers Deepcore. The taut exchange, via a CCTV link, sets up Lindsey's next action: to travel down to the rig, so that she and Bud can continue their marital feud in a conveniently-dramatic confined space. The effect of this opening sequence is to garner audience sympathy for the plight of Bud and his colleagues. Lindsey's status is further diminished through sexist sentiments in lines like the repeated "Jeez, keep your pantyhose on" and "all hurricanes should be named after women."

In contrast to the film's implicit male chauvinism, Cameron chooses to give Lindsey a technical role as a marine architect. This is an important departure in a genre that has placed many constraints on the representation of its female professionals. Since their explosion onto the science fiction screen in the 1950s, female scientists have steadily increased in number, but even today they are often confined to the natural, earthy, Mother Nature inspired disciplines the Scholes and Rabkin call "soft sciences"[31] — biology, psychology, entomology and the like. Linsdey Brigman's hard-science role is not unique, but it does suggest an attempt by Cameron to avoid this particular stereotype.

Stereotype is served to a degree by Lindsey's first appearance in the film: her sexy, legs-first exit from the aircraft echoes entomologist Nikki's arrival in *Them!* (1954). In addition, Lindsey's soft, feminine side is returned through her affinity to the aliens living in the abyss. These feminizing elements, however, are not enough to mark a return to the multi-faceted post-modern feminism of Ripley in *Aliens*; for what Cameron gives with one hand, he takes with the other. He continues to remind his audience that has created a smart, feisty, female character, through Lindsey's indignant reminders to the crew of Deepcore that this is her creation: "what have you done with my rig?," "How dare you bring that thing onto *my* rig?" But rather than enhance Lindsey's technical status, these admonishments serve to flag up insecurities and suggest weakness. Cameron's lady doth protest too much. The result is a regular undermining of her character, until it becomes clear that Cameron is telegraphing a need for Lindsey to change — to undergo a character pendulum swing before the end of the film. Despite the warning, this change comes suddenly. There is some attempt at a narrative trigger, when Linsdey fears the loss of Bud in the deep-sea trench, but it is not obvious which part of her personality this is drawn from. In his haste to reconcile his estranged husband and wife, Cameron revises Ripley's unexplained decision to return to LV-426 in *Aliens*; the sudden capitulation of Lindsey Brigman has the feeling of an un-prompted taming of the shrew.

During the writing and making of *The Abyss*, Cameron's relationship with his own wife, Gale Anne Hurd, was deteriorating. Petley's statement that "none of these problems are too evident in the final product..."[32] optimistically side-steps what might be regarded as an attack on women, through the contorted character of Lindsey Brigman. Cameron presents a strong, independent woman and then undermines her at every opportunity. However, given his record, cries of misogyny may be misplaced — especially as Hurd produced this film (as she had *The Terminator* and *Aliens*) and would go on to an executive production role on Cameron's next film, *Terminator 2*. It seems more likely that the filmmaker was using his fictional character as a form of catharsis, with what may well be a subconscious self-justification coming out through his approach to Lindsey. It may be that the real therapy offered by *The Abyss* is the opportunity for Cameron to indulge his passions for motion picture technology and diving, and to transfer his frustrations to the unique challenges of underwater filming. Perhaps, then, there is some truth behind *Halliwell's* description of *The Abyss* as "...a tedious, overlong fantasy that is more excited by machinery than people."[33]

Ironically, it is the merging of machinery and people which offers Cameron a clear opportunity to develop the characters in his next film. With his divorce out for the way, *Terminator 2: Judgment Day* (1991) would offer the filmmaker the potential to cut himself adrift of the acrimony that drives Lindsey Brigman's representation and to cement his growing reputation for strong female characters. Despite this, a lingering bitterness appears to have underpinned the development of Sarah Connor.

Sarah Connor

All you know how to create is death and destruction.[34]

Two elements potentially work in favor of the development of character in *Terminator 2*. Firstly, this is a sequel, bringing with it all the baggage that had forced Cameron to deepen Ripley's character in *Aliens*. Secondly, whilst *Terminator 2* would represent an advance in the use of CGI with its liquid-metal T-1000 Terminator, the film is not over-laden with technical innovation.[35] It is, like its predecessor, largely a straight forward action narrative. Cameron chooses, however, to channel these opportunities towards the development of a character for his T-800 cyborg, in the form of then rising star, Arnold Schwarzenegger.

The pendulum that swung to reveal the tough Sarah Connor emerging from the Hero's Journey at the end *The Terminator* appears to be stuck here now. Projected through the filter of Ripley and carrying the anger of Brigman, she is tougher than ever, a result of Cameron's efforts to test the boundaries of the masculinized female. Clearly, there can be no return to that inept waitress, but Ripley's success had relied on a process described by Christine Cornea as "gender blending,"[36] rather than a wholesale move towards the masculine — not least through her maternal role. In *Terminator 2* there is an attempt at a gender balance through the commuting of Sarah's spiritual role as a mother-of-the-future to the more corporeal mother-of-John; however, further evidence from the Special Edition suggests that Cameron is not fully committed to this deepening of his female lead.

Released on video in 1997, The *Terminator 2* Special Edition restores scenes which were deleted from the theatrical version. As with the *Aliens* Special Edition, the deletion of these scenes suggest an active de-feminization of the female character. Early in the special edition, Kyle Reese appears to Connor in a fantasy sequence. Serving once again as Joseph Campbell's *Supernatural Aid*, he lifts her spirits, encouraging her to fight on. He does this by appealing to her role as a mother: "He's all alone; you have to protect him." Through her tears, Connor tells Reese that she loves him, eventually chasing him along a corridor in her satin nightgown. This short scene at once feminizes Sarah Connor. It casts the audience back to the sex scene in *The Terminator* and it projects that femininity forward through the rest of the special edition. All of this is lost to the theatrical version.

What is left is motherhood reduced largely to an historical fact and the son merely a symbol of the survival of the human race. Sarah Connor is hellbent on ensuring that the apocalypse described by Reese never happens. Her plan is to assassinate Dyson, the computer scientist destined to create Skynet, the system which will become sentient and murderous on Judgment Day. In an echo of the actions of the T-800 in *The Terminator*, Connor breaks into Dyson's house and shoots him. Christine Cornea recognizes this new function as central to the development of Connor: "...her warrior status is written into a narrative in which, like the comic-book superheroes, she is predominantly characterized as fighting *for* patriarchy."[37] This is emphasized momentarily by Connor's violent treatment of Dyson's innocent wife, played by S. Epatha Merkerson.

As if to counteract Cornea's patriarchy claim, Connor slips towards the militant, anti-man tendencies that would later define the crudest copies of this female fighter. This radical trait is revealed fully in Connor's verbal attack on Dyson after she fails to kill him: "Fucking men like you built the hydrogen bomb. Men like you thought it up. You think you're so creative. You don't know what it's like to really create something, to create a life, to feel it growing inside you..." Whilst this speech would appear to be placing value on motherhood, its blunt radical-feminist message comes too late in the narrative to have much effect on Connor's character. It serves as superficial characterization, rather like Connor's occasional voice-over narration, which, to Rayns, "...points up the moral of the story as preachily as anything in a 30s social-problem picture: 'If a machine can learn the value of human life,' she gasps, 'then maybe we can too.'"[38]

This echo of the opening of *Xenogenesis* suggests that Cameron has retained his idealism. Indeed, Rebecca Keegan suggests that the cutting of feminizing scenes from the theatrical version of *Terminator 2* resulted from time restraints and that Cameron views it now as a mistake.[39] Coming years after the event, this admission perhaps reflects changes in the mind of a maturing director; coming in 1991, it reflects the younger Cameron's aim to create a self-contained, female, all-action hero, which works against Connor's character development. At the same time that the T-800 is reaching out, gaining humanity and a fully-rounded character through his relationship with John, Sarah is losing both, becoming more like the machine. She realizes this at the moment of her failure to kill Dyson, but, as Tony Rayns points out, it is too late: "The price she has to pay for her independence, inevitably, is exclusion from the tremulous male bonding between her son and the T-800; it's hard to project her role beyond the final fade out."[40] Rayns' prediction is proven correct, as Sarah Connor becomes just a footnote in *Terminator 3: Rise of the Machines* (2003),[41] but his observation about the power shift also points to a reason for her dropped scenes. Here in *Terminator 2*, she is being nudged into what amounts to a support role in the John Connor story. She has lost the plot.

Of course Connor never descends to the level of what Laura Miller calls the "...thin, cartoonish characters..."[42] who generally support James Cameron's films, but shifting the narrative emphasis onto John does free the director to present his female warrior. Cameron has pushed this particular envelope as far as it will go, and in so doing has created what would quickly become — for better or worse — an icon of science fiction cinema. It seems, however, that he has also become tired of his female hero. Connor can no longer represent the "fresh" approach to the female character that had driven her inception. Perhaps, then, Cameron carefully and consciously chose this zenith point to say goodbye to a female stereotype that he had helped to create.

What he replaces her with still retains residual traits of Connor, Ripley and Brigman; but those hoping that Cameron's oeuvre would continue to chart the inexorable rise of the female hero may have found *True Lies* (1994) a disappointment. Continuing the filmmaker's approach to re-inventing cinematic icons, the film was pitched with the line "What if James Bond had to come home and answer to his wife?"[43] This may suggest a central role for the female, even imply a woman in charge, but *True Lies* is another vehicle for

Arnold Schwarzenegger. Jamie Lee Curtis, as Mrs. Helen Tasker, enjoys substantial screen time, but her contribution to the plot is largely to be swept
along by circumstance, rather than to drive the narrative. All of the gains
made by these earlier women seem to dissolve in the line:

Helen Tasker

Are we gonna die?[44]

It might be argued, of course, that *The Terminator* sweeps Sarah Connor
along in a similar fashion. Indeed Leslie Felperin Sharman picks up on this
parallel trajectory: "...[Helen] has little to do apart from undergoing the standard transformation from dowdy wimp to feisty heroine."[45] It might then
also be argued that Helen makes a Hero's Journey: responding to a call away
from her mundane life and taking a plunge across the threshold to a new life.
A key difference here is that Helen never quite appears to be in danger. Despite
the bombs, guns, terrorists and her fear of death, there seems to be little jeop-
ardy for any of the central characters in *True Lies*. This is because Cameron
has built on the comic-book style alluded to by Cornea in her description of
Connor in *Terminator 2*. He has created an ideal environment for his larger-
than-life action characters. This is a comedy, so the characters are allowed to
be stereotypes. The result is a comic-book world of beefed-up men, feckless
terrorists, a femme fatale, and a working mother.

Helen's conventional role at the beginning of *True Lies* is of two-fold
importance. Firstly, it creates an effective contrast with the cool, confident
Helen at the end of the film. The same ploy, to force the appearance of a
greater character development, was employed in *The Terminator*. Secondly, it
appeals to a traditional notion of normality. Just like Helen Benson in *The
Day the Earth Stood Still* (1951), this Helen is a secretary and a mother. Whilst
there are elements of Cameron's feisty woman as the film progresses, this is
largely a surface trait, designed seemingly to draw energy from past characters,
rather than to inform this one. Ultimately, Helen Tasker is a woman tempered
by Cameron's notions of a reality that did not need to be adhered to in his
earlier science fiction films. It is still, however, an imaginary reality.

Perhaps more than any other of his films, *True Lies* exposes Cameron's
limitations when it comes to imagining real things — including women. This
distinction is identified by Sharman: "He's far less assured when dealing with
'feminine' story elements, despite the fact that the *Terminator* films, along with
the *Alien* films, are often cited by feminists as positive landmarks in the development of modern womanhood's image in film."[46] Cameron's considerable

ability to place iconic women in unfamiliar *mises en scène* appears ill-suited to the challenge of placing ordinary women in familiar places. Despite her traditional underpinning, Helen is supported by none of the visual motifs and metaphors — the dark, semi-dystopian, technological imagery — that carry Connor, Ripley and Brigman through their respective narratives. Instead, her iconic moment comes through a reference to femininity and to a female sexuality rarely used in Cameron's earlier films: the strip-tease scene.

This sequence, in which Helen performs a pole-dance for her husband, has divided critics. To some, it represents sexist objectification; to others, the slap-stick moments redeem it as a comic scene. Given Cameron's sensitive treatment of the female body elsewhere, the truth is likely to lie with the latter reading. It is, however, interesting to note that the Special Edition versions of *Aliens* and *Terminator 2*, which bring feminine elements to Connor and Ripley via their reintroduced scenes, appeared either side of this theatrical release of *True Lies*. Perhaps this trend represents a shift in Cameron's general approach to women; or perhaps it exposes the nature of the particular stereotypical crutch that Cameron looks to when he turns his attention on a more real world. Whatever its motivation, the trend (and the strip) does point to a growing attention to the feminine, which will pervade Cameron's next two films

Young Rose

I'll never let go, Jack.[47]

Despite Laura Miller's criticism of *Titanic* (1997) as "...a vulgar, clichéridden, anachronistic effort that entirely fails to capture the rigidly stratified manners of the era,"[48] this film is the closest Cameron comes to presenting reality on screen. Miller's comments are a little incautious: an attempt is clearly made to represent the class structure onboard *Titanic* and Rose is relatively well rounded for a Cameron woman. Miller's real complaint perhaps stems from the recognizable elements of universal mythology that, once again, carry the weight of Cameron's huge movie project.

Christopher Vogler takes a look at these elements in a section entitled "Drowning in Love" in the revised and expanded version of his book *The Writer's Journey*. To Vogler, Young Rose is a manifestation of the "damsel in distress" archetype. As such she is a sister of Sleeping Beauty and Snow White, princesses caught between life and death and wakened by a kiss."[49] Whilst Vogler offers no judgment as to the quality of Cameron's writing, he makes comprehensive references to his use of Campbell's hero myths and to the structural devices that "...give the audience reference points in the long story and contribute to making it a coherent design."[50]

Ultimately, it is a sense of this coherence that hobbles Cameron's female (and male) characters. That is, whilst their function has waxed and waned through his films, there remains a feeling that the audience knows who they are and what they are going to do next. Born of stereotype and archetype, they rarely have the power to surprise. Even Rose's nude scene in *Titanic*, whilst sudden, relies on notions of intense erotic femininity — an archetype as old as art itself, and one telegraphed by the script's earlier references to Bohemian Paris, impressionist art and of course by Kate Winslet's appearance as a classic pre-Raphaelite beauty.

Cameron likes women. His ability to retain good relationships with his former wives testifies to a healthy approach and, as a progressive, liberal Canadian, he wants to do what he considers to be the right thing by women. As a result, his screen females, Lindsey Brigman notwithstanding, generally avoid signs of misogyny. Whilst he has always highlighted the beauty of the female form, Cameron's approach to female nudity, like his approach to male nudity, has been driven largely by narrative demands. Kyle and Sarah's sex scene and Schwarzenegger's arrival in *The Terminator*, along with the baring of Mastrantonio's breasts during attempts to revive the dying Lindsey in *The Abyss*, are necessary to their plots. The camera does not linger gratuitously. Like Ridely Scott's use of the strip sequence in *Alien*, the female body to Cameron denotes human vulnerability, rather than objectification.

Rose's nude scene draws upon this wider picture. Critics like Laura Miller may not accept that Rose's action comes naturally from character, but this is not the point. The image, and the erotic emotion that it carries, are timeless models. Through *True Lies* and *Titanic*, Cameron introduces his audience to the notion of feminine archetypes, far removed from the masculinized female heroes of his earlier films.

In keeping with these archetypes, Rose is swept along by events and the actions of (male) others. For, even though all characters are subject to the historical events, it becomes clear at the end of *Titanic* that all that Rose has become, she owes to Jack. The photographs standing on Old Rose's bedside cabinet attest to all the things that she has achieved in Jack's name. Just as promised, she never did let go of her man.

This does at least bring hero status to Rose by framing Jack as her *Supernatural Aid*, calling her to an adventure that begins as *Titanic* sinks. It points to the residue of an independent female heroic journey that is lost completely to Cameron's biggest picture to date. As Jack becomes Jake, Neytiri, played by Zoe Saldana, becomes the facilitator in *his* journey.

Neytiri

I'm with you now, Jake. We are mated for life.[51]

A little over two hours into *Avatar*, Jake Sully, scientist Norm Spellman and Hispanic helicopter pilot, Trudy Chacon, played by Michelle Rodriguez, meet to discuss options for what will become the film's climactic battle. Throughout the scene, Chacon clutches her huge blaster rifle, a pose clearly meant as an intertextual link, to imbue Chacon with some of the no-nonsense aura created by Vasquez in *Aliens*. Added to the visual cues are Chacon's dialogue. Tough sounding lines, like "And I was hoping for some tactical plan that didn't involve martyrdom" echo Vasquez's cool "I only need to know one thing: where — they — are." These allusions suggest that Cameron has one eye on the successes of the past; however, with a budget of well over $200 million to recoup, he must also keep the other eye firmly on *Avatar*'s age classification. As a result, R-rated lines like Vasquez's "Fuck you, Man" are tempered to become Chacon's "Freakin' daisy-cutters." Despite these, albeit diluted, efforts, and the casting of Sigourney Weaver herself as Dr. Grace Augustine, the heart of *Avatar* is not with the celebrated feminist genre-icons of the 1980s. It is rooted firmly in a symbol of female cinematic representation that is as old as the genre itself: Mother Nature.

Given the nature of heroic story-telling, it is perhaps unsurprising that early science fiction cinema offered largely conventional representations of women. After all, the genre, with its heavily allegorical leanings, offers a natural home for the mothers, lovers, virgins, queens and princesses who served as metaphors for long before the arrival of cinema. Scattered amongst the dutiful wives and daughters of crack-pot inventors are cinema characters like the Queen of the Polar Regions and the Fairy of the Oceans.[52] In Georges Méliès' classic, *Le Voyage dans la Lune* (1902), the travelers reach a moon that is protected by a Mother Nature figure in the form the Queen of the Selenites — her angelic minions named after the moonstone itself. Science and sophistication converted most of the genre's overt Earth Mother figures into soft scientists and domestic mothers, leaving Mother Nature theme rarely explored — until Cameron's return to it in *Avatar*.

In fact, the notion of Mother Nature dominates *Avatar* and, unsurprisingly, it is the female characters who carry most of the weight, and are in turn dominated by, this signification. Sharing the concerns of films like Scott Derrickson's remake of *The Day the Earth Stood Still* (2008), Cameron mines the zeitgeist of ecological issues to immerse his audience in the mythologies — and imageries — of the Earth Mother. The planet Pandora is named after the first woman, the Eve, of Greek myth, formed by the gods from the soil itself.

The planet's spirit Eywa, whom the Na'vi worship, is identified throughout as female. She bestrides the film as a kind hybrid of the Force, and the Greek myth of Gaea: "'the deep-breasted,' whose soil nourishes all that exists, and by whose benevolence men are blessed with fair children and all the pleasant fruits of earth."[53] Neytiri's Mother, Mo'at, completes this picture as the personification of the natural spirit. She is the high priestess, the Keeper of the Delphic Oracle, translating the will of Eywa to her people in what Chris Hewitt calls a "...love letter to humanity and spirituality."[54]

To generate his filmic vision, Cameron catapults his audience back through Campbell and Jung to the raw cultural models that informed their studies of mythology. As Andrew Osmond observes, "In *Avatar*'s most vivid moments, the characters seem uplifted from stereotypes to archetypes ... the exotic Na'vi tiger-woman, leaping into a fire-lit glade and loosing an arrow in mid-air."[55] Cameron then has delved deeper than mere filmic stereotype, reaching into first principles of story-telling in an effort to ensure connection with a universal audience.

One of the casualties of this approach is, of course, the female narrative. For whilst Neytiri may be modelled on an Amazonian warrior woman, with a visceral femininity, and although she does save Sully's life on at least two occasions, this is clearly his story, and not hers. Despite arguably being an amalgam of residual elements from Cameron's women — smart, sassy, sexy — she must be all this from the sidelines (and take care never to reveal a nipple). In the main, Neytiri is reduced to rolling her eyes at the silly things Sully does and to teaching him to do them better. She is a facilitator in what Osmond goes on to call "...a re-spray of the hero-going-native myth...."[56] Once again, *Avatar* reveals both Cameron's debt and contribution to the cultural memory, as he positions Sully as the Broken Arrow and Neytiri as Pocahontas for generations too young to remember the 1950s television show or the 1995 Disney film. It is David Thomson's description of Walt Disney himself that explains, once again, the drive behind the latest incarnation of Cameron's female lead: "...a relentlessly ambitious man, driven more by technology than ideas or ideology."[57] The description is reflected in Cameron's own statement:

James Cameron

It's like having my own Skynet.
I love it.[58]

James Cameron's phenomenal box office success rests on his ability to marshal cinematic techniques in order to generate and present iconic imagery.

Everything is secondary to the image. When women have been central, they have become icons: Ripley and her power-loader, Connor with her guns, Rose and Jack on the prow of *Titanic*, the beautiful, blue, bow-toting Neytiri. These are powerful images, supported not by deep, nuanced character, but by the stereotypes and archetypes of filmic and narrative mythologies. Critics have argued that it is Cameron's skills as a writer that have forced a reliance on cliché and reference to what Osmond calls "...the sublime pulp territory that the he's now definitely conquered"[59]; however, there is another, more practical reason.

Cameron makes *event* films, built around his ambitions: to film underwater, to develop CGI, to rejuvenate 3-D, to improve the efficacy of motion-capture technology. As a result, his movies have become ever more expensive. Cameron knows that acceptance of new, unfamiliar cinematic concepts (in both format and content) relies on a balance of familiar characters and stories; the more universal these familiar elements, the wider the potential audience. It is the maxim that separates two titans of science fiction cinema, the esoteric masterpiece, *2001: A Space Odyssey* (1968) and the elemental phenomenon, *Star Wars*. Cameron has the power and the ability to put what he likes on the screen; but whilst he has done more on balance to develop his female characters than both Stanley Kubrick and George Lucas, he realizes that, in Hollywood, as elsewhere, risks taken must be indirectly proportional to budget size. Much as he may wish to fight the concept, the likelihood of a female hero reduces as his budgets increase.[60]

It will be interesting to observe Cameron's creative process when (or whether) he works within the confines of Yukito Kushiro's Manga creation, *Battle Angel Alita*, the source material for the director's 2013 slated project, *Battle Angel*.[61] The central character sounds familiar enough: a "small, cute, and very deadly female cyborg"[62]; however, Manga characters, especially those developed over a series of stories, offer a degree of complexity for which Cameron's characters are not necessarily noted. In a telling online review of Hiroshi Fukutomi's 1993 animated version of this work, entitled *Gunnm*, Roy Teng writes: "The movie works because it's small."[63] *Alita*'s next incarnation will doubtless be bigger; it will be forced to walk a line between chaotic density of Kushiro's female hero and practical considerations of Cameron's event-driven cinema. On the evidence so far, the position of that line, and the success of the female lead, may well depend on size of this filmmaker's budget.

NOTES

The author would like to acknowledge and thank the following for their contributions to the preparation of this essay: Alex Barnes, Jim Hawkins, Lynne Magowan and John Streets.

1. *Xenogenesis* (1978) opening dialogue [00:01:07]. This short film is not commercially available; however, it is readily accessible on the internet, including at: www.youtube.com /watch?v=T801XFmM8wc (19th November, 2010).

2. Laura Miller, review of *Titanic*, directed by James Cameron. *Sight & Sound* 8, no. 2 (1998): 52.

3. Miller, 52.

4. Tony Rayns, review of *Terminator 2: Judgment Day*, directed by James Cameron. *Sight & Sound*, 5, no. 9 (1991): 51.

5. Leslie Felperin Sharman, review of *True Lies*, directed by James Cameron. *Sight & Sound*, 4, no. 9 (1994): 50.

6. Andrew Osmond, review of *Avatar*, directed by James Cameron. *Sight & Sound* 20, no. 3 (2010): 49.

7. Similar, bipedal machines appear in *Avatar*, notably for Sully's climactic battle with Colonel Quaritch.

8. Although distributors now make much of Cameron's involvement with *Piranha II: The Spawning* (1981), very little of this is actually his work. The Greek production company merely needed an expendable American name to secure funding; it seems that the Canadian Cameron was close enough. The majority of footage, including topless women lounging on expensive yachts, is the work of director/producer Ovidio G. Assonitis. For further details, see: Rebecca Keegan, *The Futurist: The Life and Films of James Cameron* (New York: Crown, 2009), 28–35.

9. Rayns, 51.

10. *The Terminator* (1984), special edition DVD [01:04:45].

11. For more on the genesis of *Xenogenesis*, see: Keegan, 14/5.

12. For a deeper discussion of Lucas' use of hero myths, see: John Shelton Lawrence, "Joseph Campbell, George Lucas, and the Monomyth," in *Finding the Force of the Star Wars Franchise: Fans, Merchandise and Critics*, eds. Matthew Wilhelm Kapell and John Shelton Lawrence (New York, Peter Lang, 2006), 21–34. For *Star Wars*, Lucas also borrows liberally from Akira Kurosawa's *The Hidden Fortress* (1958). For more on this, see: Dean Conrad, *Star Wars: The Genesis of a Legend* (London: Valis, 1996), 20-24.

13. "('because it's perfect,' Cameron explains, tellingly)," Keegan, 218.

14. James Cameron quoted verbatim in Keegan, 44.

15. Christopher Vogler, *The Writer's Journey: Mythic Structure for Storytellers and Screenwriters* (Basingstoke and Oxford: Pan/Macmillan, 1999), xviii.

16. See: Vogler, 14.

17. Joseph Campbell, *The Hero with a Thousand Faces* (London: Fontana, 1993), 33 (emphasis in the original).

18. Campbell, 97.

19. Julian Petley, review of *The Terminator*, directed by James Cameron. *Monthly Film Bulletin* 52 (1985): 59.

20. *Aliens* (1986) theatrical release version [01:24:27].

21. Whilst the original *Planet of the Apes* was well received, and represented a considerable boost for science fiction cinema in 1968, the next four films garnered increasingly negative critical reception. In addition, box office receipts slipped from around $32.5 million to a little under $9million for the final film of the series, *Battle for the Planet of the Apes*. Source: www.boxofficemojo.com (19th November 2010).

22. Ximena Gallardo C. and C. Jason Smith, *Alien Woman: The Making of Lt. Ellen Ripley* (New York and London: Continuum, 2004), 62.

23. John Pym, review of *Aliens*, directed by James Cameron. *Monthly Film Bulletin* 53 (1986): 263.

24. Jim Hawkins in conversation with the author for a forthcoming retrospective.

25. Harvey R. Greenberg, M.D., "Reimagining the Gargoyle: Psychoanalytic Notes on 'Alien.'" *Camera Obscura* (fall 1986): 97.

26. Gallardo C. and Smith, 54.

27. James H. Kavanagh, "Feminism, Humanism and Science in 'Alien,'" in *Alien Zone: Cultural Theory and Contemporary Science Fiction Cinema*, ed. Annette Kuhn (London: Verso, 1995), 80.

28. *The Abyss* (1989), theatrical release version [01:49:43].

29. Petley, 329.

30. James Pallot and the editors of CineBooks, eds., *The Virgin Film Guide*, 3d ed (London: Virgin Books, 1994), 3.

31. Robert Scholes and Eric S. Rabkin, *Science Fiction: History, Science, Vision* (New York: Oxford University Press, 1977), 136. The notion of female characters in "hard" and "soft" science roles is explored further in Dean Conrad, "Where Have All the Ripley's Gone?" *Foundation: The International Review of Science Fiction* 38, no. 105 (2009) 55–72.

32. Petley, 329.

33. John Walker, ed., *Halliwell's Film & Video Guide 1999* (London: HarperCollins, 1999), 3.

34. *Terminator 2: Judgment Day* (1991), special edition (1997) [01:38:56].

35. Many of the effects assumed to be CGI in this film (like the wounded T-1000) are in fact traditional in-camera shots using make-up and prosthetics produced by Stan Winston and his award-winning team.

36. For a wider discussion of this notion, see: Christine Cornea, "Gender Blending and the Feminine Subject in Science Fiction Film," Chapter 5 in Christine Cornea, *Science Fiction Cinema: Between Fantasy and Reality* (Edinburgh: Edinburgh University Press, 2007), 146–74.

37. Cornea, 163.

38. Rayns, 51.

39. Keegan, 118.

40. Rayns, 51.

41. It should be noted that Linda Hamilton suffered for many years with a bipolar disorder, which may have made her unavailable for the next *Terminator* film. However, she also made many other screen appearances between 1991 and 2003. She was married to James Cameron for much of this time, so his withdrawal from the *Terminator 3* project may also have been a factor.

42. Miller, 52.

43. Keegan, 142.

44. *True Lies* (1994) theatrical release version [01:34:22].

45. Sharman, 50.

46. Sharman, 50.

47. *Titanic* (1997) theatrical release version [02:50:15].

48. Miller, 52.

49. Vogler, 259.

50. Vogler, 259.

51. *Avatar* (2009), 155 minute, single-disk, DVD release (2010) [01:20:58].

52. In, for example, *The Voyage of the Arctic* (1903) and *Deux Cent Milles Lieues sous les Mers* (1907) respectively. For further details, see: Phil Hardy, ed., *The Aurum Film Encyclopedia—Science Fiction*, 2d ed. (London: Aurum, 1991), 24, 28.

53. Félix Guirand, ed., *New Larouse Encyclopedia of Mythology*, trans. Richard Aldington and Delano Ames (London: Hamlyn, 1993), 89.

54. Chris Hewitt, review of *Avatar*, directed by James Cameron. *Empire* 248 (2010), 54.

55. Osmond, 48.

56. Osmond, 49.

57. David Thomson, *A Biographical Dictionary of Film*, 2d ed. (London: Andre Deutsch, 1995), 198.

58. James Cameron quoted verbatim in *Empire* 244 (October 2009), inside-cover gatefold.

59. Osmond, 49.

60. Quoted budgets vary between sources, but the upward trend is consistent. *The Terminator.*

$6.4m; *Aliens*: $18.5m; *The Abyss*: $69.5m; *Terminator 2*: $102m; *True Lies*: $120m; *Titanic*: $200m; *Avatar*: $237. Source: *The Internet Movie Database*, www.imdb.com (24th November, 2010).

61. The release date of this project is slated for 2013. At the time of writing, neither this date nor the budget have been fixed. For further details, see: "Battle Angel," *The Internet Movie Database*, www.imdb.com/title/tt0437086/ (19th November 2010).

62. Theron Martin, "Battle Angel Alita: Last Order," *Anime News Network*, 2005, www.animenewsnetwork.com/review/battle-angel-alita-last-order-gn-6 (19th November, 2010).

63. Roy Teng, online user review of *Gunnm* (aka: *Battle Angel Alita*), directed by Hiroshi Fukutomi, *Internet Movie Database*, www.imdb.com/title/tt0107061/usercomments (24th November, 2004).

WORKS CITED

Campbell, Joseph. *The Hero with a Thousand Faces*. London: Fontana, 1993. First edition, Princeton University Press, 1949.

Conrad, Dean. "Where Have All the Ripley's Gone?" *Foundation: The International Review of Science Fiction* 38, no. 105 (Spring 2009) 55–72.

_____. *Star Wars: The Genesis of a Legend*. London: Valis Books, 1996.

Cornea, Christine. *Science Fiction Cinema: Between Fantasy and Reality*. Edinburgh: Edinburgh University Press, 2007.

Gallardo C., Ximena, and C. Jason Smith. *Alien Woman: The Making of Lt. Ellen Ripley*. New York and London: Continuum, 2004.

Greenberg, Harvey R., M.D. "Reimagining the Gargoyle: Psychoanalytic Notes on 'Alien.'" *Camera Obscura* 15 (Fall 1986): 86–109. Also in *Close Encounters: Film, Feminism and Science Fiction*. edited by Constance Penley, Elisabeth Lyon, Lynn Spigel and Janet Bergstrom, 82–105. Minneapolis and Oxford: University of Minnesota Press, 1991.

Guirand, Félix, ed. *New Larouse Encyclopedia of Mythology*, translated by Richard Aldington and Delano Ames. London: Hamlyn, 1993. First published: 1959; in this edition: 1968.

Hardy, Phil, ed. *The Aurum Film Encyclopedia—Science Fiction*, 2d ed. London: Aurum Press, 1991. Original edition: 1984.

Hewitt, Chris. Review of *Avatar*, directed by James Cameron. *Empire* 248 (February 2010), 54/5.

Jezewski, Mary Ann. "Traits of the Female Hero." *New York Folklore* 10 (1984): 1/2.

Kavanagh, James H. "Feminism, Humanism and Science in 'Alien,'" in *Alien Zone: Cultural Theory and Contemporary Science Fiction Cinema*, edited by Annette Kuhn, 73–81. London: Verso, 1995. Original edition, 1990.

Keegan, Rebecca. *The Futurist: The Life and Films of James Cameron*. New York: Crown, 2009.

Lawrence, John Shelton. "Joseph Campbell, George Lucas, and the Monomyth," in Matthew Wilhelm Kapell and John Shelton Lawrence, eds., *Finding the Force of the Star Wars Franchise: Fans, Merchandise and Critics*, 21–34. New York: Peter Lang, 2006.

Martin, Theron. "Battle Angel Alita: Last Order." *Anime News Network*, 2005. www.animenewsnetwork.com/review/battle-angel-alita-last-order-gn-6 (Access date, 19th November, 2010).

Miller, Laura. Review of *Titanic*, directed by James Cameron. *Sight & Sound* 8, no. 2 (February 1998): 50-2.

Nathan, Ian. "Where We're Going ... We Don't Need Roads." *Empire* 254 (August 2010): 78–90.

Osmond, Andrew. Review of *Avatar*, directed by James Cameron. *Sight & Sound* 20, no. 3 (March 2010): 48/9.

Pallot, James, and the editors of CineBooks, eds., *The Virgin Film Guide*, 3d edition. London: Virgin Books, 1994.

Petley, Julian. Review of *The Abyss*, directed by James Cameron. *Monthly Film Bulletin* 56 (1989): 328-9.

_____. Review of *The Terminator*, directed by James Cameron. *Monthly Film Bulletin* 52 (1985): 328–9.

Pym, John. Review of *Aliens*, directed by James Cameron. *Monthly Film Bulletin* 53 (1986): 263–4.

Rayns, Tony. Review of *Terminator 2: Judgment Day*, directed by James Cameron. *Sight & Sound* 5, no. 9 (September 1991): 50-1.

Scholes, Robert, and Eric S. Rabkin. *Science Fiction: History, Science, Vision*. New York: Oxford University Press, 1977.

Sharman, Leslie Felperin. Review of *True Lies*, directed by James Cameron. *Sight & Sound* 4, no. 9 (September 1994): 49–50.

Teng, Roy. Online user review of *Gunnm* (aka: *Battle Angel Alita*), directed by Hiroshi Fukutomi. *Internet Movie Database*, 29th April, 1999. www.imdb.com/title/tt0107061/usercomments (Access date, 24th November, 2004).

Thomson, David. *A Biographical Dictionary of Film*, 2d ed. London: Andre Deutsch, 1995.

Vogler, Christopher. *The Writer's Journey: Mythic Structure for Storytellers and Screenwriters*. Basingstoke and Oxford: Pan/Macmillan, 1999.

Between *Aliens* and *Avatar*:
Mapping the Shifting Terrain
of the Struggle for Women's Rights

ELISA NARMINIO *and*
MATTHEW WILHELM KAPELL

> *What is told is always in the telling.*
> —Roland Barthes, 1974
> *Identity is not a personal project but a political one.*
> — Richard Ned Lebow, 2011

Aliens (1986) and *Avatar* (2009) are films about human beings fighting for their survival in outer space, both as individuals and as a species. In *Aliens*, the human colony on LV-426 has been eradicated by extraterrestrials which threaten to soon spread to Earth. In *Avatar*, humans turn to the planet Pandora as a source of the mineral unobtanium which is a necessity to the human species' survival on Earth. Each film carries characters that have become central to James Cameron's reputation as a filmmaker — strong women. With *Aliens*, a film that the American news magazine *Time* described upon its release as an "electrifying parable of two righteous single mothers, one an earthling ... the other a mammoth uggy bug,"[1] we find James Cameron has quite deftly captured the high mark of second wave feminism. It is a film that *Time* called a "story of a woman who keeps finding ways to transcend the limits that unexamined custom often imposes on her sex."[2]

There is a similarly strong woman twenty-three years later with *Avatar*'s Neytiri. But she is neither as central to the plot as Sigourney Weaver's Ripley in *Aliens*, nor as well-developed. *Aliens* offered a hero(ine) that re-wrote the rules of who can and should be the lead in Hollywood action films, and captured the cover of *Time* magazine as a result. After *Aliens*, Cameron continued in an analogous vein, making his career, in part, on the presentation of similarly strong women. In Cameron's *Terminator* films, *The Abyss*, and even *Titanic*, Cameron's women are, quite simply, different from their usual representation in film. Traditionally, the female leads were, as *Time* noted, "supposed to swoon or retreat to a safe corner (or, at best, praise the Lord and pass the ammunition) while the male lead protects them and defends Western civilization as we know it."[3] Cameron's message, replayed in his films through *Titanic* but especially with the character development of Ripley in *Aliens* and Sarah Connor in the first *Terminator* film, was a message of transformation. Cameron's women were in every way the equal of the men they shared the screen with, without losing their status as actual, real *women*. And Cameron's stories had these women, more often than not, transforming themselves to meet the challenges of his narratives.

Yet, for *Avatar*, that same American news magazine could only note that in the character of Neytiri "we find a strong woman seeking a man whose strength she can tap."[4] It would seem that the difference between the Ripley of 1986 and the Neytiri of 2009 was a difference in Cameron's desire to project his female lead to the apex of his story. It would be a simplistic argument to note that between 1986 and 2009 Cameron seems to have backed away from his desire to center his narratives on strong female characters and that somehow the 2009 Cameron is a betrayal of his earlier convictions. However, the difference between these two Camerons may be far more the result of the changes between the 1986 and 2009 feminisms. The 1986 Cameron could fashion a story of the transformation of his main character, Ripley, because the second wave feminism of the era made such a transformation possible — and desirable. Cameron's *The Terminator* had done much the same thing in presenting the transformation of Sarah Connor, but it was with *Aliens,* and the establishment of a pattern, that Cameron seemed to declare himself an ardent feminist of a sort. The transformation of his main character in *Avatar* cannot pull off the same feat because the dominant third wave feminism of the early twenty-first century is not nearly as amenable to the concept. Thus, that transformation is assigned to a male in the narrative, though the change the character experiences remains significant for feminists.

While a majority of Cameron's films depict strong female characters, a direct comparison of *Aliens* and *Avatar* allows for two, related examinations. Both films show strong female characters, and both films show those characters dealing with the military. As the military remains "a gendered organization and [one] that is gendering," thus shaping the social representations of gender, both films serve as benchmarks by which to contrast the evolution not just of women, but of feminism between the 1980s and the early twenty-first century.[5] *Aliens* was written in the early 1980s and released at the transition between second and third wave feminism — but at the height of the influence of the second wave on popular culture. *Avatar,* the product of a more successful filmmaker, may likewise present a powerful female character, but can also be seen as an indicator of the less influential third wave in mass media and society in general. Gender equality has progressed and an increasing number of women are participating in military and political life. However, feminism has simultaneously become institutionalized — bureaucratic structures run by paid staff have become the watchdogs of gender equality — and marginalized. The international enthusiasm, the networking and the shifts in legal and political practices of second wave feminism have given way to the mainstreaming of political issues, a loss of sense of urgency and a disengagement from the public.

Thus, while the majority of Cameron's films contain strong female roles, a comparison of his early work in *Aliens* to his most recent in *Avatar* allows both an examination of how Cameron presents women, and how feminism has changed during the period of Cameron's career. The films epitomize the challenges faced by feminism on theoretical and policy levels, and the difficulties of the West to escape patriarchy's cultural traditions, institutional structures and linguistic gender hierarchies. As a result, James Cameron's work presents us with a unique opportunity: we can examine the work of a filmmaker who clearly relishes placing strong women characters in important roles, and we can simultaneously interrogate how various kinds of institutionalized feminisms have developed over the same period.

"Get away from her, you bitch!"
Liberating the Body from Gender

One of the major struggles of feminist movements was the right for women to have control over their own bodies. This was epitomized in the recurrent question of "family planning"— the soft-spoken and less controversial version of birth control. It is at the heart of relationships between men and women and is a topic of great emotional depth built around ideas of both gender and sexual difference. And, it is a topic that all of the *Alien* films confront in differing ways. In discussing *Alien* (1979) popular culture scholars Ximena Gallardo-C. and C. Jason Smith approached the issue of gender and reproduction by focusing on exactly how the Aliens reproduced themselves. In their book, *Alien Woman: The Making of Lt. Ellen Ripley*, it is the image of the alien facehugger orally raping the character of Kane (John Hurt) that fully prepares viewers for an attack on gender norms. "[T]he facehugger is a monstrously embodied sex act," specifically confronting issues of reproduction and, in "its very existence challenges human notions of biology, sex, and gender."[6] This is an argument also offered by multiple film scholars, perhaps most famously by the American film critic Amy Taubin. She described it in her summation of the themes of the first three films: "the aliens didn't bother about the niceties of sexual difference. When the baby alien burst from John Hurt's chest [in *Alien*], it cancelled the distinction on which human culture is based."[7] At the same time, as James H. Kavanagh has described it, *Alien* is a film "about feminism as a collective and potentially radical force, a force which opposes traditional gender roles [and] the sexual division of labour."[8] Going further, Kavanagh also notes, *Alien* is "almost post-feminist" with a crew whose skills and strengths do not seem to devolve to their gender.[9] *Alien* was a film released at exactly the right moment to capture what the feminist sociologist Ann Brooks called that aspect of the 1960s and 70s Women's Movement that allowed for "a range of women and feminist writers offering a critical voice to discourses in literature, art, politics and social theory."[10] Yet, where *Alien* is keen to dwell on those aspects of feminism that dominated institutional discourses in the late 1970s — discourses allowing its "fascination with the maternal body — its inner and outer appearance, its functions, its awesome powers"[11] as Barbara Creed put it — Cameron's *Aliens* takes its discussion of such topics further. Where in *Alien* reproduction represents "a monstrously embodied sex act,"[12] *Aliens* advances the metaphor and becomes the fight between two single mothers. Indeed, if Kavanagh is correct that *Alien* is almost post-feminist, *Aliens* certainly is post-feminist and, at the same time, ignores institutionalized feminism completely.

Aliens comments on the debates around birth control and motherhood. Tellingly, Ellen Ripley is a single mother who devotes her attention to only one child. Amanda, her daughter, dies two years before Ripley is found drifting in space at the beginning of the film. Ripley later steps into the role of mother for Newt, the little girl who survived the Alien attack on LV-426: her maternal instincts are triggered from the moment the expedition team discovers her hiding in the air ducts of the bunker-like metal and concrete buildings of the colony. Janice Hocker Rushing notes that "when the Marines get no response to their interrogations from the shell-shocked little girl, Ripley substitutes nourishment (hot chocolate) for questions."[13] From that moment on, Ripley establishes a maternal bond with Newt, whom she promises never to abandon.

Aliens presents several ends of the family spectrum: the alien queen is the hyperbolic representation of the woman enslaved to her body, whose sole function is child bearing. Her mechanical and incessant laying of eggs emphasizes both the biological and cultural enslavement of women to childbearing and is portrayed as being wholly monstrous, degrading women to mere beasts. During the final showdown with the alien queen, Ripley, coming to the aid of her now clearly adopted daughter Newt, shouts, "Get away from her, you bitch!" The word "bitch" resonates both as a reference to the animal nature of the alien, and as a stark critique of her offspring-producing function. The female Marines are at the other end of the spectrum; they embody both extremist feminist stances advocating women's complete liberation of their bodies, and the stereotypes of feminists as wannabe men. In the middle, there is Ripley: a single mother caring for a single child. Ripley shows extreme courage and determination to save Newt from the aliens' den, which results in the confirmation of the strong bond linking the two characters when Newt calls her "Mommy." Likewise, in *Avatar*, the heroes realize their full potential as newly only child Jake (Sam Worthington) steps into the role vacated by his dead twin brother, Tommy, while the additional scenes of the extended cut of *Avatar* tell us that Neytiri's (Zoe Saldana) sister, Sylwanin was killed by the humans.

Single children appear to be favored in both films allowing characters, freed from biological and social child bearing functions, to have control over their bodies, work and positioning in the social realm. Cameron underlines this by graphically blurring the boundaries between female and male bodies. In *Aliens*, the Marines — men and women alike — wear similar khaki uniforms, and have the same short haircuts. Ripley, the "consultant," is pictured a little differently: her clothes are grey, and her hair is slightly longer. But apart from that, she fits very much into the masculine warrior-type: she is muscular and her hips are narrow.

In *Avatar* a comparable aesthetic reigns. The Na'vi people, the military contingents and the scientists are all represented in a similarly gender-neutral fashion. The clothes are large and shapeless, for all characters in the army and in the science lab alike. The Na'vi wear only a loincloth and a few ornaments. The most visible difference is a slight disparity in the width of each character's torso and in the length of their necklaces, hiding the females' barely visible breasts. Apart from that, their naked bodies are built in the same ways. These representations in both films mirror the evolution of people's relationship to gendered appearance in Western society. Women have been wearing masculine clothing for quite some time now as Ripley does in *Aliens*, but what is new is that since the mid–1990s, it goes both ways. The metrosexual fashion trend in Western culture sees an increasing number of men wearing feminine accessories: make-up, handbags, and fitted clothes. The images in both films are disruptive of conventional conceptualizations of sex and gender by presenting the very leading edge of these cultural shifts.

Once again, it is the military and the political arenas that offer the best gauge for assessing the place of women in societies — imaginary or not. Cameron's films tackle the "double standards" protest[14] from the outset, arguing that men and women score the same in the army. Even when it comes down to upper body strength,[15] the female combatants in Cameron's movies are up to standards. This is emphasized in a specific scene of *Aliens* featuring

Private Vasquez (Jenette Goldstein). Upon waking from hypersleep, Vasquez is among the first soldiers to begin exercising while her comrades are still complaining about the situation. Cameron allows a close-up on Vasquez' arms, her grimacing face and the metallic bars she exercises on, conveying an image of cold masculinity. The camera executes a tracking movement, tilting up and down, mirroring fascination for the tough female body. After a pause, the camera tilts right and Vasquez starts doing pull-ups again, along with Private Drake (Mark Rolston), who gives up before she does. Cameron's script emphasizes this point when Private Hudson (Bill Paxton) asks, "Have you ever been mistaken for a man?" and Vasquez quickly replies, "No, have you?" On one level this is simply a moment of amusing character development, but on another it serves to emphasize that the physical capabilities of men and women in combat positions are presented as equal in Cameron's films. In a similar fashion, *Avatar*'s Neytiri is presented as Jake's protector and educator. He comes to her "ignorant as a child" and she teaches him how to become a part of the Na'vi society, ultimately assessing his readiness to enter the clan as a hunter when he performs a "clean kill."

However, this equality in combat does not completely smoothen out gender differences. Cameron offers a balanced representation of gender interaction, as he allows romance to develop between his characters. In *Aliens*, after their pull-up session, Vasquez and Drake slap each other in the face and walk away from each other, laughing. But for a moment, their heads are crossed as if they were kissing. In *Avatar*, Jake and Neytiri fall in love and seal their bond when they mate before Eywa.

In both *Aliens* and *Avatar*, then, the female characters' bodies appear to grant them the same place in combat as the male characters. Preparation for battles becomes not a way to separate the genders, but to bring them together. Physical training becomes a site of shared bonding, thus undermining the argument that "unit cohesion is degraded by double standards"[16] and simultaneously exonerating women of accusations of "unprofessionalism."[17]

Women Saving Their Worlds: Guns, Trucks and Shrewdness

This ability for combat is a necessity on both Pandora and LV-426. The humans and "aliens" on both planets are fighting for the survival of their species: on LV-426, the aliens need human bodies to gestate their young, while the humans need to stop the rapid destruction of their population. On Pandora, humans are seeking unobtanium — a material mainly located under the Na'vi Home Tree and necessary to the humans' survival on earth — and thus are threatening the habitat of the Na'vi people. In both films these situations create a narrative of conflict and war, and allow space for the female characters to grow beyond roles that would seem familiar and traditional to viewers. The characters adopt the masculine roles of protectors, leaders and fighters.

Yet even the names of the planets in *Avatar* and *Aliens* bring an undercurrent of the ideology of women's rights. LV-426 is renamed Acheron by the colonists on the planet.[18] While LV-426 is a neutral number, Acheron has many resonances. It is a river located in Greece's Epirus region, which in ancient Greek mythology was known as the river of pain. In Homer's poems, the Acheron was one of the five rivers of Hades, the Greek underworld,[19] which the newly dead had to cross with Charon in order to enter.[20] The name has a dangerous resonance, but does not conjure up gendered representations. Pandora, however, is a tale of the danger women represent for humanity. Pandora, the "all-gifted," was the first woman on earth in Greek mythology. Tales, recounted over centuries, from Hesiod to Albert Camus, tell us that when Prometheus stole the secret of fire from the gods to give it to mankind, the gods punished humanity by sending Pandora to Earth, whom they had endowed with the most seductive qualities. Her vice was her curiosity, and she opened the one jar that she must keep sealed. The theodicy tells us that Pandora opened the jar, spreading all evils on earth, keeping only Hope inside. Quaritch, *Avatar*'s personification of the patriarchy, insists that Pandora is the most hostile environment known to man, and that "if there is a hell, you might want to go there for some R&R after a tour on Pandora," conveying the image that women — and femininity in particular — are lethal dangers to men.

Thus *Aliens* and *Avatar* present two models through which Cameron can explore the roles of women. When Cameron's female characters take on masculine characteristics and social roles they force viewers to react to their own understanding of gender roles. Big guys with big trucks and big guns are clichéd images in modern cinema and, indeed, all of contemporary popular culture. Yet, Ripley's technical skills locate her in the space traditionally reserved for masculinity. In both *Aliens* and *Avatar*, the military uses the same machines — humanoid walking robots or biomechanical suits piloted by humans that serve as both travelling device and as weapon. *Aliens'* Sergeant Apone (Al Matthews) enacts patriarchy's skepticism towards the technical utility of women when he answers Ripley's question, "is there anything I can do?" with a sarcastic, "I don't know, is there anything you can do?" The pun plays on the polysemy of the verb "to do" — Ripley means *action* whereas Apone implies *capacity*.

When Ripley uses technical language, affirming she can operate the "loader" (a biomechanical suit), Apone's and Corporal Hicks' (Michael Biehn) attitude must immediately change — in much the same way, and for the same reason, that Cameron forces viewers' attitudes to change. The scene neatly encapsulates Maggie Humm's description of second-wave feminism, which "takes as its starting point the politics of representation," while minimizing gender differences.[21] Ripley's use of the suit, then, allows Cameron to present her with what Judith Evans calls "adequate similarity." Ripley shows, "no differences that could justify discrimination on the grounds of sex."[22]

Ripley takes charge of the biomechanical suit that she will later use in her confrontation with the alien Queen in a way specifically designed to confront the viewer with her competence. This entire scene builds up a technicality of the female body. The first five establishing shots are quite long (five to seven seconds each), but from the moment Ripley straps in, the shots become extremely short (fourteen one to two-second shots). They feature mechanical parts of the loader and Ripley's body parts setting it in motion. Ripley's body is meshed into technical tools with the machine she controls. The focus on her fingers, hands and feet, the close-ups on the loader's arms and buttons, added to the shortness of the shots give the audience a strong sense of action. The viewer is left with an image of Ripley as a woman, but one filled with meanings usually associated with the male form in popular film.

Where Ripley becomes a fierce combatant during *Aliens*, in *Avatar* Neytiri is presented from the beginning as a skilled hunter, and one of the only Na'vi people portrayed in the act of killing before the assault of Colonel Quaritch (Stephen Lang) and his soldiers on the Tree of Souls. During the battle, Neytiri fights alongside other warriors. The thanator — whose name stems from the Greek word *thánatos*, the personification of death — that threatened to kill Jake upon his arrival on Pandora bows to her, and lets her ride him during the battle. Cameron's other female characters are similarly presented. The skilled pilot Trudy embodies the tough, fearless woman, sacrificing herself by attacking Colonel Quaritch's assault ship. Grace is the lead scientist, director of an entire laboratory, who fends for herself, her team and the Na'vi population. Yet, Colonel Quaritch, the film's allegory of the patriarchy, kills them both.

Where Ripley achieves combat competence through the course of *Aliens*, Neytiri has it from the outset. When Caporal Hicks gives Ripley a rifle, showing her how to use it, Ripley states matter-of-factly, "show me everything, I can handle myself." Hicks replies "Yeah, I noticed." This process is later confirmed to the audience when Ripley arms herself to the teeth before going on a mission to rescue Newt from the alien's den. Cameron uses tropes of masculine action to portray the potency of women. The only human male character that survives LV-426 is Hicks, who articulates the up-and-coming acceptance of Western societies at that time that women were equal to men. When Ripley destroys first the alien's nest, then the alien queen herself, she does so by co-opting the weapons brought by the marines, then the biomechanical loader. Cameron allows Ripley to become proficient with the technological tools of the patriarchy in precisely the fashion second-wave feminism envisions. To use the terms of Judith Evans' argument again, Ripley expresses the paradigm of true second-wave ideology in that she seems to be claiming for women, "we deserve to be equal with you, for we are in fact the same. We possess the same capabilities."[23] In the mean time, this game of mimesis is an attempt, as Luce Irigaray notes, "to locate the place of [woman's] exploitation by discourse, without allowing herself to be simply reduced to it."[24] And, in her use of the biomechanical suit, flamethrowers, and big guns Ripley is offering proof of exactly that.

When Neytiri confronts a similar device, another biomechanical suit — this time worn by Quaritch — she does not co-opt the technology, but rather fights it. Where Ripley showed her skill through her ability to use the technology of the patriarchy, Neytiri directly confronts it, battles it, and destroys it. While *Avatar*'s hero, Jake, lies incapacitated, it falls to the woman warrior to enact a final victory. This is not all that different than the narrative relationship between Hicks and Ripley in *Aliens*. What is different — and what highlights the changes between the second-wave feminism of *Aliens* and the third-wave of *Avatar* — is that this time the female hero does not require the tools or technology of the patriarchy to achieve victory. Ripley achieved victory by using a biomechanical suit to kill the alien queen and, in the process, minimizing any perceived gender differences. Neytiri's victory is through the destruction of just such a suit. Neytiri's competence is in no way dependant on using the technology associated in patriarchal values to masculinity — Luce Irigaray reminds us that the human species is divided in two sexes, and that equality must be attained not through a process of gender neutralization, but through an acceptance of difference.[25] Her aptitudes exist wholly independently of that technology and, very much in line with third-wave perspectives, fully emphasize those aspects that make her different. At the same time, Neytiri's skills have little to do with her gender. As Imelda Whelehan has noted, a significant criticism of second-wave feminism was "its tenacious reliance upon gender difference as the single most important analytical category,"[26] and Neytiri's skills as a warrior, regardless of either her sex or gender, emphasize this very critique. Her skills are neither because she is female, nor in spite of that fact. Where such a narrative would have negatively suggested deviance in a mid–1980s film like *Aliens* by the twenty-first century such a character is presented as celebratory.

Discourses of Deviance in a Transitional Social System

Yet, as celebratory as Neytiri's representation in *Avatar* might appear, the patriarchal values system remains very much in place in the film's narrative. The French philosopher Michel Foucault asserted that order and identity are created and sustained through "discourses of deviance."[27] While Foucault would turn this analysis on sexuality and mental illness rather than gender categories, his insight implies precisely why the character of Ripley in *Aliens* so strongly captured the zeitgeist of second wave feminism whereas Neytiri in *Avatar* fully misses a similar resonance with the third wave. Ripley as a character—and by extension, Cameron as the writer-director of *Aliens*—is fully aware of the gender norms she is deviating from throughout the film. She is violating the established norms of the mid–1980s action film simply by being a woman, after all. At the same time, Neytiri is merely occupying the position of "powerful female warrior" and not deviating from that role at all.

The feminist philosopher Jana Sawicki uses Foucault's terms in a fashion that captures this distinction. By "deviancy," she claims, a discourse is created in which "norms are established through the very process of identifying the deviant as such, then observing it, further classifying it, monitoring and 'treating' it."[28] The "deviance" of Ripley is only deviant in the historical moment of the film. Coming at the fruition of second wave feminism, such deviance was in the process of being re-defined as a new "normal." Ripley's deviance, then, is ephemeral. Indeed, the characters of Ripley and Neytiri have to be considered from the perspective of the historical moment of their creations by Cameron. *Aliens* was released at a crest in the influence of the second wave—and, indeed, is part of the evidence of that crest. As such, it typifies a new form of gender representation. *Avatar*, however, is a film caught within the eddies of the third wave. As such, the historical moment of the latter film is altogether different than it was for the former.

Foucault presented his own way of considering this difference in a general discussion of the history of ideas, but one that specifically applies here to the differences between Ripley and Neytiri. There are "two categories of formulation" that must be distinguished from each other, he noted. First are "those that are highly valued and relatively rare, which appear for the first time, which have no similar antecedents, which may serve as models for others, and which to this extent deserve to be regarded as creations." It is under this rubric that we classify the character of Ripley. Neytiri, on the other hand, must be classified among "those, ordinary, everyday, solid [things] ... which derive, sometimes going so far as to repeat it word for word, from what has already been said."[29] So much of *Avatar* seems to "repeat word for word" from Cameron's previous films that it seems almost *sui generis* of Cameron rather than part of a wider discourse about gender.

However, the discourse of deviance in *Avatar* and *Aliens* tells us much about the fundamental values and beliefs of the fictional societies Cameron describes — as well as much about the society of the filmmaker. Despite the overt discourse of gender equality, the ancestral fear of the powerful woman remains, especially in Cameron's latest film. Social research moreover shows that discrimination is most pronounced in situations where groups compete for political power or physical resources,[30] and both films engage with this scenario.

The only powerful female character that is truly successful in both movies is Ripley. Her image corresponds to the feminist and political discourses of the 1980s, which were full of hope for the access of men and women to a gender neutral society, in which each person could contribute depending on individual abilities rather than gender. The character has "no similar antecedents" — at least, no similar recent antecedents (with the exception of Cameron's own Sarah Connor). Turning again to the scene in which Ripley drives the loader does bring out one antecedent, however, in that it recalls religious imagery. The only three medium distance shots of the scene are filmed from a significant low angle putting on-screen Ripley's whole body positioned on the loader. The audience is looking up at Ripley's face. The surroundings are dark, bringing out her face bathed in light, with her eyes half-closed in all three shots, which very much recalls Italian Renaissance paintings of the Virgin Mary, while her position on the loader evokes images of the Christ on His cross. The image of the savior pervaded through the staging of Ripley in *Aliens* reflects upon the enthusiasm of the time — she is saving the earth, twice-fold: first intradiegetically by eradicating the aliens, second metatextually, by presenting a new model of womanhood to the public.

However, this female character remains exceptional. It was the 1980s ideal, which has not been replicated in Cameron's films since, although this seems at odds with the normalization of the concept of gender in Western societies over the past few decades. Society still presents women in combat and in political roles as something exceptional, although political and military institutions are more open to women than ever before in history. Yet in Cameron's moral universe, the female characters that are the toughest and present the most masculine traits are eliminated: they are deviant as they are socially unsustainable and thus disrupt the order in place. William Connolly, echoing Foucault, argues that in the western world, the quest for a perfectly ordered society can only be sustained by casting out or destroying everything that does not fit in.[31]

The fascination implied by the camera's movement in *Aliens* at Vasquez' physical strength, and the agency, courage and leadership of Trudy and Grace in *Avatar* are disruptive of commonsense representations of womanhood and lead to their deaths. The portrayed deviance of these characters recalls Foucault's description of mental illness. Referring to Milton Rokeach, Richard Ned Lebow reminds us that it is increasingly attributed to "disturbance of the sense of identity,"[32] which in itself is an arbitrary notion based on the social identities imposed on individuals. The woman adopting masculine attitudes and taking on power in traditional male-reserved domains is thus portrayed as "abject" in Julia Kristeva's sense. She is simultaneously captivating and terrifying[33] — and must therefore be eliminated. This process of casting out what is deviant in the patriarchy's norms underlines the difficulties of the Western world to come to grips with the social changes it initiated mid–twentieth century.

It should not be surprising, then, that the character of Neytiri cannot easily replicate the feminist success of Ripley — for Ripley *is* Neytiri's "similar antecedent." At the same time, the respect of women's rights and of gender equality implies not only a shift in mentalities, but also an architectural change of society, as it pervades all aspects of family life, institutional organization, labor and access to agency in the form of political and military power. Neytiri cannot possibly represent such a monumental societal shift because such a shift has yet to happen in the broader culture. And, certainly, such a shift was not hinted at through the character of Ripley, either — Cameron's moral universe would not allow it.

By 2009, although tremendous changes have given women equality in law and access to education and jobs they had never occupied before, the enthusiasm of the 1980s has plummeted. Cameron's mass-mediated film *Avatar* does not present us with a revolutionary social model, but with confused societies that have integrated the norms of gender equality while still promoting a patriarchal model. Tellingly, while *Aliens* featured an avant-garde family structure — a strong and successful single mother in a "blended family"—*Avatar* promotes a very traditional, even backwards, family model. The partners are "mated for life," and the men chose their women.

Sharing Power? Women Stepping Out of Leadership Roles

The emphasis on traditional gender roles is central to the narrative of *Avatar* and makes the film far more regressive than we should expect from the writer-director who gave us *Aliens*. All the female alien figures on Pandora occupy overly familiar roles: family, education, spirituality, and dependence upon men for the more "serious" matters such as politics and survival. Neytiri is cast in the role of a combined wife and mother figure. She educates Jake — who is "like a baby," "ignorant like a child" — to the values and customs of Na'vi society, and shows him how to live on Pandora. She has the role of educator and protector of the vulnerable one, a role classically reserved to women. She educates Jake until he is ready to take his place within the Na'vi society, thus giving him the knowledge and tools necessary to save the Na'vi from the humans. When the time comes for Jake to accomplish his heroic acts, Neytiri steps back and allows him free rein.

This is hardly a new position for a female — even a female alien — to find herself in. As early as 1552, La Boétie claimed in his *Discourse on Voluntary Servitude* that any form of rule is dependent upon the "voluntary servitude" of the people.[34] Feminists have picked up on this in later centuries, asserting that patriarchal systems are upheld not only by men, but also by women finding security and comfort in the discrimination operated against them. These patterns of discrimination are institutionalized through education and socialization. Children raised in such a system must adapt to the prevailing ideology of the patriarchy.[35]

Cameron, however, seems to argue through his films that such a system of education and socialization should not force a relapse into traditional discrimination toward women. If this is indeed the case, then something else seems to be at play in the different representations of women between *Aliens* and *Avatar*. The distinction between the powerful figure of Ripley and the women of the Na'vi strongly implies that female agency is less important as of 2009 than it was in 1986. Even in some of their reserved domains, female figures in *Avatar* are stripped off their credibility and agency. The division of ruling is clear in Na'vi society — Eytukan (Wes Studi), the clan leader, is in charge of political and military decisions, while his wife Mo'at (CCH Pounder) is the *tsahik*, the spiritual leader who interprets the signs of the deity Eywa. From what the audience understands, this role is transmitted to girls from one generation to the next. But Neytiri misunderstands Eywa's will, whereas Jake's prayers are heard, thus supplanting Neytiri in her role. Likewise, Mo'at is a character presented as willful, rational and courageous throughout the movie. She appears to take joint decisions with Eytukan; she has the final word over Jake's destiny when he arrives in the Na'vi society: "It is decided. My daughter will teach you our ways." However, during the assault, she turns to Jake crying, asking him to help the Na'vi people.

The military and political agency remains firmly in the hands of the male characters in *Avatar*. As he is dying, Eytukan, the Na'vi clan leader and Neytiri's father, hands his political and military power over to his daughter by handing her his bow and using the injunctive sentence "Protect the People." The chaos of the situation can be read three ways: that Eytukan has chosen Neytiri because of her familial connection, yes, but also because he believes she will best guide the Na'vi people and that the urgency of the situation — he is dying, after all — demands that he pass on his power immediately and only Neytiri is present.

Visually, the transmission of power between the two characters is strongly staged. The father and daughter's heads are alternatively off- and on-screen, visually beheading them by turns — Eytukan is filmed from a high angle and his face slowly disappears. The ash of the burning forest is floating in the air, passing from Eytukan to Neytiri, implying that his life is passed on to her. Neytiri has become the political leader and the protector of the Na'vi, a role traditionally incumbent to the men. However, this empowerment of the female figure is completely overlooked in the remainder of the film. Norm will ignore the shift in power and simply declare that Tsu'tey (Laz Alonso), a Na'vi man who was betrothed to Neytiri during their childhood, "is *olo'eyktan* now." Tsu'tey is in turn ousted by Jake who takes the lead of the Na'vi people by affirming that *he* has "over fifteen clans out there." Jake becomes a hypertrophied hero figure, blotting out all other characters. Significantly, however, the erasure of Neytiri's political and military role is already suggested in the scene where her father dies. The camera movements are jittery; the angles are changing constantly, heralding the unstable nature of her empowerment.

Neytiri herself gives in to patriarchal stereotypes of protective men when Jake appears as Toruk Macto on the Great Leonopteryx and welcomes him by asserting: "I was afraid Jake, for my people. I'm not anymore." Neytiri is definitely set aside when Jake fully ignores the fact that Neytiri was given the bow by her father and asks Tsu'tey for the permission to speak to the Na'vi people, inciting them to fight back against the humans. Jake takes Neytiri by the hand to place her behind him in the scene. Jake, Tsu'tey and Neytiri are spatially standing in a triangle. Jake and Tsu'tey are standing in the front; one speaking, the other translating, while Neytiri is placed in the background. This triangular organization is used to marginalize Grace in the film as well: when standing with Quaritch and Selfridge, she is ridiculed and dismissed for being irrational and emotional while placed in a similar visual relationship to both. In the triangle, both Grace and Neytiri are silenced by two males and their relationship to the single woman present.

Lene Hansen pointed out the importance of voice for the construction of subjectivity in her analysis of the Little Mermaid tale. Hansen notes that "those who like the Little Mermaid are constrained in their ability to speak security are therefore prevented from becoming subjects worthy of consideration."[36] Neytiri is deprived of agency simply by being deprived of her voice.

She is rarely granted an articulate speech by Cameron — she moans, wails, grunts, growls, hisses, screams — thus losing her agency while simultaneously emphasizing the emotive aspects of the feminine. When she speaks, often it is to repeat what the men have just said or to fulfill her traditional feminine role of socializer and educator within the Na'vi culture.

The price to pay for women accessing a wider range of roles, *Avatar* tells us, is their silence and their retreat into patriarchal gender hierarchies. The revolution of female emancipation is aborted before it has started — worse, it leaves the audience feeling that it has been completed and is not a matter for continued debate. Where in *Aliens* Ripley seems to be fully engaged in the examination of what a woman can accomplish, in *Avatar* the women have already seen that question answered for them, and are no longer concerned with anything other than the roles traditionally assigned to them. The American feminist Barbara Epstein has emphasized this dilemma. After the active awareness of women's rights during the second wave, a feeling that we have changed all we could has lead to a disengagement of the public from debates around gender roles.[37] The mainstreaming of gender issues into the broader Western culture[38] and the disengagement of the public has allowed for recurring patriarchal hierarchies of gender to re-emerge more strongly within both the public and private realm. In Cameron's *Avatar*, Richard Ned Lebow's allegation that "individuals who join countercultures are likely to find themselves under just as much social pressure to conform to another"[39] identity sheds light on Neytiri's abandonment of her political responsibilities to Jake. Quite simply, and through a very well-established sense of ideological normalcy, she just feels more secure when he is in charge.

Avatar reflects upon the period of transition Western societies are experiencing at the dawn of the twenty-first century. The achievements in terms of gender equality have been enormous in a short period of time, but it will take no less effort to institutionalize equal rights of women and men in practice, be it in the public sphere or in their homes. This will require a more important shift in mentalities — and in the visual and linguistic common-sense signs we use to communicate and which *Avatar* uses to establish a sense of gender normality. As Wittgenstein's famous dictum holds, language is not an image of the world; it is "part of an activity, a way of life."[40] Human agency can thus not take place outside of language; it is intrinsically linked to it.[41] *Avatar* is a fictional universe still ruled by a male-dominated language and a male-dominated set of visual cues, even though it is also staged as being critical of patriarchal gender hierarchies. Thus, *Avatar* epitomizes the difficulties of Western cultures — and of many cultures worldwide — to break out of gendered visual representations and gendered language.

Avatar, however, represents a regressive perspective on such issues. Where

Aliens' Ripley forced a reevaluation of gender roles, Neytiri does not. In a period where most military organizations have long-since adopted new regulations for the service of women, gay men, and lesbians in their ranks, *Avatar* presents an image of the military as just another white male patriarchal structure — even when that "white, male" structure is organized around blue, male aliens. In a period when the U.S. military was in the process of eliminating their long-standing "don't ask, don't tell" policy, which was repealed mid–December 2010, *Avatar's* narrative convincingly keeps women, at least, relegated to the rear of both power-structures and visual images. While *Avatar* may not be intentionally presenting itself as a film intent on the marginalization of its female characters, its net effect is precisely that.

Conclusion: "I was afraid, Jake. I'm not anymore."

The political scientist William Connolly has noted that only seldomly "does a policy of repression or marginalization present itself as such."[42] Whether by conscious intent or not, James Cameron has emphasized this precise point through his films. In his early films, and especially in *Aliens*, Cameron worked at criticizing gendered domination. But by reintroducing visual, linguistic and socio-political systems depriving women of agency in *Avatar* he seems to have fully contradicted the inherent feminism of his early work. Examining both films in tandem shows us that no social improvement is definitive; no right is vested and change is not always progressive. From *Aliens* to *Avatar*, the institutionalization of feminine roles in military and political leadership roles seemingly has become contradictory — so much so that the later film seems far less advanced than its predecessor. In *Aliens* the female and male characters of these futuristic gender-egalitarian societies are represented as gender-neutral, while in *Avatar* the women are traditional wives and mothers, relying on male leaders for their survival.

It should be a simple thing to conclude, then, that this shift in Cameron's gender paradigm is one of the personal changes of a specific filmmaker. However, these profound changes in the representation of female characters might also serve to highlight the huge gap that remains to be bridged between law and political reality, between ideals and cultural norms. *Aliens* has become emblematic of a cultural shift in the representation of women in film and gender norms more generally. At the time, it constituted almost a gender deviancy, thus emphasizing a turning point in feminism itself. While no similar claims can be made for *Avatar* this might have less to do with the prevailing images of women and more to do with the effectiveness of institutionalized feminism in the twenty-first century.

Indeed, this reflects upon the fact that, for cultural, historical and philosophical reasons, we are often too quick to grant ontological status to identities; although this is a mistake.[43] Identities are not fixed, they are socially established and have a performative character — they are enacted practices, but they can also resonate as calls to action. As much as *Aliens* encapsulated the call to action of second wave feminism, *Avatar* mirrors what the Western world is experiencing at the moment. It is difficult, in Giddens' words, to "keep [the] particular narrative going" through the internecine battles of third wave feminist debates.[44] At a time when, as Imelda Whelehan has noted, "feminist debates continue and become increasingly complex and diverse in the scholarly arena," *Avatar* steps away from Cameron's tradition of interrogating female roles and presents a different transformative narrative in its place.[45] As contemporary feminists have adopted increasingly postmodern categories in an attempt to overcome the "tenacious reliance upon gender difference as the single most important analytical category," Cameron has presented a wholly different category of his own in *Avatar*.[46] The use of these new tools for feminists have revolved around a need to offer the kind of "fluidity of the self [that] feminists seek; that postmodernism brings," and which are also offered, after a fashion, by Cameron in *Avatar* as well.[47]

Yet both *Aliens* and *Avatar* do present certain aspects of hope for those concerned with social change. While *Aliens* does this by capturing the significant successes of second wave feminism, *Avatar* is not wholly bereft of such qualities. There is a powerful fluidity of identity in the film which is epitomized in Jake first moving from being a "jarhead" Marine to being "a cup that is already full" (an equal with the scientists) and then changing species — the ultimate barrier that can be crossed. Richard Ned Lebow insists upon the fact that "science fiction regularly probes identity at the species level" while some works take "the next logical step and explore 'post-species' identities."[48] In *Avatar*, the process of Jake's change concerns the entire Na'vi society — it takes time and necessitates social rites of acceptance, but ultimately it is a success. His radical transformation echoes the Hope left in Pandora's jar after all evils escaped it. This metamorphosis is, to use the Foucauldian categories of Jana Sawicki, wholly about overcoming the "disciplinary power" inherent in the cultural control of the body. What Jake accomplishes in the final scenes of *Avatar* "is a knowledge of and power over the individual body — its capacities, gestures, movements, location, and behaviors."[49] Although it recounts the identity change of a male character, it bodes well for a radical change in mentalities and behaviors, allowing for women to concretely obtain the same place, agency and power as men within society.

Where *Aliens* brought to the forefront those issues of the second wave that had become central to Western culture in the two decades before its release, it remains difficult to criticize *Avatar* for being overly regressive. Since *Aliens*, the surge of feminism has given way to the "reality that feminism as a political movement with a mass following has waned in both Europe and the United States."[50] A critique of women characters in *Avatar*, then, might say more about the current status and role of institutional feminism than it can possibly say about James Cameron.

Both *Aliens* and *Avatar* bring to our attention the contradictions that still need to be overcome in the Western world in order to promote women's rights from the legal to the policy world — and they tell us that it is possible to reinvent a differently structured "we," although it needs to happen at the community level. *Avatar* and *Aliens* offer, if not a new language, an incentive to find one that will encourage new social structures and the abrogation of gender-based roles.

NOTES

Elisa Narminio would like to thank Kimberly Hutchings for her intellectual generosity, her communicative enthusiasm and her dedicated support. She would also like to thank Richard Ned Lebow for kindly sharing his manuscript *In Search of Ourselves* with her. Both authors thank Stephen McVeigh for his dedicated reading(s) of drafts.

1. *Time Magazine*, "Cinema: The Years of Living Splendidly," July 28, 1986. Available at: www.time.com/time/magazine/article/0,9171,961869-1,00.html (Access date January 26, 2011).

2. *Time Magazine*, "Help! They're Back!" July 28, 1986. Available at: http://www.time.com /time/magazine/article/0,9171,961839-1,00.html (Access date January 26, 2011).

3. *Time Magazine*, "Help! They're Back!"

4. Richard Corliss, "Corliss Appraises *Avatar*: A World of Wonder," *Time Magazine*, December 14, 2009. Available at: http://www.time.com/time/arts/article/0,8599,1947438,00. html (Access date January 12, 2011).

5. Gerhard Kümmel, "When Boy Meets Girl: The 'Feminization' of the Military An Introduction Also to be Read as a Postscript," *Current Sociology* 50:5 (2002), 630; see also Irene Padavic "The Re-Creation of Gender in a Male Workplace," *Symbolic Interaction* 14:3 (1991); Robert W. Connell, *Masculinities* (Polity Press, 1999); Regina Titunik "The First Wave: Gender Integration and Military Culture," *Armed Forces and Society* 26:2 (2000); Sylvia Wilz "'Gendered Organizations': Neuere Beiträge zum Verhältnis von Organisationen und Geschlecht," *Berliner Journal für Soziologie* 11:1 (2001).

6. Ximena Gallardo-C and C. Jason Smith, *Alien Woman: The Making of Lt. Ellen Ripley* (New York: Continuum, 2005), 37.

7. Amy Taubin, "Invading Bodies: *Aliens³* [sic] and the Trilogy." *Sight and Sound* (July-August 1992): 9.

8. James H. Kavanagh, "Feminism, Humanism and Science in *Alien*," In *Alien Zones: Cultural Theory and Contemporary Science Fiction Cinema*, Ed. Annette Kuhn (London: Verso 1990): 87.

9. Kavanagh, 77.

10. Ann Brooks, *Postfeminisms: Feminism, Cultural Theory and Cultural Forms* (New York: Routledge 1997), 118.

11. Barbara Creed, "Gynesis, Postmodernism and the Science Fiction Horror Film," In *Alien Zones: Cultural Theory and Contemporary Science Fiction Cinema*, Ed. Annette Kuhn (London: Verso, 1990): 215.

12. Gallardo-C. and Smith, *Alien Woman*, 37.

13. Janice Rushing Hocker, "Evolution of 'The New Frontier' in *Alien* and *Aliens*:

Patriarchal Co-optation of the Feminine Archetype," In *Screening The Sacred: Religion, Myth, and Ideology in Popular American Film*, Eds. Joel W. Martin and Conrad E. Ostwalt (Boulder, CO: Westview, 1995), 111–112.

14. Carol Cohn, "'How Can She Claim Equal Rights When She Doesn't Have to Do as Many Push-Ups as I Do?': The Framing of Men's Opposition to Women's Equality in the Military," *Men and Masculinities* 3 (2000).

15. Cohn, 138. "The one irreducible difference for the majority of women is that as a group, most women have less upper body strength."

16. David Buckingham, "The Warrior Ethos" (Newport, RI: Naval War College, 1999), 17.

17. Carol Cohn, "War, Wimps and Women: Talking Gender and Thinking War," in *Gendering War Talk*, ed. Miriam Cooke and Angela Woollacott (Princeton University Press, 1993), 231.

18. James Cameron, *Aliens* (Screenplay), is available in multiple print and online sources. Available at: http://www.avpoe.org/amr/html/scripts/aliens2.txt (Access date January 12, 2011).

19. Homer, *The Odyssey* (London: Penguin Classics, 2003).

20. Virgil, *The Aeneid* (Oxford: Oxford Paperbacks, 2008).

21. Maggie Humm, *Feminism and Film* (Edinburgh: Edinburgh University Press, 1997), 197.

22. Judith Evans, *Feminist Theory Today*, 13.

23. Evans, *Feminist Theory Today*, 13.

24. Luce Irigaray, *Speculum of the Other Woman*. Trans. Gillian C. Gill (Ithaca: Cornell University Press, 1985), 76.

25. Luce Irigaray, *Je, tu, nous. Pour une culture de la différence* (Paris: Grasset, 1990).

26. Imelda Whelehan, *Modern Feminist Thought*, 195.

27. Michel Foucault, *Madness and Civilization: A History of Insanity in the Age of Reason* (Vintage, 1988).

28. Jana Sawicki, *Disciplining Foucault: Feminism, Power, and the Body* (New York: Routledge, 1991), 39.

29. Michel Foucault, *The Archaeology of Knowledge* (New York: Pantheon Books, 1972), 141.

30. Muzafer Sherif and Carolyn Sherif, *Groups in Harmony and Tension* (New York: Harper, 1953); Robert A. LeVine and Donald T. Campbell, *Ethnocentrism: Theories of Conflict, Ethnic Attitudes, and Group Behavior* (New York: Wiley, 1971); Donald L. Horowitz, *Ethnic Groups in Conflict* (Berkeley: University of California Press, 1985).

31. William E. Connolly, *Political Theory and Modernity* (Ithaca: Cornell University Press, 1993/1988), 13–14.

32. Milton Rokeach, *Three Christs of Ypsilanti* (New York: NYRB Classics, *forthcoming*), 310. Cited in Lebow, *In Search of Ourselves*.

33. Julia Kristeva, *For Teresa Brennan*, in *Living attention*, ed. Alice Jardine, et al. (SUNY Press, 2007).

34. Étienne de la Boétie, "Discours de la Servitude Volontaire," in *Œuvres Complètes* (Slatkine Reprints, 1967/1552).

35. Fraser, "Becoming Human: The Origins and Developments of Women's Human Rights." *Human Rights Quarterly* 21 (1999), 855; Cynthia Enloe, "Gender Makes the World Go Round," in *Bananas, Beaches and Bases: Making Feminist Sense of International Politics* (London: Pandora Press/Rivers Oram Press, 1989), 16.

36. Lene Hansen, "The Little Mermaid's Security Dilemma and the Absence of Gender in the Copenhagen School," *Millenium* 29:2 (2000): 285.

37. Barbara Epstein, "What Happened to the Women's Movement?" *Monthly Review* 51:1 (2001), Available at: http://www.monthlyreview.org/0501epstein.htm (Access date Dec 25, 2010).

38. Barbara Epstein, "Feminist Consciousness After the Women's Movement?" *Monthly Review* 54:4 (2002), Available at: http://www.monthlyreview.org/0902epstein.htm (Access date December 25, 2010).

39. Richard Ned Lebow, *In Search of Ourselves: The Politics and Ethics of Identity* (Cambridge: Cambridge University Press, forthcoming).

40. Ludwig Wittgenstein, *Philosophische Untersuchungen*, in *Werkausgabe Band 1* (Frankfurt: Suhrkamp, 1993/1952), 250.

41. Roland Bleiker, *Popular Dissent, Human Agency and Global Politics* (Cambridge: Cambridge University Press, 2000), 41.

42. William E. Connolly, *Identity/Difference: Democratic Negotiations of Political Paradox* (Ithaca, NY: Cornell University Press, 1991), 159.

43. Pierre Bourdieu and Loïc Wacquant, *An Invitation to Reflexive Sociology* (Chicago: Chicago University Press, 1992), 228; Rogers Brubacker, *Ethnicity Without Groups* (Cambridge: Harvard University Press, 2004), 23.

44. Anthony Giddens, *Modernity and Self-Identity: Self and Society in the Late Modern Age* (Stanford University Press, 1991), 54, 75.

45. Imelda Whelehan, *Modern Feminist Thought*, 2.

46. Whelehan, *Modern Feminist Thought*, 195.

47. Judith Evans, *Feminist Theory Today*, 23.

48. Richard Ned Lebow, *In Search of Ourselves: The Politics and Ethics of Identity* (Cambridge: Cambridge University Press, forthcoming), introduction.

49. Jana Sawicki, *Disciplining Foucault*, 67.

50. Imelda Whelehan, *Modern Feminist Thought*, 2.

WORKS CITED

Bleiker, Roland. *Popular Dissent, Human Agency and Global Politics*. Cambridge: Cambridge University Press, 2000.

Bourdieu, Pierre, and Loïc Wacquant. *An Invitation to Reflexive Sociology*. Chicago: Chicago University Press, 1992.

Brooks, Ann. *Postfeminisms: Feminism, Cultural Theory and Cultural Forms*. London: Routledge, 1997.

Brubacker, Rogers. *Ethnicity Without Groups*. Cambridge: Harvard University Press, 2004.

Buckingham, David. "The Warrior Ethos." Newport, RI: Naval War College, 12 March 1999.

Cameron, James. *Aliens* (Screenplay). Available at:http://www.avpoe.org/amr/html/scripts/aliens2.txt (Access date January 12, 2011).

Cohn, Carol. "'How Can She Claim Equal Rights When She Doesn't Have to Do as Many Push-Ups as I Do?': The Framing of Men's Opposition to Women's Equality in the Military." *Men and Masculinities* 3 (2000): 131–151.

_____. "War, Wimps and Women: Talking Gender and Thinking War," in *Gendering War Talk*, ed. Miriam Cooke and Angela Woollacott. Princeton: Princeton University Press, 1993.

Connell, Robert W. *Masculinities*. Cambridge: Polity Press, 1999.

Connolly, William E. *Identity/Difference: Democratic Negotiations of Political Paradox*. Ithaca, NY: Cornell University Press, 1991.

_____. *Political Theory and Modernity*. Ithaca, NY: Cornell University Press, 1993/1988.

Corliss, Richard. "Corliss Appraises *Avatar*: A World of Wonder." *Time Magazine* (December 14, 2009). Available at: http://www.time.com/time/arts/article/0,8599,1947438,00.html (Access date 12 January 2011).

Creed, Barbara. "Gynesis, Postmodernism and the Science Fiction Horror Film." In *Alien Zones: Cultural Theory and Contemporary Science Fiction Cinema*, ed. Annette Kuhn, 214–218. London: Verso, 1990.

Enloe, Cynthia. "Gender Makes the World Go Round." In *Bananas, Beaches and Bases: Making Sense of International Politics* (collected essays), 1–18. London: Pandora Press/Rivers Oram Press, 1989.

Epstein, Barbara. "Feminist Consciousness After the Women's Movement." *Monthly Review* 54:4 (2002). Available at: http://www.monthlyreview.org/0902epstein.htm (Access date December 25, 2010).

_____. "What Happened to the Women's Movement?" *Monthly Review* 51:1 (2001). Available at: http://www.monthlyreview.org/0501epstein.htm (Access date December 25, 2010).

Evans, Judith. *Feminist Theory Today: An Introduction to Second-Wave Feminism*. London: Sage, 1995.

Foucault, Michel. *The Archeology of Knowledge.* New York: Pantheon Books, 1972.

_____. *Madness and Civilization: A History of Insanity in the Age of Reason.* Vintage, 1988.

Fraser, Arvonne. "Becoming Human: The Origins and Developments of Women's Human Rights," *Human Rights Quarterly*, 21 (1999): 853–906.

Gallardo-C., Ximena, and C. Jason Smith. *Alien Woman: The Making of Lt. Ellen Ripley.* New York: Continuum, 2004.

Giddens, Anthony. *Modernity and Self-Identity: Self and Society in the Late Modern Age.* Stanford: Stanford University Press, 1991.

Hansen, Lene. "The Little Mermaid's Security Dilemma and the Absence of Gender in the Copenhagen School." *Millenium* 29:2 (2000): 285–306.

Hocker Rushing, Janice. "Evolution of 'The New Frontier' in *Alien* and *Aliens*: Patriarchal Co-optation of the Feminine Archetype." In *Screening The Sacred: Religion, Myth, and Ideology in Popular American Film*, eds. Joel W. Martin and Conrad E. Ostwalt, Jr., 94–117. Boulder, CO: Westview Press, 1995.

Homer. *The Odyssey.* London: Penguin Classics, 2003.

Humm, Maggie. *Feminism and Film.* Edinburgh: Edinburgh University Press, 1997.

Irigaray, Luce. *Je, tu nous. Pour une culture de la différence.* Paris: Grasset, 1990.

_____. *Speculum of the Other Woman.* Trans. Gillian C. Gill. Ithaca, NY: Cornell University Press, 1985.

Kavanagh, James. "Feminism, Humanism and Science in *Alien*." In *Alien Zones: Cultural Theory and Contemporary Science Fiction Cinema*, ed. Annette Kuhn, 73–81. London: Verso, 1990

Kristeva, Julia. *For Teresa Brennan*, trans. Shannon Hoff, in *Living Attention*, ed. Alice Jardine, Shannon Lundeen, and Kelly Oliver. Albany: State University of New York Press, 2007.

Kümmel, Gerhard. "When Boy Meets Girl: The 'Feminization' of the Military An Introduction Also to be Read as a Postscript." *Current Sociology* 50:5 (2002): 615–639.

La Boétie, Étienne de. "Discours de la Servitude Volontaire," ed. P. Bonnefon in *Œuvres Complètes.* Geneva: Slatkine Reprints, 1967/1552.

Lebow, Richard Ned. *In Search of Ourselves: The Politics and Ethics of Identity.* Cambridge: Cambridge University Press, forthcoming.

Padavic, Irene. "The Re-Creation of Gender in a Male Workplace." *Symbolic Interaction* 14:3 (1991): 279–294.

Rokeach, Milton. *Three Christs of Ypsilanti.* New York: NYRB Classics, *forthcoming*.

Sawicki, Jana. *Disciplining Foucault: Feminism, Power, and the Body.* New York: Routledge, 1991.

Sherif, Muzafer, and Sherif, Carolyn. *Groups in Harmony and Tension.* New York: Harper, 1953.

Taubin, Amy. "Invading Bodies: *Aliens³* [sic] and the Trilogy." *Sight and Sound* (July-August 1992): 8–10.

Time Magazine. "Cimena: Help! They're Back!" (July 28, 1986). Available at: http://www.time.com/time/magazine/article/0,9171,961839-1,00.html (Access date January 26, 2011).

_____. "Cinema: The Years of Living Splendidly" (July 28, 1986). Available at: www.time.com/time/magazine/article/0,9171,961869–1,00.html (Access date Jan 26, 2011).

Titunik, Regina. "The First Wave: Gender Integration and Military Culture." *Armed Forces and Society* 26:2 (2000).

Virgil. *The Aeneid.* Oxford: Oxford Paperbacks, 2008.

Welehan, Imelda. *Modern Feminist Thought: From the Second Wave to "Post-Feminism."* Edinburgh: Edinburgh University Press, 1995.

Wilz, Sylvia. "'Gendered Organizations': Neuere Beiträge zum Verhältnis von Organisationen und Geschlecht." *Berliner Journal für Soziologie* 11:1 (2001): 97–107.

Wittgenstein, Ludwig. *Philosophische Untersuchungen*, in *Werkausgabe Band 1.* Frankfurt: Suhrkamp, 1993/1952.

FILMS CITED

Aliens. Directed by James Cameron. Twentieth Century–Fox, 1986.

Avatar. Directed by James Cameron. Twentieth Century–Fox, 2009.

The Terminator. Directed by James Cameron. Hemdale Films, 1984.

Terminators, Aliens, and Avatars: The Emergence of Archetypal Homosexual Themes in a Filmmaker's Imagination

ROGER KAUFMAN

In a grim future on Earth after nuclear holocaust, a motley crew of survivors courageously fights the brutal machines that relentlessly hunt them down. Farther into the future, on a verdant moon in a distant solar system, diverse species of resplendent animal life rise up in concert to help expel rapacious human invaders. These are just two of the many visionary scenes in James Cameron's science fiction films that have stretched the limits of what kinds of imagery can be realistically rendered on screen. However, his movies are much more conventional when it comes to the presentation of erotic relationships, overtly showing only heterosexual dynamics, with no same-sex romance or gay-identified individuals ever openly portrayed. To counterbalance this creative limitation, a gay-centered psychoanalytic amplification of selected components of Cameron's work may reveal signature qualities of homosexual love just below the surface, with consequential symbolic import for receptive viewers of the films.

In previous essays, I have identified meaningful themes of same-sex romantic love, including its distinctive function as a forceful catalyst for self-realization, in many popular films, including the six-part *Star Wars* saga, *The Lord of the Rings* trilogy, *E.T.: The Extra-Terrestrial,* and *The NeverEnding Story,* as well as in the television series, *Star Trek: Voyager.*[1] In line with this earlier work, a hypothesis to be considered in the forthcoming analysis is that homosexual urges, feelings, and images are intrinsic, influential elements of the transpersonal human psyche generally, and that in any serious work of art inevitably drawing inspiration from such fecund depths, emblematic features of same-sex love will naturally appear in the metaphorical warp and woof of the resulting tapestry, even if the filmmaker is heterosexual. Perhaps Cameron does have a primary attraction to women, as evidenced by his succession of five wives,[2] but he also has acknowledged how his work has been significantly inspired by his own unconscious, suggesting a rich possible source for underlying homosexual motifs. In a 1986 interview about *Aliens*, the innovative writer/director described this important wellspring for his artistic vision:

> I get a lot of imagery from my own dreams, and I find them to be a cathartic experience and a good inspiration for images and concepts and situations... Dreams are a shared experience, it's a way for us all to leave this plane and explore around a little bit and that's what movies do as well, especially in the science fiction context.[3]

As Cameron opens to the rich visions of his own mind to conjure his futuristic worlds, he may inadvertently draw up homosexual material, which becomes masked perhaps by a more conscious heterosexist bias on the filmmaker's part. Yet, evocations of same-sex love do become increasingly prominent, as I hope to show, in the evolution of this auteur's oeuvre as his maturing creative process has presumably provided access to ever-deeper levels of the transpersonal psyche.

Tools for Excavation: A Gay-Centered Analytical Method

To uncover same-sex-loving motifs in Cameron's work, I will employ the gay-centered modality called *contemporary Uranian psychoanalysis*, the development of which has been spearheaded over the past three decades by psychologist Mitch Walker.[4] This syncretistic theory and practice integrates Freudian, Jungian, and gay liberation concepts to break through Western civilization's longstanding homophobia and heterosexism in order to appreciate same-sex romantic love on its own experiential and symbolic terms.

A Uranian psychoanalytic attitude recognizes that homosexual desire has its own momentous validity as a purposeful phenomenon, not something to be deconstructed as many postmodern critical approaches attempt,[5] but rather a vital experience to be fully felt, honored and explored for its many nuanced pleasures as well as its generative possibilities, including when expressed in relationships and/or serving as the center of a foundational personal identity.

Freed from the power differential found in virtually all heterosexual relationships, romance between two individuals of the same sex can, at least in its ideal form, have a profound characteristic of mirroring equality, where both parties are appreciated as sacred individuals rather than objects to be conquered. Released from the biological imperative for literal reproduction, same-sex partners can focus their regard on the perceived inner and outer beauty of the beloved as a satisfying goal in its own right, and may subsequently be thus so inspired, as Plato wrote, to produce "immortal" children of the mind in the form of intellectual and creative achievements.[6] Fascination with the mysterious source of such ecstasy and ingenuity can lead an individual further inward in an effort to understand this powerful force of attraction, thereby encouraging the development of a psychological attitude and subsequent spiritual awakening.

Although he was unable to fully comprehend the many growthful aspects of same-sex love, C. G. Jung was the only early psychological pioneer to develop a terminology for identifying the felt experience of transpersonal levels of the unconscious, including a territory of inner symbolic meaningfulness below the conscious ego that he called the *soul,* which can be seen to personify itself as an erotically charged autonomous figure in the mind.[7] Due to his heterosexist limitations, Jung suggested that this soul-figure appeared as the opposite sex, what he called *anima* in men and *animus* in women. He further proposed that heterosexual intercourse provided a primary symbol for the forging of a vital center of aliveness, a *coniunctio oppositorum,* where all paradoxical opposites — female and male, good and evil, life and death, and so on — are harmonized in a fulfilling ideal of psychological wholeness.

To rectify the heterosexist restrictions of Jung's ideas, Mitch Walker has suggested the universal presence of a same-sex sibling to anima and animus called the *double,*[8] which can be seen to provide a frame for close relationships between individuals of the same gender, either in the positive variation of the *partners* or the *youth-adult* form, but also sometimes in the negative motif of the *competitors.* Where a person's libido is organized homosexually, relationships structured by the double become genitally awakened, and the soul personifies itself as an alluring *same-sex* figure. Homosexual romance is ignited when this soul-twin is projected onto another person of the same gender. If this projection can be consciously reclaimed, one can make contact with a mesmerizing inner lover, an internal muse who draws the individual magnetically into an initiatory odyssey of fuller self-actualization. By this route, a *same-sex coniunctio* becomes the primary symbol pointing toward the mystery of psychological wholeness, simultaneously achieving a union of sames *and* a reconciliation of the opposites,[9] leading to enhanced realization of what Jung called the archetypal Self, the all-encompassing "god-image" in the psyche.[10]

Moving backward briefly into the early stages of erotic development, it can be seen how a young boy's homosexual desire will likely be first activated in the psyche, though not necessarily consciously, by interaction with his own father, usually between the ages of 4 to 6.[11] This same-sex oedipal dynamic is not exclusively limited to those boys who will grow up to self-identify as gay, but is naturally particularly heartfelt for them. A parallel occurrence can also be seen to transpire for young girls with their mothers. As it would always be traumatic for such incestuous wishing to be physically consummated, the child's desire must be caringly thwarted by the parent, though in our homophobic culture, this is virtually always handled poorly. Yet nevertheless, the child's frustrated libido turns back inward, sparking the "birth" of a new inner figure: the enchanting double soul.

In my earlier discussion of the double in the *Star Wars* saga, I identified seven particular qualities consistently prominent in many of the same-sex partnerships portrayed, and which are also important distinctive attributes of same-sex romance.[12] This strong correlation led to the implication that, even though homosexual intent is never blatantly shown on the screen, many relationships are indeed infused with such eros and thus evocative of the spiritual realizations that same-sex romantic love can inspire. In the *Star Wars* films, significant same-sex relationships are repeatedly shown to be *mutual, primary, enduring, lifesaving, transformative, transmissive,* and *transcendent.* For my subsequent consideration of female same-sex affiliations in *Star Trek: Voyager,* I employed these categories again, while also adding two more: *passionate* and *affectionate.*[13]

I will refer to all the characteristics just named as relevant in the following consideration of James Cameron's films, with the goal of illuminating living symbols which may have a homosexual resonance. For Jung, a true symbol is a "transformer" of libido which pushes the individual's internal psychodynamics into a particular alignment toward some otherwise as-yet inexpressible experience or goal.[14] Through associative amplification, certain aspects of the deeper meaning of symbols may be perceived. Such a method of analysis works best if the analogical process stays in close contact with the original symbolic image, which must be accurately apprehended, relatively unencumbered by defensive twisting or muffling. For example, the double as erotic soul-figure likely points toward a different underlying significance than the double as non-sexual friend. In particular, as noted above, a homosexual valence implies the possibility of a same-sex *coniunctio,* potentially stimulating the greatest possible unfolding of conscious self-awareness.

This essay focuses exclusively on Cameron's science fiction movies,[15] which, as he himself intimates in the earlier statement quoted, are able to hew more closely to the unconscious imaginal dreamworld than a pop-culture-oriented action-comedy such as *True Lies* or the historical epic, *Titanic,* although these films are by no means devoid of archetypal patterns.

The Terminator *and* Terminator 2: *Judgment Day*

The main action of the first movie that Cameron had creative control over, *The Terminator,* begins numinously with two handsome, naked men — the first massively muscular (Arnold Schwarzenegger) and the other more leanly athletic (Michael Biehn)—appearing out of thin air at two different Los Angeles locations with a commotion of lightning flashes and wafting steam. Such imagery calls forth various fantasies for viewers, who might ask themselves, for example, what would I do if confronted by such a strange appearance? The nudity immediately provokes erotic possibilities. But the story moves quickly in a contrasting direction, as the two male characters proceed to struggle against one another in a classic *competitor* scenario of brutal ferocity. The larger of the two men is actually a T-800 cyborg, hellbent on murdering a young woman named Sarah Connor (Linda Hamilton), while his lithe human adversary, Kyle Reese, is determined to stop him.

The clashing competitor theme continues in *Terminator 2: Judgment Day*, the energetic sequel Cameron co-wrote and directed in 1991, which features another devastating conflict, this time between two Terminators, the T-800 (Arnold Schwarzenegger) and the T-1000 (Robert Patrick). However, another prominent theme in this second movie is the humanization of the mechanical monster, as the T-800 Terminator villain from the previous film has been transformed — an identical model or "twin" of the first was re-programmed — into a beneficial figure, as one who will die if necessary to *protect* Sarah Connor's son, an adolescent John Connor (Edward Furlong), who is destined to grow up to become the leader of the resistance against the machines in the dark future. William Wisher, co-writer with Cameron of both *Terminator* screenplays, recalls that Schwarzenegger only reluctantly consented to the idea of becoming a positive figure during sequel script development, and added a caveat by remarking, "Just don't make me gay,"[16] demonstrating that at least one member of the production team was conscious of possible homosexual themes erupting to the surface. Perhaps Schwarzenegger intuitively sensed there could be something really "gay" about the mean bad guy becoming a caring good guy!

Especially when viewed together as a continuous narrative, the *Terminator* films find a relevant mythological precursor in the saga of the ancient Egyptian brother-gods Horus and Seth, who are fierce rivals in the earthly realm, representing opposites such as day and night respectively, but who are eternally united in the heavenly realm, in what was called "the Secret of the Two Partners."[17] Surviving stone reliefs show Horus and Seth together tying a ritual marital knot, and the two fraternal lords are also sometimes depicted as a single, two-headed deity.[18] As Mitch Walker has described in his exploration of this mythology, here is "a sacred union animated by male-male eros, which leads to the reconciliation of the opposites," demonstrating how a same-sex *coniunctio* can integrate conflicting forces.[19] In the first *Terminator* movie, the more stark antagonism of the earthly realm is depicted, where Kyle Reese fills the role of daylight Horus and the Terminator embodies the dark god Seth. In the second film, the Terminator "twin" of the first, still capable of terrible destruction and initially terrifying to young John Connor, is soon revealed to be dedicated to the boy's safety and eventually a reliable partner, eclipsing his prior destiny as a ruthless killing machine, suggesting that a harmonizing union of Horus and Seth energies could be occurring.

Another relevant aspect of this Egyptian mythic narrative is that, as one of many machinations in their constant rivalry, including bawdy sexual dynamics, Seth was tricked into eating Horus's semen on a leaf of lettuce, and then a golden disc emerged from his forehead, understood by the Egyptians to signify the birth of the wisdom god Thoth, "son of the two Lords."[20] At the same time, Thoth was seen to be the procreative cause of Horus and Seth's ultimate reunion in his role as "the pacifier of the gods."[21] Paradoxically, then, Thoth is both father and son to himself through Horus and Seth. Likewise, in the *Terminator* films, John Connor is really father to himself, in that his future self sends his birth father, Kyle, back through time to impregnate his mother-to-be so he himself can be born. Kyle then dies to protect John's pregnant mother, Sarah, so in *Terminator 2*, the future John Connor re-formats a captured T-800 and sends him back in time to protect his own adolescent self from the T-1000, and in so doing intentionally provides his younger self with a virtually indestructible father-figure and companion. The two male characters become inseparable and increasingly fond of each other as the narrative progresses. In a voice-over internal monologue, Sarah reflects on this unique relationship as she observes her son playfully teaching the Terminator how to act less robotic:

> Watching John with the machine it was suddenly so clear. The Terminator would never stop, it would never leave him, and it would never hit him, never shout at him or get drunk and hit him, or say it was too busy to spend time with him. It would always be there, and it would die to protect him. Of all the would-be fathers who came and went over the years, this thing, this machine, was the only one who measured up. In an insane world, it was the sanest choice.

Sarah is thinking "father" here, but actually it is young John who is instructing the physically larger Terminator in the ways of humanity, almost reversing the paternal role, thereby equalizing their dynamic.

Thus, this boy-cyborg alliance is truly a *mutual* relationship, in which the T-800's vastly superior physical strength is exquisitely balanced by John's ability to command and educate him. Their bond is also *primary* during their time together, more stable and supportive than John's relationship with his overtly traumatized mother or his foster parents. This same-sex alliance is also clearly *lifesaving*, as the Terminator protects John successfully from the relentless, murderous drive of the T-1000. We witness a *transformative* affiliation, as John quickly grows from a parentless juvenile delinquent to a promising young leader, and the killing machine is humanized to the point of understanding the emotions which engender tears. At the end of the film, when the Terminator realizes he must sacrifice himself so his destructive technology is not used for nefarious purposes, he says to John, "I know now why you cry," meaning his mechanical "heart" has opened, and loving feelings have developed out of a machine. Here we see that their relationship is both *passionate* and *affectionate*, and the ubiquitous cultural prohibition, "Boys don't cry," does not apply here at all, as John's face is frequently wet with tears during peak moments throughout their bonding process. Their connection is also *transmissive*, in that the Terminator downloads all the information he has about how present-day technological advances lead to future catastrophe. Finally, their bond is *transcendent*, as the would-be arch-rivals of adolescent boy and cyborg, linked through time travel, exceed their individual limitations and together change the course of history for the better. As Sarah says in a voice-over at the end of the film, "If a machine, a Terminator, can learn the value of human life, maybe we can too." Although the "father-son" paradigm is explicitly invoked in the film, what we actually witness also has the feeling tone of a romantic partnership. These contrasting positions can be reconciled by recognizing how the erotic oedipal feelings between fathers and sons described earlier can continue to reverberate into adulthood.

Looking back at the full narrative of the two *Terminator* films, we find the origin story of a hero, John Connor, who, using time-travel "magic," can orchestrate his own existence as humanity's savior, echoing the originative powers of mythic figures like Thoth, Hermes, Mercurius, Jesus, and Buddha.[22] John's journey is not one propelled by heterosexual romance, but rather of creating himself by designating his own fathers, who also become his steadfast companions, birth-father Kyle as a loyal soldier with the future John, and the T-800 in adolescence. The implications go both ways here, in reference to Cameron's protagonist and humanity's most enlightened spiritual leaders, which is that ardent same-sex relationships, especially in their function as internalized catalyzing symbols, provide critical inspiration to spur the internal growth necessary to achieve the farthest reaches of psychological development and enhanced consciousness.

Aliens: *Twins Bonding Against the Terrible Mother*

The rich mix of transmutational father-son and double themes in the *Terminator* films has a resonant parallel in *Aliens*, which Cameron wrote and directed in between his creation of the two cyborg movies. As I have discussed in a previous essay,[23] *Aliens* is a rare example of a science-fiction film where the relationship between two female persons is central to the narrative.

Fifty-seven years ago, as seen in Ridley Scott's film, *Alien*,[24] Ellen Ripley (Sigourney Weaver) barely got away with her life after being attacked by a vicious extraterrestrial monster with acid blood and multiple, telescoping, teeth-laden jaws. As Cameron's sequel opens, we learn that Ripley has just been found and revived out of bio-stasis after floating in her small escape craft through space for decades, but at first no one believes her report about the attack of the horrific alien. The same planet, LV-426, where her crew first encountered the creature has since been colonized without incident, but then the loss of any communication from that terraforming community offers evidence that there may be credence to Ripley's tale after all, and the traumatized, nightmare-ridden heroine is corralled into revisiting the distant planet for a second confrontation with the demonic beast.

Upon her return to LV-426 with a military contingent, Ripley rescues a traumatized young human girl, Newt (Carrie Henn), the only colonist to have survived an infestation by the destructive, relentless aliens, now greatly multiplied in numbers. Ripley is the only new arrival who understands from her own prior experience the horrors that Newt has witnessed. As the frightened group of humans become besieged by the creatures, Ripley and Newt grow ever-more tightly bonded.

Ripley employs considerable skill in comforting Newt, and at one climactic moment, the frightened girl even calls Ripley "Mommy." But there is another dimension implicit in this situation, I would suggest, which is that Ripley and Newt form what is better described as a twinning partnership, one more of equals than of a parent and child. Whenever Ripley is patronizing toward Newt, the young girl quickly corrects her. For example, when Ripley is tucking Newt into a cot so the young girl can finally get some sleep, Newt tells her she has scary dreams. Ripley picks up the doll head named Casey that Newt has been carrying around, and while looking up into the doll's empty interior from its open neck, she says, "I bet Casey doesn't have scary dreams." Newt replies, with perfect condescension, "Ripley, she doesn't have bad dreams because she's just a piece of plastic," at which point Ripley promptly apologizes. Later in the conversation just described, Newt says, "My mommy always said there were no monsters, no real ones, but there are." Ripley's response: 'Yes, there are, aren't there?" And a little later, when they are together defenselessly facing an approaching alien, Newt says, "Ripley, I'm scared," and Ripley responds, without a hint of a parental tone, "Me, too."

The deepening connection between Ripley and Newt intensifies when together they face the queen of the alien hive, an even more awful creature than the others, with a huge, bulbous egg-laying sack and an imposing black exo-skeletal "crown" which frames her hideous, drooling, multi-jawed head. An archetypal Terrible Mother akin to the Hindu goddess Kali, the queen brings her victims to near-suffocation with her gooey webbing, using people as mere vessels for incubating her multitude of crab-like babies. Ripley musters every ounce of her considerable courage to rescue Newt from the queen's lair. Here the alien queen and Ripley could be seen as the dark and light aspects of Newt's mother complex, but the story is perhaps even more meaningful when Newt is viewed as Ripley's own inner twin whom she must embrace in order to heal from the suffocating, annihilating horrors of her own negative mother complex. Cameron spoke in a 1986 interview about the deep psychological doubling between Ripley and Newt:

> A film like *Aliens* is basically just one long bad dream... It ties into a lot of primal and subconscious fears that are very universal for people... It was also a way in this specific film, in *Aliens*, of unifying the Ripley character and the Newt character. They both have the same nightmare, and that bonds them, it makes them the same person in a way, and watching *Aliens* is a lot like their experience in the film, which is you're going through this long dark tunnel, and you come out at the other end, and you're going to be okay — they can dream again.[25]

As Cameron describes here so clearly, Ripley and Newt have a potent, *mutual* partnership of closely mirrored experience. It is also a new *primary* affiliation for both of them, utterly committed, *passionate*, and *affectionate*, a bond which is *enduring* beyond the horrors of the confrontation with the monsters. Clearly, this is a *lifesaving* attachment, where Ripley literally rescues Newt, but Newt in turn helps Ripley heal her own parallel trauma, thus making the relationship *transformative* and also *transmissive*, in the sense that Ripley and Newt mirror one another's psychological wounds and survival skills, spurring a new integration of emotional pain for each of them. Finally, the relationship is *transcendent*, where they both step beyond their former roles as mother and daughter to discover something more magical, a powerful evocation of two tightly linked equals, a manifestation of the double in its most libidinally vital form.

The Fairies of The Abyss

Between the filming of *Aliens* and *Terminator 2*, Cameron created his underwater adventure, *The Abyss*. This descent into the dark liquid depths of the Atlantic Ocean, offering a rich metaphor for the emotionally challenging exploration of the unconscious psyche, focuses its dramatic attention on a man and woman in the process of a divorce, who through much trial and tribulation rediscover their love for one another. Thus, the film is heavily weighted around heterosexual tension and reconciliation. However, at the climax of the film, the hero Bud Brigman (Ed Harris) dives alone deeper than any human ever before in a valiant effort to shut down an errant nuclear device. What appears to be a suicide mission becomes a rebirth, as Bud makes friends with a beautiful phosphorescent underwater alien creature, who rescues him and brings him back to a glowing colony of inhabited alien dwellings on the ocean floor. These are highly intelligent beings who have both "masculine" and "feminine" characteristics, much like many gay men and lesbians who comfortably straddle gender expressions. These entities are also evocative of the mythic *fairies* of Celtic folk heritage, which homosexual people have long been associated with, often in a pejorative sense, but also in a reclaimed positive affinity with such creatures' enchanting attributes. In the late 1970's, many gay men in the western U.S. spawned a grassroots spiritual movement around such an understanding called the Radical Faeries, of which Mitch Walker was one of three principal co-founders.[26] In symbolically amplifying this link between fairies and homosexual men, Walker quotes an Irish mystic who reported seeing:

> a tall figure with a body apparently shaped out of a half-transparent or opalescent air, and throughout the body ran a radiant, electrical fire, to which the heart seemed the centre. Around the head of this being and its waving luminous hair, which was blown all around the body like living strands of gold, there appeared flaming wing-like auras.[27]

In *The Abyss*, very similar diaphanous, luminescent creatures, who have been living quietly under the ocean for quite some time, go on to not only save Bud, but also his crew. Moreover, they effectively warn all humanity to stop its relentless path of violence by generating massive tidal waves which almost — but finally do not — crash ashore. The relationship between Bud and the alien fairies is clearly *passionate, lifesaving, transformative, transmissive,* and *transcendent*, with growing feelings of being *affectionate*, though not *mutual*, due to the clear imbalance in power, nor *primary*, as Bud re-unites with his wife at the end, and it is unknown if his affiliation with the aliens is *enduring*. Thus, in *The Abyss* we are left with some tentative fairy-like impressions of same-sex love rather than clear correlations.

Avatar: *Metamorphic Same-Sex Coniunctio*

Cameron's imaginative palette has reached a whole new order of abundant colorfulness in his most recent film, *Avatar,* an expansive epic, set in the year 2149, about a cynical paraplegic ex–Marine who transmutes himself into a graceful alien tribal leader deeply engaged in and committed to his new life. The theme of a transfigurational same-sex *coniunctio* in an electrifying twin-ship dynamic is critical to the story throughout, notably more prominent than in Cameron's earlier work.

Avatar opens with a black screen and sonorous, ominous tribal-themed music that builds anticipation for the visual/aural plunge into deep fantasy which is about to begin, substantially enhanced in the theatrical version by the live-action 3-D illusion Cameron has pioneered. As the camera flies over a lush, tropical, mist-covered rainforest, a voice-over monologue alerts us to the nocturnal source of the forthcoming experience: "When I was lying there in the V.A. hospital, with a big hole blown through the middle of my life, I started having these dreams of flying. I was free." This is the voice of Jake Sully (Sam Worthington), suddenly given the opportunity to step into the life of his twin brother, Tommy, who was murdered "for the paper in his wallet" just a week before he was scheduled to ship out on a research mission to the luminous alien moon called Pandora. Jake's brother had been training to be the "driver" of an avatar, which means temporarily transferring one's consciousness into a living biological body grown into the form of the indigenous Na'vi people, but synthesized with one's own DNA, thus retaining aspects of the individual's human visage in the Pandoran body. Since they were identical twins with the same genetic code, Jake is the only other person who could inhabit the avatar created for his now-dead brother. Yet their life choices have up till now been radically different: Tommy was a scientist, and was planning to operate the avatar as part of a peaceful effort to study the moon's profuse eco-system, including the aboriginal humanoids, while Jake is just a military grunt, a now-disabled member of the "Jarhead Clan." Here are familiar echoes of the Horus-Seth-Thoth myth earlier found in the *Terminator* films. The twin brothers here are identical yet also opposites — scientist vs. soldier — and it takes the two of them to create a third, their "son," the avatar/Jake hybrid who becomes a reborn Na'vi savior by the conclusion of the film.

When Jake first sees his avatar fully grown floating in a fluid-filled incubator tank, it is a marvelous sight, a huge 12-foot naked blue male humanoid body with "great muscle tone," as the scientist Max (Dileep Rao) remarks. Jake maneuvers his wheelchair to get up close and looks pensively at his avatar's face through the glass wall, which he says resembles his brother. "It looks like *you!*" replies Norm (Joel David Moore), another new avatar operator. The numinous feeling in this scene, where a fascinating male form is admired at length with awe, shows the creative distanced traveled since Cameron's first film, *The Terminator*, in which the naked male body is almost immediately disfigured by violence.

For Jake, the initial experience of relocating his consciousness into the avatar is not only about becoming an interesting alien, but is more profoundly also about regaining his mobility and vitality after being doomed to life in a wheelchair, and in his first joining with his avatar, he cannot resist the immediate joyful ecstasy of being able to walk —*and run*— again, or actually better than before, in this nimble new body.

In his Na'vi form, Jake struts through the film with increasing gymnastic confidence, soon almost completely naked save for a small loincloth in front, with broad shoulders, slender waist, handsomely shaped pectorals, flat stomach, uncovered muscular buttocks, and an agile, phallic tail. His physique seems to have been lovingly designed to provide maximum sex appeal, muffled only perhaps for some by the odd cyan color of his skin. For male viewers of any sexual orientation, watching Jake in his Na'vi form throughout the film provides a virtually unprecedented dose, in a major motion picture, of masculine body worship, all of it potently enhanced in 3-D!

To better understand Jake's sensuous experience of having — and himself becoming — an avatar, a dictionary definition of the word may be helpful:

1. The descent to earth of a Hindu deity, esp. Vishnu, in human or animal form.
2. An embodiment, as of a quality or concept: an archetype.
3. A temporary manifestation or aspect of a continuing entity.[28]

Thus, an avatar can be seen as an archetypal divine presence entering into a person's mundane life, with all the galvanizing implications of such an event. Indeed, Jake's all-consuming connection with his avatar fully revolutionizes his existence. Taking a step further, I would suggest that the joining of Jake and avatar could be described in colloquial terms as the best possible kind of wondrous "mind-fuck." Every time Jake links with his avatar, a rushing light tunnel opens in his mind, like a wormhole in the space-time fabric of his inner universe, with strong intimations of sexual receptivity as the thrill of existing inside a Na'vi body floods his awareness with exquisite sensations and powerful vitality. This is a most transformative same-sex *coniunctio*, a union of sames which also reconciles the opposites in a boundary-breaking experience of wholeness and vastly expanded, newly embodied consciousness.

But what are we to make of Jake's romance with the indigenous woman, Neytiri (Zoe Saldana)? Although it is true that their relationship is consummated in *Avatar*, this union is secondary to the primary relationship Jake has with his avatar and his own self-realization. From this gay-centered perspective, Neytiri's role is somewhat similar to how many gay men experience the anima, as sisterly support for the homosexual individuation process, much like Prince Leia's relationship with her brother, Luke Skywalker, in *Star Wars*. Likewise, Neytiri serves as emotional guide and support to Jake's psychological and even physiological metamorphosis from human to Na'vi, which is the primary narrative superseding the heterosexual love story depicted.

It seems to me that Jake's same-sex neural union with particular Pandoran animals is more visibly passionate than his romance with Neytiri, and helps amplify key themes in his relationship with his own avatar body. Although it may appear we are entering the realm of bestiality rather than homosexuality, I would suggest that this is in part due to the inevitable heterosexist context of the movie's creation, which pushes the more graphic aspects of same-sex love out of the humanoid realm. However, another way to explore this material is to appreciate Jung's criteria for an activated symbol as integrating the two experiential poles of human existence, the animal and the spiritual.[29] Furthermore, the Na'vi develop intimate relationships with animals which are much different and more equal than the mundane domestication humans have employed.

In fact, the Na'vi have a remarkable capacity to neurologically connect with other sentient beings and the planetary web-like consciousness called Eywa that links all living things on Pandora. Each Na'vi individual has a long black pony-tail, at the end of which is a lively grouping of neural tendrils called a *queue*,[30] which when linked with the queue of another animal or person allows for intuitive and sometimes even verbal communication. It is also used for sexual union between humanoids.

Jake's first experience relating to another creature through the queue is not with Neytiri but with a female dire-horse, a blue Pandoran six-legged horse-like creature. But she throws him into the mud almost immediately when he attempts to ride her, and his second effort is only temporarily more successful.

Jake has a vastly better experience becoming the rider of what the humans call a *banshee*, a flying pterodactyl-like creature with giant, multi-colored wings. He learns from Neytiri that each of these beautiful beasts only links with one person for life, evoking the image of a sacred marriage, and in the film this is always portrayed as a same-sex bond: Neytiri's banshee is female and Jake's is male. The relationship between banshee and rider is in many ways the most ardent, joyful kind of affiliation shown in the film.

The vital bond between Jake and his banshee is vividly portrayed through the drama of their initial connection. Along with the other Na'vi adepts, Jake must climb high into the floating Hallelujah Mountains to the resting ground of the banshees. Here he must be chosen by one of the creatures, who will then attempt to kill him, but if Jake can successful join their queues, then they will be linked together for life. Jake starts hissing animalistically at a particularly active banshee, and then he says, "Let's dance!" invoking a mating ritual. Jake then grabs onto the long, muscular, phallic neck of the banshee with his bare legs, holding onto the banshee's head, attempting to wrestle the banshee into communion, while Neytiri urgently yells out, in her role as sisterly guide, *"Make the bond!"* But when Jake brings his queue around to connect with the banshee's, he is thrown off, and is just barely able to grab a protruding root before going off the edge of a cliff. Undaunted, Jake quickly climbs back up and hops on the creature's long thick neck again, this time successfully linking his tendrils with the banshee's, whose big round eyes suddenly pop wide open, having a moment of great receptivity as if being penetrated sexually, and then relaxing. Jake looks into the eyes of his newfound soulmate, and says, "You're mine!" And then off they go for their first flight together to "seal the bond." At first it is harrowing, but Jake quickly learns how to communicate with his banshee through the queue union, and soon he can gracefully, playfully fly on the back of his male banshee, in great, obvious contrast with how clumsy he was on the female dire-horses. Jake exclaims in voice-over while flying: "I may not be much of a horse guy, but I was born to do this!"

Jake's keen connection with his banshee allows them later in the story to together accomplish a huge heroic act, which features an extraordinary same-sex *coniunctio*. This sequence begins when Jake reaches the lowest moment in his journey, after the other humans have heinously destroyed the massively monumental tree that was the Na'vi's home. Jake is subsequently banished by the Pandorans, and he is lost amongst the ashes of the ruined, abandoned community. But Jake's banshee intuitively finds him, and their reunion brings new hope. Jake realizes that, with his banshee's aid, he must "make the bond" with the great *Toruk*, similar in shape but much, much bigger than the banshees, known to humans as *Leonopteryx*, which means "flying king lion,"[31] and who, as the "baddest cat in the sky," never needs to look up for fear of a higher predator. This gives Jake an opportunity to soar on his banshee unnoticed above Toruk, allowing him to take this royal animal by surprise and jump on his back, quickly joining their queues, thereby becoming only the sixth *Toruk Makto*, or "rider of the last shadow," in the whole history of the Na'vi people. It is this exceedingly brave maneuver, exuding fleshy sensual gravitas, which allows Jake to re-unite with the Na'vi people, suddenly elevated from hated exile to the new leader of their tribe. After a climactic battle and victory fighting on the side of the Na'vi against the invading humans, Jake releases Toruk, and, though it is not shown on screen, presumably resumes his bond with his original banshee.

Thus, Jake's relationship with his banshee, further amplified by his more temporary bond with Toruk, is most definitely *passionate* and increasingly *affectionate*, generating a *mutual* affiliation. Their alliance is *enduring*, as they are married in a "monogamous" relationship for life, though Jake briefly steps outside of the commitment for his necessary liaison with Toruk. The attachment between Jake and his banshee is truly *lifesaving*, as Jake is shown in an early scene guiding his banshee to safety away from an earlier, more vulnerable encounter with Toruk, and his banshee locates him in his lowest moment of ashen despair. Their link is *transformative*, giving Jake wings to fly, as he had long dreamed, and *transmissive*, as they communicate directly with one another through the neural queue. Finally, their relationship is *transcendent*, moving beyond the divide between animal and person to become a unified twinship pair, and empowering Jake to become a truly responsible, enlightened leader. Thus, almost all of the most resonant attributes of same-sex romantic love are strongly evoked in this vigorous partnership.

Now returning to Jake's ever-deepening connection with his avatar, he ultimately decides to abandon his human body and permanently transfer his consciousness through the planetary neural net into his Na'vi body. The film ends not with a heterosexual embrace but rather with Jake's big Pandoran eyes opening for the first time without the support of the human technological interface, looking directly at the viewer. For men especially, this is a striking moment of being salutarily confronted by the avatar as inspiring reflection soul.

Now it can be seen that Jake's relationship with his avatar, featuring the DNA of his twin brother, is both *mutual* and *primary*, since, by the end of the story, one cannot live without the other. Even his romance with Neytiri, as noted above, is dependent on the foundational relationship between man and avatar. Along these same lines, the union between Jake and his Na'vi body-self is *enduring*, especially because in the end of the film, as just mentioned, he shifts his consciousness permanently into his avatar. This moment, as well as many others, is *lifesaving*, and clearly *transformative*, from human to Na'vi, and even *transmissive*, in both directions, as Jake brings his human attributes into his avatar and his new community, while also receiving the wisdom of Na'vi interconnectedness through his avatar body, and specifically through the connection made possible by the lively queue at the end of his braid. Finally, the relationship is *transcendent* as Jake goes beyond human and Na'vi to create a third entity, a new synthesis. He surpasses his own personality as well as all aspects of being human, but also brings a sense of individuality to a highly communal culture which needs the spark of a monad to stand up successfully to the human invaders. Here I would propose that Jake's experience in having and becoming an avatar is a wonderful symbol for the conscious realization of one's erotic double soul, a magnetic union of the sames that also reconciles the opposites, in an ebullient libidinal self-awakening. In *Avatar,* the result is that a man is lifted out of amoral, nihilistic destructiveness into harmonious, ethical living in a state of fulfilling relatedness with self, other beings, and a vital eco-system. The film's effulgent imagery can inspire an analogous developmental trajectory for all of us.

Conclusion

In this essay, I have used concepts from Uranian psychoanalytic theory and my previous explorations of many different fantasy films to uncover feeling-laden images that evoke homosexual love and its symbolic meaning in James Cameron's movies. Now, looking back over the distance travelled, a clear arc of development can be seen in his work, where same-sex dynamics shift from largely antagonistic in *The Terminator* to those in subsequent films that are increasingly *passionate, affectionate, mutual, primary, enduring, life-saving, transformative, transmissive,* and *transcendent.* Thus, the relationships between John Connor and the T-800, Ripley and Newt, and Jake with his own avatar and banshee all elicit some of the most meaningful characteristics of homosexual love, and offer increasingly overt hints at its symbolic power as a catalyst for spiritual transmutation and creative rebirth.

This discussion has also demonstrated how significant homosexual themes can be uncovered in cultural products that at first glance appear completely heteronormative, thereby providing support for the hypothesis that same-sex romantic love has deep roots in the universal human psyche. Yet having to dig for such motifs in Cameron's films also reveals one of their key limitations, which is that overt homosexual romance remains "the love that dare not speak its name,"[32] its magnificent capacity for sublime revelation still mostly hidden below the surface. This is a creative failure which deserves to be redressed, either by Cameron or those who follow him, because as his films show all too well, humanity faces a bleak, apocalyptic future if we do not find alternative, non-destructive ways of living. And the egalitarian attributes of same-sex love highlighted in this analysis may actually serve as the crucial, beneficial inspiration needed to achieve a more humane future.

At least Cameron understands the source of our possible demise when in a recent interview reflecting on his *Terminator* films, he commented on humanity's probable fate: "It is not the machines that will destroy us, it is ourselves."[33] The filmmaker's awareness of the ramifications of humanity's shadow-side is an essential factor, it seems to me, in giving his films some psychological and political heft beyond average blockbuster quality. Jung also feared for humanity's future, having had a vision just before he died in 1961 in which "a large part of the world was destroyed,"[34] perhaps not unlike the post-nuclear doom portrayed in *The Terminator* movies. But Jung also highlighted in a positive way how confrontation with the shadow can lead to much fuller access to the shimmering treasures of the unconscious psyche, and likewise, at their best, Cameron's films show the results of such ingenuity, hopefully now more fully fleshed out with the revelation that homosexual patterns can be found within his work.

By way of its lifesaving capacity to inspire psychological transformation, same-sex romance offers a robust symbolic pathway toward the alchemical integration of light and dark necessary for better human progress. A crucial aspect of this growthful gay journey is the recognition that there is already a Pandora-like, luminescent paradise in each of us called the imagination, which when responsibly cultivated, can liberate us all and lead to new creative vistas, rich with pulsating aliveness and divine homosexual love.

NOTES

1. Roger Kaufman, "How the *Star Wars* Saga Evokes the Creative Promise of Homosexual Love: A Gay-Centered Psychological Perspective," in *Finding the Force in the Star Wars Franchise: Fans, Merchandise & Critics*, ed. Matthew Wilhelm Kapell & John Shelton Lawrence (New York: Peter Lang, 2006); Roger Kaufman, "Heroes Who Learn to Love Their Monsters: How Fantasy Film Characters Can Inspire the Journey of Individuation for Gay and Lesbian Clients in Psychotherapy" in *Using Superheroes in Counseling and Play Therapy*, ed. Lawrence Rubin (New York: Springer, 2007); Roger Kaufman, "Evocations and Evasions of Archetypal Lesbian Love in *Star Trek: Voyager*," in Star Trek *as Myth: Essays and Archetype at the Final Frontier*, ed. Matthew Wilhelm Kapell (Jefferson, NC: McFarland, 2010).

2. Deborah Keegan, *The Futurist: The Life and Films of James Cameron* (New York: Crown, 2009), 55.

3. James Cameron and Don Shay, "Interview with James Cameron." James Cameron, *Aliens: Special Edition*, DVD. Directed by James Cameron (1986; Beverly Hills, CA: Twentieth Century–Fox, 2005).

4. Mitch Walker, *Gay Liberation at a Psychological Crossroads* (Los Angeles: Institute for Contemporary Uranian Psychoanalysis, 2009).

5. Nancy Sullivan, *A Critical Introduction to Queer Theory* (New York: New York University, 2003).

6. Plato, *Symposium,* trans. Robin Waterfield (New York: Oxford University Press, 1994), 53.

7. C. G. Jung, *Psychological Types* (Princeton, NJ: Princeton University Press, 1971), 463.

8. Mitchell Walker, "The Double: An Archetypal Configuration," *Spring* (1976).

9. Mitch Walker, "Jung and Homophobia," *Spring* (1991), 64.

10. C. G. Jung, *Aion: Researches into the Phenomenology of the Self* (Princeton, NJ: Princeton University Press, 1969), 31.

11. Walker, "Gay Liberation," 14.

12. Kaufman, "*Star Wars.*"

13. Kaufman, "Lesbian Love."

14. C. G. Jung, *Symbols of Transformation* (Princeton, NJ: Princeton University Press), 1956.

15. James Cameron with Gale Anne Hurd, *The Terminator: Special Edition*, DVD. Directed by James Cameron (1984; Los Angeles: MGM Home Entertainment, 2001); James Cameron, *Aliens: Special Edition*, DVD. Directed by James Cameron (1986; Beverly Hills, CA: Twentieth Century–Fox Home Entertainment, 2005); James Cameron, *The Abyss: Special Edition*, DVD. Directed by James Cameron (1989; Beverly Hills, CA: Twentieth Century–Fox Home Entertainment, 2002); James Cameron and William Wisher, *Terminator 2: Judgment Day: The*

Ultimate Edition, DVD. Directed by James Cameron (1991; Santa Monica, CA: Artisan Home Entertainment, 2000); James Cameron, *Avatar*, Blu-Ray DVD. Directed by James Cameron (2009; Beverly Hills, CA: Twentieth Century Home Entertainment, 2010).

16. Keegan, *Futurist,* 114.
17. Walker, "Jung," 63.
18. Walker, "Jung," 63.
19. Walker, "Jung," 64.
20. Cited in Mitchell Walker, "The Uranian Coniunctio: A Study of Gay Identity Formation and the Individuation Model of C. G. Jung" in *The Uranian Soul: A Gay-Centered Jungian Psychology of Male Homosexual Personhood for a New Era of Gay Liberation Politics with Universal Implicational Import* (Unpublished manuscript, 2008), 239.
21. Cited in Walker, "Uranian," 239.
22. Walker, "Uranian," 240-241.
23. Kaufman, "Heroes."
24. Dan O'Bannon, *Alien*, DVD. Directed by Ridley Scott (1979; Twentieth Century–Fox Home Entertainment, 1999).
25. Cameron and Shay, "Interview."
26. Harry Hay, *Radically Gay*, ed. Will Roscoe (Boston: Beacon, 1996), 238.
27. Mitch Walker, *Visionary Love: A Spirit Book of Gay Mythology* (San Francisco: Treeroots Press, 1980), 89.
28. Cited in Keegan, *Futurist*, 231.
29. Jung, *Psychological Types*, 478.
30. Maria Wilhelm and Dirk Mathison, *Avatar: A Confidential Report on the Biological and Social History of Pandora* (New York: It Books/HarperCollins, 2009), 28–29.
31. Wilhelm and Mathison, *Avatar*, 78.
32. Lord Alfred Douglas, "Two Loves," in *The Columbia Anthology of Gay Literature*, ed. Byrne Fone (New York: Columbia University Press, 1998), 341.
33. Keegan, *Futurist,* 56.
34. Barbara Hannah, *Jung: His Life and Work* (Wilmette, IL: Chiron, 1997), 347.

Works Cited

Douglas, Lord Alfred. "Two Loves." In *The Columbia Anthology of Gay Literature*, edited by Byrne Fone, 341. New York: Columbia University Press, 1998.
Hannah, Barbara. *Jung: His Life and Work*. Wilmette, IL: Chiron, 1997.
Hay, Harry. *Radically Gay*, edited by Will Roscoe. Boston: Beacon, 1996.
Jung, C. G. *Aion: Researches into the Phenomenology of the Self.* Princeton, NJ: Princeton University Press, 1969.
_____. *Psychological Types*. Princeton, NJ: Princeton University Press, 1971.
_____. *Symbols of Transformation*. Princeton, NJ: Princeton University Press, 1956.
Kaufman, Roger. "Evocations and Evasions of Archetypal Lesbian Love in *Star Trek: Voyager*." In *Star Trek as Myth: Essays and Archetype at the Final Frontier*, edited by Matthew Wilhelm Kapell, 144–162. Jefferson, NC: McFarland, 2010.
_____. "Heroes Who Learn to Love Their Monsters: How Fantasy Film Characters Can Inspire the Journey of Individuation for Gay and Lesbian Clients in Psychotherapy." In *Using Superheroes in Counseling and Play Therapy*, edited by Lawrence Rubin, 293–318. New York: Springer, 2007.
_____. "How the *Star Wars* Saga Evokes the Creative Promise of Homosexual Love: A Gay-Centered Psychological Perspective." In *Finding the Force in the Star Wars Franchise: Fans, Merchandise & Critics*, edited by Matthew Wilhelm Kapell and John Shelton Lawrence, 131–156. New York: Peter Lang, 2006.
Keegan, Deborah. *The Futurist: The Life and Films of James Cameron*. New York: Crown, 2009.

O'Bannon, Dan. *Alien*. DVD. Directed by Ridley Scott. 1979; Twentieth Century–Fox Home Entertainment, 1999.

Plato, *Symposium,* trans. Robin Waterfield. New York: Oxford University Press, 1994.

Sullivan, Nikki. *A Critical Introduction to Queer Theory.* New York: New York University, 2003.

Walker, Mitchell. "The Double: An Archetypal Configuration." *Spring* (1976): 165–175.

_____. *Gay Liberation at a Psychological Crossroads.* Los Angeles: Institute for Contemporary Uranian Psychoanalysis, 2009.

_____. "Jung and Homophobia." *Spring* (1991): 55–70.

_____. "The Uranian Coniunctio: A Study of Gay Identity Formation and the Individuation Model of C. G. Jung" in *The Uranian Soul: A Gay-Centered Jungian Psychology of Male Homosexual Personhood for a New Era of Gay Liberation Politics with Universal Implicational Import.* Unpublished manuscript, 2008.

_____. *Visionary Love: A Spirit Book of Gay Mythology.* San Francisco: Treeroots Press, 1980.

Wilhelm, M., and Dirk Mathison. *Avatar: A Confidential Report on the Biological and Social History of Pandora.* New York: It Books/HarperCollins, 2009.

FILMS CITED

The Abyss: Special Edition. DVD. Directed by James Cameron. 1989; Beverly Hills, CA: Twentieth Century–Fox Home Entertainment, 2002.

Aliens: Special Edition. DVD. Directed by James Cameron. 1986; Beverly Hills, CA: Twentieth Century–Fox Home Entertainment, 2005.

Avatar. Blu-Ray DVD. Directed by James Cameron. 2009; Beverly Hills, CA: Twentieth Century Home Entertainment, 2010.

The Terminator: Special Edition. DVD. Directed by James Cameron. 1984; Los Angeles: MGM Home Entertainment, 2001.

Terminator 2: Judgment Day: The Ultimate Edition. DVD. Directed by James Cameron. 1991; Santa Monica, CA: Artisan Home Entertainment, 2000.

"I see you":
Colonial Narratives and the
Act of Seeing in *Avatar*

JOHN JAMES *and* TOM UE

In a pivotal moment in *Avatar,* Norm tries to explain to Jake the complexity of the expression "I see you": "But it's not just, 'I'm seeing you in front of me,' it's 'I see into you. I see you.' ... I'm accepting you. I understand you." As one reviewer writes, it means, "I see into you and know your heart."[1] The greeting is an acknowledgment of differences. Seeing, however, is not an indifferent act, and the narrative structure of *Avatar* may encourage us to sympathize with and overlook the central focaliser Jake's ethical flaws. In his avatar, Jake can walk like the Na'vi, he can look and move like them, but he will always retain the clandestine memories and consciousness of a human being. As Manohla Dargis has put it, "With his avatar, Jake will look just like one of the natives, the Na'vi, a new identity that gives the movie its plot turns and politics."[2] Indeed, Jake's disguised identity often complicates the plot for both the Na'vi and the humans, and this analogy works on several levels. Although the Na'vi recognize that Jake is a human from the outset, the Jake they think they know maintains ulterior motives. In this context, the deep sense of betrayal expressed by the Na'vi becomes more than warranted when Jake confesses he has known all along about the Colonel's plan to destroy Hometree. While we, as viewers, sympathize with the betrayal of the Omaticaya, and more so than with Jake's betrayal of his own race, the latter merits more critical attention.

The "avatar," however, is not the only symbol in the film whose true reality remains largely beneath the surface. In fact, all of Pandora is connected by Eywa, a network of botanical neurons beneath the planet's surface, functioning, as Dr. Grace Augustine suggests, much like synapses in the human brain. While the presence of Eywa is almost entirely invisible, its role in the ecosystem of Pandora is invaluable to the Na'vi. Its role in their culture is sacred. How, then, do we read "seeing" as such a blatant metaphor, when what is seen is so emphatically not reality? This article argues that seeing is not an indifferent act, and that someone — the one doing the seeing — is always privileged, while the seen (the greeting's "you") becomes objectified. The process of seeing operates only as an acknowledgment, neither as perception or understanding. The gap between the privileged and the objectified becomes increasingly salient when the human-Na'vi relationship is considered in terms of colonizer and colonized, for that is precisely the social process beginning to take place on Pandora. When the seer (the greeting's "I") becomes the objectifying colonizer, the seen (the greeting's "you") takes up a position of cultural, economic and racial subservience. Through this dynamic, not only does the "I" occupy the position of colonizer, but also, by necessity, each of its members must be branded with that identity.

This article analyzes Jake's character and his privileged position as one who knows and understands the perspectives of both the humans and the Na'vi, and his appropriation of narrative for his own agendas. We will discuss Jake's representation of a frequent cinematic plot identified as the "Messiah Complex." And finally, this article's conclusion places *Avatar* in conversation with Steven Spielberg's *Indiana Jones and the Kingdom of the Crystal Skull* (2008) and Neill Blomkamp's *District 9* (2009), two recent films at the time of writing that are, like *Avatar*, self-conscious about colonialism. In so doing, we aim to show how all of these films, despite their attempts at satire, actually reaffirm the colonial prejudices they seek to challenge thematically. Ultimately, this analysis suggests, Western culture's failed attempts at anticolonialism point to continued Eurocentric values of superiority which, though rarely discussed openly, remain latent in the public consciousness. Only by discussing this phenomenon, and the ways it continues to manifest itself in our culture's artistic endeavors, can critics, filmmakers, and theatergoers seek change.

Colonial Rooting

Even from the film's outset, Cameron establishes a clear-cut case against the humans as colonizers and exploiters: they extract from the Na'vi both materially and ideologically. More often than not, it becomes not only the mission of Parker Selfridge and his compatriots to educate and provide for the Na'vi, but their burden to do so.[3] Selfridge, the corporate administrator of RDA's mining operation, claims he has attempted to give the Na'vi medicine, education and roads. Ultimately, however, Selfridge desires a healthy quarterly statement and, unsurprisingly, none of his efforts gain cooperation from the Omaticaya. All of his contributions are obvious bribes to the Omaticaya, aimed at gaining their cooperation in order to acquire the mysterious mineral, "unobtanium." Cameron's naming of Selfridge, which sounds almost like "self-*ish*," one's unmovable ridge, or the department store Selfridges, is an obvious jab at the insatiable greed of the humans in the film, as well as today's corporate culture, which is, as many critics note, a major focus of the film's satire. Nothing is new about the colonial dynamic Cameron fashions between the humans and the Na'vi. The relationship centers on constructed notions of cultural superiority derived from various cultural establishments. Humans have come to objectify the Na'vi based on academic, governmental and, especially, military institutions, not unlike what Edward Said has described in *Orientalism*: "The Orient that appears in Orientalism [...] is a system of representations framed by a whole set of forces that brought the Orient into Western learning, Western consciousness, and later, Western empire."[4] These representations are forged by "an influential academic tradition," as well as by "travelers, commercial enterprises, governments, military expeditions, readers of novels and accounts of exotic adventure." If we simply replace the words "Orient" and "Orientalism" with "Pandora" and, say, "Pandorism," the humans' relationship with the Na'vi closely parallels the experiences of nineteenth-century colonizers with their subjects.

Faithful to record, Cameron's colony is a brutal place, where violent resistance is tempered with even stronger violent acts. Like Selfridge and the humans, imperial countries historically established a system of institutions and classes in the colonies. Those at the top benefitted, at least superficially and quite often materially, from the imperial system, and in turn maintained and internalized the order established by the mother country. Jean-Paul Sartre provides a brief explanation of this process:

> The European élite undertook to manufacture a native élite. They picked out the most promising adolescents; they branded them, as with a red-hot iron, with the principles of western culture; they stuffed their mouths full with high-sounding phrases, grand glutinous words that stuck to the teeth.[5]

Colonial rooting extends deeper than speech, and sometimes deeper than conscious thought, to the point where colonial peoples look and talk and desire to be like their imperial oppressors. One's desires to think and speak for oneself are policed, as Frantz Fanon reveals, in *The Wretched of the Earth*: "In the colonies it is the policeman and the soldier who are the official, instituted go-betweens, the spokesmen of the settler and his rule of oppression."[6] Policemen and soldiers and, indeed, even citizens are rewarded for internalizing and reinforcing the control of the colonizing presence or the puppet government it has established. Fanon goes on to elaborate:

> In capitalist societies the educational system, [...] the structure of moral reflexes handed down from father to son, the exemplary honesty of workers who are given a medal after fifty years of good and loyal services, and the affection which springs

from harmonious relations and good behaviour — all these esthetic expressions of respect for the established order serve to create around the exploited person an atmosphere of submission and of inhibition which lightens the task of policing considerably.[7]

Colonization, with all of its institutional structures, is undoubtedly taking root in Pandora. Cameron's depiction is largely in keeping with what Fanon, Sartre and Said describe. We see this most evidently in Grace Augustine's English-language school. Selfridge and his big-armed, big-gunned lackeys may encourage us to overlook Grace's complicity and downright participation in fostering racial and imperial prejudices; but even Grace's well-meaning efforts are meant to understand the Na'vi, and to expand human scholarship on them, ultimately fail. Although she seems to mean well, Grace is not so different from Selfridge: she benefits through the reputation she gains as a leading scholar and the author of an authoritative book on the Na'vi. Moreover, rather than help the Omaticaya, Grace's school works only to further the human's colonial project. Even before Jake Sully arrives, the humans control the Na'vi through violence, as we learn from the Special Edition Re-Release and Collector's Extended Cut of the film. In these versions, she shows to Norm and Jake the closed school. "This was our school," she explains: "Now it's just ... storage. The kids were so bright. Eager to learn. They picked up English faster than I could teach it." When Jake asks about the bullet holes on a wall, Grace refuses to explain, and it is not until the Collector's Extended Cut that she tells him about the violence that ultimately put a stop to her school:

> Neytiri's sister, Sylwanin, stopped coming to school. She was angry about the clear-cutting. And one day, she and a couple of other young hunters came running in all painted up. They had set a bulldozer on fire. I guess they thought I could protect them. The troopers pursued them to the school. They killed Sylwanin in the doorway. Right in front of Neytiri. And then shot the others. I got most of the kids out. But they never came back.

The violent incident helps to suggest the complexity of Cameron's project. While Grace confides to Jake that her ten years' work in the school prevents her from retaining the objectivity that a good scientist requires, we, as viewers, recognize that the school only teaches the Na'vi English so they can trade away their natural resources and become better colonial subjects. The classroom setting reinforces a kind of obedience that makes them unlike Sylwanin and the other hunters — the same submissive obedience of which Fanon speaks.

Really, the only person who succeeds in gaining the Na'vi's trust is Jake Sully, and this is only after living with the Omaticaya for long enough to be initiated into the tribe. However, Jake's relationship with the Omaticaya is tainted by his ambiguous allegiance. Jake's position as a foreigner, coupled with his uncanny ability to prevail over Omaticaya natives in athletic feats, positions him not only as an unlikely savior of the Na'vi, but a self-indulgent one for your average theatergoer.

Jake Sully: Problematic Leader of the Omaticaya

Throughout *Avatar*, viewers follow Jake Sully's metamorphosis from "Jarhead" marine, lost in the jungles of Pandora, to fearless leader of the Omaticaya and organizer of the Na'vi people. "The story," as Philip Horne has put it, "brings together multiple myths and archetypes and political and movie references: messianic redemption stories, Vietnam and Iraq, the War on Terror, rainforests, the genocide of American Indians; and *Apocalypse Now*, *The Last of the Mohicans*, *The Emerald Forest*."[8] Jake's transformation is not seamless: he faces opposition from members of the Omaticaya, and the harsh environment of Pandora, as well as members of his own race. Jake triumphs over these challenges, which hastens the Omaticaya to accept him as one of their own; however, the rapid change resonates unconvincingly, particularly in light of Jake's shaky assimilation into Na'vi culture. For one, his limited understanding of the Na'vi language illustrates a linguistic hierarchy between humans and the Na'vi — a gap which persists, even as Jake rallies the Na'vi against his own race.[9] It seems indicative of Jake's role as the privileged outsider that, even after he has lived with the Omaticaya for several months, clan members must cater to Jake's linguistic shortcomings. An active witness whose ignorance of both science and the world of Pandora allots him to a role of bicultural gaucheness, Jake Sully occupies what over the last twenty or so years in film has developed into what David Brooks identifies as "the Messiah Complex."[10] Plots like the Messiah Complex have always been part of cinematic history, as Ella Shohat and Robert Stam have suggested in *Multiculturalism and the Media*:

> The colonial domination of indigenous peoples, the scientific and esthetic disciplining of nature through classificatory schemas, the capitalist appropriation of resources, and the imperialist order of the globe under a panoptical regime, all formed part of a massive world historical movement that reached its apogee at the beginning of the twentieth century. Indeed, it is most significant ... that the beginnings of cinema coincided with the giddy heights of the imperial project, with an epoch where Europe held sway over vast tracts of alien territory and hosts of subjugated peoples.[11]

Shohat and Stam go on to illustrate how these early films have provided, to viewers, access to a mythology that sought "to neutralize the class struggle and transform class solidarity into national and racial solidarity."[12]

The Messiah Complex is a familiar plot, one in which a virile young male adventures "into the wilderness in search of thrills and profit. But, once there, he meets the native people and finds that they are noble and spiritual and pure. And so he emerges as their Messiah, leading them on a righteous crusade against his own rotten civilization."[13] Brooks cites such examples as Kevin Costner's *Dances with Wolves* (1990), Bill Kroyer's *FernGully: The Last Rainforest* (1992), Mike Gabriel's and Eric Goldberg's *Pocahontas* (1995), and Edward Zwick's *The Last Samurai* (2003). *Avatar* is one of many films that satisfy audiences by seeming to be environmentally conscious, culturally aware, and pleasantly satirical; however, such films, while striving for political correctness, cause audiences to grow complacent. Cameron's film repeatedly gestures towards the consequences of capitalism, a system that drives humans, often out of desperation, into colonizing places like Pandora, as we will examine in some detail below. Yet, the film only reaffirms the colonial, social, and economic paradigms that it seeks to undermine by suggesting the natives' inability to liberate themselves from the forces of oppression, industry, and colonization, thereby conferring power to a privileged colonizer, in this case, a white American male. As Brooks puts it, when he draws upon the language of teenagers:

> [Jake] goes to live with the natives, and, in short order, he's the most awesome member of their tribe. He has sex with their hottest babe. He learns to jump through the jungle and ride horses. It turns out that he's even got more guts and athletic prowess than they do. He flies the big red bird that no one in generations has been able to master.[14]

The "big red bird" to which Brooks refers is, of course, the Great Leonopteryx, Toruk, whom only five members of the Omaticaya have mounted throughout the entire history of the tribe. Having learned the tribe's lore and their mixed-feelings of reverence and fear for the great bird, Jake utilizes this information to regain their trust following the destruction of Hometree. He mounts and rides on Toruk to display his skill, and fortifies himself in the eyes of the Omaticaya. Following his rise in the Omaticaya clan, Jake leads the Na'vi to freedom by going to war against the humans. Jake's revolt is Fanonian in its violent rhetoric, particularly in his speeches, but Cameron's perpetuation of the Messiah Complex plot remains to be reconciled.

Racial Memory and the Problems of Ending

Stuart Hall complicates our reading of Jake Sully further in his discussion of cultural identity as an ongoing production in his essay "Cultural Identity and Cinematic Representation." He writes, "[I]nstead of thinking of identity

as an already accomplished historical fact ... we should think, instead, of identity as a 'production,' which is never complete, always in process, and always
constituted within, not outside, representation. But this view problematizes
the very authority and authenticity to which the term, 'cultural identity,' lays
claim."¹⁵ Cultural identity is, for Hall, an interactive narrative, one to which
we contribute by engaging with it and imbuing it with our geographical, historical, and cultural perspectives:

> It is *something*— not a mere trick of the imagination. It has its histories — and his-
> tories have their real, material, and symbolic effects. The past continues to speak
> to us. But this is no longer a simple, factual "past," since our relation to it is, like
> the child's relation to the mother, always-already "after the break." It is always
> constructed through memory, fantasy, narrative and myth. Cultural identities are
> the points of identification, the unstable points of identification or suture, which
> are made within the discourses of history and culture.¹⁶

Jake, in his incorporation of Omaticaya lore, obeys the clan's traditions
only when it benefits him, ignoring the customs that fail to satisfy his own
objectives. Ultimately, he removes the lore from its historical and cultural
contexts, as we may infer from his romance with Neytiri. While Jake respects
Neytiri by asking her if she reciprocates his romantic feelings, this alliance
undermines the clan's hierarchal system which had predetermined Tsu'tey's
and Neytiri's marriage and their eventual succession of her parents' places as
the clan's elders, and Jake's "brotherly" duty towards Tsu'tey. If Jake values
the Na'vi customs much less than his individual desires, the language with
which he rallies the Na'vi may strike the viewer as being deeply problematic,
triggering us to reassess his culpability.

In fact, a comparison between Jake's and the Colonel's battle speeches
betrays striking similarities. After the Colonel destroys Hometree, Jake tells
the Omaticaya:

> The Sky People have sent us a message[:] that they can take whatever they want
> and no one can stop them. Well, we will send them a message. You ride out as
> fast as the wind can carry you. You tell the other clans to come. You tell them
> Toruk Makto calls to them. And you fly now with me! My brothers! Sisters! And
> we will show the Sky People that they cannot take whatever they want, and that
> this, this is our land!

If Jake strives to send the humans a message, so too does the Colonel, who
uses, after only minutes of narrative time in the film, similar language to
mobilize his troops:

> Our only security lies in pre-emptive attack. We will fight terror with terror. Now,
> the hostiles believe that this mountain stronghold of theirs is protected by their
> ... their deity. And when we destroy it, we will blast a crater in their racial memory
> so deep that they won't come within 1,000 klicks of this place ever again. And
> that, too, is a fact.

It is no coincidence that the Colonel selects the culturally- and socially-important symbol of the Tree of Souls to launch his attack, just as Jake selects Toruk: this war transcends the physical, and moves to the level of symbols and narratives. However, both characters ignore the graver social realities that drive humans to colonize Pandora in the first place, even though this ghostly and largely unseen world is as important as Pandora. By the end of *Avatar*, Jake tells us in a voiceover, which we later discover to be a video log: "The aliens went back to their dying world. Only a few were chosen to stay. The time of great sorrow was ending. Toruk Makto was no longer needed." Jake's use of the term "alien" may recall the prejudiced words of Eytukan, chief of the Omaticaya and Neytiri's father: "I have said no dreamwalker will come here. His alien smell fills my nose."

Jake's description of the human world as a dying one and his echoing of Eytukan's profound hostility may prompt us to examine more closely what this human world really embodies. Early on in the film, we learn that most of the soldiers working in Pandora were formerly "army dogs, marines, fighting for freedom"; however, they have now descended to become "hired guns, taking the money, working for the company." In the Collector's Extended Cut of the film, we see footage of this overpopulated and overdeveloped world in which Jake's attempt at heroism at a bar is not only unrewarded but also puts him in a physically vulnerable position. Again and again, we are reminded of the social and economic crises in the human world, one in which Jake's brother Tommy is killed for his money, and in which, as Jake tells us: "They can fix the spinal if you got the money, but not on vet benefits, not in this economy." The economy of this dystopian world, then, is one that spurs soldiers, including Jake, to barter away their individual and independent dignity and beliefs, one that makes any individual a potential victim of armed robbery and violence, and one that prevents Jake from acquiring medical treatment even from his benefits. In fact, this economy is bad enough to drive soldiers to Pandora despite the Colonel's assurance to the new recruits, at the start of the film, that he will not be able to keep them all alive.

Although Jake is correct in arguing for the need to speak to the humans, his violent "response" forges a disparity in the fields of experience between us, as the film's viewers, and Jake, despite his privileged position as a human who supposedly sees and knows the perspectives of both the humans and the Na'vi. During the attack on Hometree, we witness the immediate reactions of everyone including, perhaps, the Colonel, while Jake is in his avatar with the Na'vi. He cannot know that, during the bombing, even Parker is disturbed, and the Colonel turns away from the image of the bombed tree after promising his troops the first round of drinks later that night. In fact, when the Colonel launches his full-scale attack on the Tree of Souls, Parker is visibly disturbed.

While we might attribute his concern to the reactions of his shareholders, narratives have a way of moving us to different ethical ends, even unpredictable ones.[17] Jake's conviction, despite his limited viewpoint, reveals the markedly little difference between Jake's and the Colonel's violence — and the idioms that they use to narrate it. While Jake triumphs over the Colonel, he has only managed to implant this defeat on the humans' memory. This defeat, combined with the sheer desperation of the human world, will certainly move them to wage another war, one with even better military strategy and more ammunition.[18] Thus, although the Na'vi have triumphed for the time being, at the level of ideology, they have lost the war over their comparatively peaceful beliefs.

Conversations

Several films from the last few years have conversed with *Avatar* in provocative ways. Chris Sanders' and Dean DeBlois' *How to Train Your Dragon* (2010) and Tim Burton's *Alice in Wonderland* (2010) present colonial relationships similar to that between the seer and the seen in *Avatar*, and Kathryn Bigelow's *The Hurt Locker* (2008) places audiences within a recognizably colonial, and politically relevant context, which Cameron pokes fun at in his film with phrases lifted directly from Bush Administration propaganda (recall the line, "fight terror with terror"). That said, we would like to investigate two recent films in close detail: Steven Spielberg's *Indiana Jones and the Kingdom of the Crystal Skull* and Neill Blomkamp's *District 9*, both of which present colonial scenarios comparable to those appearing in *Avatar*. Examination of these films in tandem with Cameron's may evince certain peculiarities concerning our culture's understanding of its role in the postcolonial, or perhaps neocolonial, world. Particularly given Brooks' observation of a developing Messiah Complex among contemporary filmmakers and audiences, it seems pertinent to assess, if briefly, the frequency of this and similar cinematic plots. In so doing, we will attempt to shed light on Cameron's phrase, "I see you," rendering it a hopeful yet problematic greeting, which serves — like the whole of Cameron's film, and those discussed by Brooks — to perpetuate notions of cultural hegemony.

In Spielberg's latest installment of the *Indiana Jones* franchise, viewers will notice a clear differentiation between the colonizers and natives. Throughout the film, the titular hero and his allies seek to locate the crystal skull — an alien device with supernatural powers — and return it to its rightful place in the mountains of Peru, and then into the hands of its alien creators. Jones' enemies, Soviet operatives led by Dr. Irina Spalko, are motivated by their desire to triumph over the Americans by securing and acquiring the knowledge promised through access to these skulls. All of these outsiders, the American and the Russians, can be considered colonizers. Like Selfridge and his team, the Jones crew and the Soviets are consistently rational in their objectives; though, in contrast to the colonizers in *Avatar*, they battle one another, taking some of the pressure off the colonized natives. The efficiency of these characters is metaphorically represented through the colonizers' use of guns and other technologically advanced weapons that are accurate, minimize the users' exposure to danger, and are extremely lethal. By contrast, and in comparison with the Na'vi, the natives prey on all foreigners entering their territories, using their superior physical agility and deadly, though inefficient weaponry (often, poison darts). Near the film's conclusion, the juxtaposition of a medium close-up shot of Spalko surrounded by native corpses suggests that the Russians with their machine guns, unsurprisingly, violently triumphed over the natives.

Even though Indiana Jones and his allies are not responsible for these natives' murder, the Americans do not seem troubled that so many native people have been killed. It is as if, to come back to Cameron, they simply are not "seen." Certainly they are not recognized as equals, as the greeting is meant to suggest. Later, the inclusion of alien beings suggests yet another level of hierarchy: the aliens, by dint of force, require the invading humans to locate and return the skull. The inherent superiority of the aliens may cause viewers to feel less critical toward the means by which Jones and company justify their ends. Setting aside that *Indiana Jones* is an action flick, and so adopts Hollywood's conventional "anonymous bad-guy" routine, by lending so little face-time to these characters Spielberg fashions a world where non-white people generally go unregarded and undervalued. Moreover, given the film's South American setting, Spielberg's treatment of natives begins to feel reminiscent of that of Francisco Pizarro and other Spanish conquistadors of the fifteenth and sixteenth century. Of course, this could be said of many films within this particular genre, and we should not fault Spielberg specifically for adopting this feature in any installment of the *Indiana Jones* series, and countless other films from the 1980s to the present. Still, the disregard for human life, demonstrated by careless slaughter of indigenous people, illustrates the small life-value Jones, his team, and the Soviets ascribe to non–European, non-white beings.

If *Indiana Jones and the Kingdom of the Crystal Skull* stages and repeatedly reaffirms this unbridgeable divide between the colonizers and the natives, one in which true understanding and communication seem impossible, so too does *District 9*. By the end of the film, Wikus van de Merwe, field officer of Multinational United (MNU), is transformed into an alien after coming into contact with a mysterious fluid. He thus becomes one of the 2.5 million aliens that make up District 10. If Jake's resort to violence and his replication of the

Colonel's vocabulary spur us to question his "victory," Wikus' quest is still more doubtful. He shows his assistant and trainee Fundiswa, the prospective viewer of the MNU footage, and the viewer of *District 9* how to destroy an alien nursery. Wikus begins by detaching the feeding apparatus that supplies the alien egg with nutrients — an act that moves Fundiswa to mutter "Oh, God"— before detaching another tube and telling the trainee: "The little guy has gone to a nice little sleep now." Wikus hands an apparatus to a soldier "as a souvenir for [his] first abortion," and it is interesting to note that Fundiswa has moved away from him. This method of killing individual aliens, however, is too slow for Wikus and his team, so they set fire to the nursery. The smiling Wikus asks his viewer in graphic imagery: "Do you hear that? That's a popping sound that you're hearing. It's almost like a popcorn. What the egg does is, it pops up. The little guy, what's left of him, pops out there. So that's the sound that you are hearing with the popping." Both Wikus' knowledge of how to kill the aliens and his carefree — and just creepy — use of the popcorn simile may spur us to question his status as "victim" later in the film, particularly if we are watching the film with containers of popcorn on our very laps.

Wikus' complicity in a holocaust is rendered only more pronounced when he confesses to aliens Christopher Johnson and his son, after realizing that they are his only hope of changing back to a human: "You don't wanna go to the tents [of District 10]. They're not better. They're smaller than the shacks. Actually more like a concentration camp." Despite Wikus' knowledge that these camps promise confinement and death for the aliens, he is perfectly content to take charge of the eviction initiative, and he would have been pleased to continue doing his job had he not come into contact with the alien fluid. While Wikus does not know about the medical experiments on aliens that are going on in the MNU laboratories, his fundamental selfishness, and his direct involvement in this abortion and doubtless many others make it difficult for viewers to identify with him. Unlike Jake, however, even when Wikus begins to be transformed into an alien, he refuses to self-identify as one. After seeing that his arm is changing into an alien's and deducing that he must have come into contact with the transformative fluid that fuels their ship, Christopher Johnson and his son help conceal Wikus from the MNU. However, when Johnson's son compares his arm with Wikus' and says, "We are the same," Wikus reveals his persisting conviction that these aliens are inferior: "Fuck off, man. I'm not the same. Not the fucking same." Yes, Wikus helps Christopher Johnson and his son escape back to the mother ship, yet he is motivated by his desire to transform back into a human rather than to recompense the aliens for all the wrongs he has personally committed. Wikus' motivation toward his human identity is evidenced by the film's conclusion, when Wikus gives his wife a metal rose. The gift places greater emphasis on the relationship between Wikus and his wife, and reconfigures what began as an examination of colonial relations into a romance between two humans.

Through excellent command of cinematic language and narrative strategies, these filmmakers transport us to lands as far away and exotic as Pandora or the Peruvian Andes, and as close to home as a fictionalized Johannesburg. In all cases, a colonizing protagonist force is pitted against a less technologically advanced civilization. *Avatar* stands out, however, in the protagonist Jake's adoption of indigenous morals, which he uses to defeat his own culture. Yes, indigenous values are championed — this is more than can be said of *Indiana Jones*— but Cameron's use of a human liberator, let alone a white male, illustrates the insistence of the West on Eurocentric racial and cultural power structures. *Avatar* is a step in the right direction; Cameron does not condone the colonial process taking place on Pandora. However, that step continues to be a self-indulgent one for theatergoers, whose own economic choices perpetuate colonial practices in the postcolonial third world. Only when filmmakers cease to congratulate audiences for their pseudo-cognizant efforts, and hold them actively accountable for their actions, will this phenomenon be resolved.

NOTES

For their insightful reading, encouragement, and suggestions, the authors would like to thank Julia Guez, Charles Hatten, Tamar Heller, Philip Horne, Tyler Shores, and Neil ten Kortenaar. John James would like to thank Columbia University School of the Arts, and Bellarmine University, and Tom Ue would like to thank University College London, the Social Science and Humanities Research Council of Canada, McGill University, and the University of Toronto at Scarborough. The analysis of *Indiana Jones and the Kingdom of the Crystal Skull* builds on a journal prepared by Tom Ue for the ENGC70HY LEC 01: The Imperial Imaginary in Film course at the University of Toronto at Scarborough. Unless otherwise specified, all references are to the Original Theatrical Edition of *Avatar*.

1. Kirk Honeycutt, *"Avatar*— Film Review," *The Hollywood Reporter*, December 10, 2009, http://www.hollywoodreporter.com/hr/film-reviews/avatar-film-review-1004052868.story.

2. Manohla Dargis, "A New Eden, Both Cosmic and Cinematic," *New York Times*, December 18, 2009, http://movies.nytimes.com/2009/12/18/movies/18avatar.html.

3. Readers might find Selfridge's treatment of the Na'vi in keeping with Rudyard Kipling's "The White Man's Burden." The poem refers to indigenous peoples as "Half-devil and half-child" (8), and insists that it is the responsibility of the white, educated European to enlighten the undeveloped, "savage" people of the colonies.

4. Edward Said, *Orientalism* (New York: Pantheon Books, 1978), 60.

5. Jean-Paul Sartre, "Preface," *The Wretched of the Earth* (New York: Grove, 1966), 7.

6. Frantz Fanon, *The Wretched of the Earth.* (New York: Grove, 1966), 31. Fanon interchanges the terms "colonizer" and "settler." Both refer to a conquering, imperial presence.

7. Ibid., 31.

8. Philip Horne, *"Avatar*, DVD review," *The Telegraph*, April 27, 2010, http://www.telegraph.co.uk/culture/film/dvd-reviews/7624833/Avatar-DVD-review.html.

9. The Na'vi language is extremely difficult to master, as evidenced by the five years of

study Dr. Norm Spellman must endure just to be able to speak it with textbook competency. Of course, language does not exist in a vacuum, and Jake should acquire the language much more quickly via immersion to the cultural environment in which Na'vi is spoken.

10. David Brooks, "The Messiah Complex," *The New York Times*, January 7, 2010, http://www.nytimes.com/2010/01/08/opinion/08brooks.html.

11. Ella Shohat and Robert Sham, *Multiculturalism and the Media* (London: Routledge, 1994), 100.

12. Ibid., 100.

13. David Brook, "The Messiah Complex," *The New York Times*, January 7, 2010, http://www.nytimes.com/2010/01/08/opinion/08brooks.html.

14. Ibid.

15. Stuart Hall, "Cultural Identity and Cinematic Representation," in *Ex-iles: Essays on Caribbean Cinema*, ed. Mbye B. Cham (Trenton: Africa World Press, Inc., 1992), 220.

16. Ibid., 224.

17. See Tom Ue, "Metanarratives and the Representation of Violence in Quentin Tarantino's *Inglourious Basterds*" (paper, 31st Annual Southwest/Texas Popular & American Culture Associations, Albuquerque, New Mexico, February 12, 2010). As Tom Ue has pointed out in his analysis of *Nation's Pride* in *Inglorious Basterds*, the embedded film moves Fredrick emotionally. Still, it does not teach him to make more ethical choices. In the premiere of *Nation's Pride*, we get not one or two, but five reaction shots of Fredrick, the character who hunted down Russian soldiers, and the actor of the film. As he watches his actions represented on screen, he is repeatedly depicted as looking disturbed and shaking his head. In the last of these shots, in response to both his watching of the film and his witnessing of Hitler and Goebbels laughing as they enjoy it, Fredrick leaves to look for Shosanna. While *Nation's Pride* elicits a strong reaction from him, he is only slightly better as a reader than the viewers of the embedded film, who applaud at every soldier Fredrick kills as one does at a soccer match. When he finds Shosanna, he does not behave with any more courtesy towards her, and disrespects her repeated and increasingly forceful attempts to show her inability to reciprocate his romantic affections."

18. Mathias Uy has made this case after watching the film. See Dean DeBlois' and Chris Sanders' *How to Train Your Dragon* (2010). If an economic crisis motivates the human population of *Avatar* to begin a colonial project in Pandora, and the questions that precipitate regarding this situation are left unanswered, so too are the questions about food in the animated feature. A persisting problem for Hiccup's Viking community is that the dragons are capturing sheep and other food supplies, and causing substantial damages. As the film unfolds, Hiccup learns that everything that is known about dragons is wrong, and that a large dragon named Red Death is bullying the others into stealing for him. In order to prevent themselves from being eaten by the larger dragon, the smaller ones are plaguing the Viking population. Although Red Death is destroyed by the end of the film, the Vikings must now provide for themselves as well as all of these dragons, so that the concern over food-shortage persists.

WORKS CITED

Brooks, David. "The Messiah Complex." *The New York Times*. January 7, 2010. http://www.nytimes .com/2010/01/08/opinion/08brooks.html.

Dargis, Manohla. "A New Eden, Both Cosmic and Cinematic." *The New York Times*. December 18, 2009. http://movies.nytimes.com/2009/12/18/movies/18avatar.html.

Ebert, Roger. "Avatar." *Chicago Sun Times*. December 11, 2009. http://rogerebert.suntimes.com /apps/pbcs.dll/article?AID=/20091211/REVIEWS/912119998/1023.

Fanon, Frantz. *The Wretched of the Earth*. New York: Grove, 1966.

Fitzpatrick, Lisa. *The Art of Avatar*. New York: Abrams, 2009.

Hall, Stuart. "Cultural Identity and Cinematic Representation." In *Ex-iles: Essays on Caribbean Cinema*, edited by Mbye B. Cham, 220-36. Trenton, NJ: Africa World Press, 1992.

Honeycutt, Kirk. "Avatar — Film Review." *The Hollywood Reporter.* December 10, 2009. http://www.hollywoodreporter.com/hr/film-reviews/avatar-film-review-1004052868.story.

Horne, Philip. "Avatar, DVD review." *The Telegraph.* April 27, 2010. http://www.telegraph.co.uk/culture/film/dvd-reviews/7624833/Avatar-DVD-review.html.

Kipling, Rudyard. "The White Man's Burden." In *Rudyard Kipling Complete Verse*, 321. New York: Anchor, 1988.

Said, Edward. *Orientalism.* New York: Pantheon Books, 1978.

Sartre, Jean-Paul. "Preface." In *The Wretched of the Earth*, 7–26. New York: Grove, 1966.

Shohat, Ella, and Robert Sham. *Multiculturalism and the Media.* London: Routledge, 1994.

Ue, Tom. "Metanarratives and the Representation of Violence in Quentin Tarantino's *Inglourious Bastards*." Paper, 31st Annual Southwest/Texas Popular & American Culture Associations, Albuquerque, NM, February 12, 2010.

Wilhelm, Maria, and Dirk Mathison. *James Cameron's Avatar: A Confidential Report on the Biological and Social History of Pandora.* New York: It Books–HarperCollins, 2009.

FILMS CITED

Alice in Wonderland. Directed by Tim Burton. Walt Disney Pictures, 2010.

Apocalypse Now. Directed by Francis Ford Coppola. United Artists, 1979.

Avatar. Directed by James Cameron. Twentieth Century Fox, 2009.

District 9. Directed by Neill Blomkamp. Sony Pictures Home Entertainment, 2009.

Emerald Forest, The. Directed by John Boorman. Embassy Pictures Corporation, 1985.

FernGully: The Last Rainforest. Directed by Bill Kroyer. Twentieth Century Fox, 1992.

How to Train your Dragon. Directed by Chris Sanders and Dean DeBlois. Paramount, 2010.

Hurt Locker, The. Directed by Kathryn Bigelow. Voltage Pictures, 2008.

Indiana Jones and the Kingdom of the Crystal Skull. Directed by Steven Spielberg. Paramount, 2008.

Inglorious Bastards. Directed by Quentin Tarantino. Universal Studios, 2009.

Last of the Mohicans. Directed by Michael Mann. Twentieth Century Fox, 1992.

Gonzalo Guerrero and the Maya Resistance to the Spanish Conquistadors: A Sixteenth Century "Avatar" of *Avatar*

C. SCOTT LITTLETON

It is, I think, fair to say that the great majority of American film critics have compared James Cameron's technologically brilliant movie *Avatar* (2009) to Kevin Costner's *Dances with Wolves* (1990).[1] And with good reason. Like Cameron's renegade Marine hero Jake Sully, vis-à-vis the Na'vi, fictional inhabitants of the equally fictional moon Pandora, Costner's Custer-era character Army Lieutenant John J. Dunbar, deserts and casts his lot with the indigenous culture his compatriots are attempting to subjugate: the Lakota Sioux, who freely roamed the high plains of South Dakota and elsewhere in the American West until they were forced onto a reservation toward the end of the nineteenth century.[2] Other critics have noted a marked resemblance between *Avatar* and a more recent film, *The Last Samurai* (2003), in which Tom Cruise's character, Nathan Algren, a burnt-out, former Union Army officer in the employee of the newly established Imperial Japanese Army, becomes not only an admirer of another vastly different and technologically inferior culture — the samurai, who are resisting Japan's modernization in 1876 and bravely but futilely charging the Imperial Army's Gatling guns with their swords — but also, like Sully and Dunbar, falls in love with a beautiful female member of that culture.[3]

Still others have suggested that Cameron's film, which focuses on Sully's romantic relationship with a Na'vi "princess," called Neytiri, is in some respects an updated retelling of the story of Captain John Smith and Pocahontas in early seventeenth century Virginia[4] — despite the fact that the famed "Indian princess" eventually married tobacco planter John Rolfe rather than Captain Smith, whose life she had saved, and that neither of these two Englishmen saw fit to renounce his own culture and become a Powhatan Indian. Indeed, it was Pocahontas who shifted cultures and, bearing her baptismal name

"Rebecca," accompanied her husband to London in 1617 and died there of a European disease for which she had no immunity.[5]

The critical response to *Avatar*, by focusing on narratives that focus upon nineteenth century American renegades — after all, both *Dances with Wolves* and *The Last Samurai* feature Civil War veterans — tends to obscure the fact that the narrative presented in *Avatar* is actually timeless. To be sure, the film is about a former American fighting man thrust into a future colonial situation involving the United States. But as we shall shortly see, the history of soldiers like John Dunbar, Nathan Algren, and Jake Sully is *far* older than the United States.

Moreover, there is in all of these narratives, fictional and otherwise, a common thread: what I have come to call "embracing the other." It is an intense eagerness to embrace an exotic culture, an "other," either dominant or subordinate, with which one's own culture has recently come into intense contact. Pocahontas, of course, enthusiastically embraced the technologically superior, already dominant English culture, personified by Smith and Rolfe.

But the direction I'm primarily concerned with in this essay is the opposite one, where a member of a technologically dominant culture "goes native," as it were, and wholeheartedly embraces a simpler culture, like that of the Na'vi, the Lakota Sioux, and the Samurai, whose very existence is threatened his (or her) compatriots. And in my estimation, the most dramatic example of such a situation — that is, the most striking single "avatar" of *Avatar*— was a historical event that long predates the fictional milieux of *Dances with Wolves* and *The Last Samurai* and which seems to have totally eluded the critical establishment.[6] It occurred almost a century *before* the English settled at Jamestown in 1607. The location was the Yucatán Peninsula, the native culture in question was that of the ancient Maya,[7] and the prototypes of the former Marines who were tasked with "pacifying" the Na'vi were the Spanish Conquistadors.

Geronimo de Aguilar and Gonzalo Guerrero

Our story begins in Spain shortly before the turn of the sixteenth century and involves two very different men who would become shipmates on an ill-fated voyage in 1511. One of them, Geronimo de Aguilar, was born ca. 1489 in the Andalusian town of Ejica and later educated for the Church. The other, Gonzalo Guerrero, about whom we will have much to say shortly, appears to have born ca. 1470 in the port city of Palos, near modern Cadiz; it was the port from which Columbus left on his first voyage in 1492. Indeed, Guerrero, who as a youth had been a soldier in the Spanish army that drove the Moors from the Iberian Peninsula once and for all in the same year, appears to have been a part of that epic voyage, having served, it is said, as a crewman aboard the *Niña*.[8] I suspect that, with the Reconquista finally at an end, he found himself at loose ends and signed on with the Genovese explorer. But the high probability that he had had military experience before and perhaps after becoming a sailor — it is also said that he served as an *arcabucero* (a soldier who carried an arquebus, a long-barreled firearm of the era) in the Spanish army under "*Gran Capitán*" Gonzalo Fernández de Córdoba y Aguilar at Naples in the late 1490s[9]— will loom large in what follows. A decade or so later, probably ca. 1505–1508, Guerrero was back in the New World, this time for good.

By the time Geronimo de Aguilar (no relation to the "*Gran Capitán*," I presume) reached the Indies, which I suspect was several years after Guerrero, he seems to have taken preliminary vows and was thus on track to becoming a Franciscan friar. His reasons for making the journey are unclear, although he probably wanted to help convert the heathen natives to the True Faith. Unlike his compatriot, he almost certainly had had no military experience whatsoever.

In any case, in the spring of 1511 both men, whose lives would thenceforth be intertwined, found themselves in the Darién colony in what is today Panama, and both joined a ship's company bound for the city of Santo Domingo on the Island of Hispaniola. According to the Spanish chronicler Bernal Diaz de Castillo,[10] it was captained by a Conquistador named Juan de Valdivia and was loaded with 10,000 crowns of gold, as well as two women, several slaves, and reports for the governor of Hispaniola concerning a dispute between Valdivia and a man named Encoso.

Why Guerrero, who was then about forty years of age, was in Darien at that point and why he signed on with this particular crew is unknown, although he was a soldier of fortune and perhaps had decided to return to Santo Domingo so as to join another exploratory/free-booting expedition. De Aguilar, on the other hand, appears to have been reassigned to another clerical institution — perhaps a monastery — on Hispaniola.

At first, the voyage went well. The weather was fine, and they made good time. But as so often happens in that part of the world, a powerful storm — or possibly even a hurricane — suddenly appeared out of nowhere and drove the heavily laden little ship onto a shoal south of Jamaica called Las Viboras (the vipers). Valdivia and seventeen or eighteen others, including de Aguilar, Guerrero and the two women, managed to escape the sinking ship and drifted westward on the Yucatán current for about two weeks in a small boat.

By the time they reached the Yucatan coast, probably just to the south of Cozumel Island near the modern resort town of Akumal, seven of the survivors had died of starvation, and of those who did make it ashore four, including Valdivia, were immediately killed by local Mayan *caciques*, or chiefs, who divided them up to be sacrificially consumed in a cannibalistic ritual. The rest were locked in cages so they could be fattened up for a similar fate. But a handful of Spaniards managed to escape, and after stumbling around in the jungle for a few days they were captured by another Mayan *cacique* called Aquincuz, the lord of a town called Xamanzana. Although this time they were held as slaves rather than as potential sacrificial victims, all but de Aguilar and Guerrero soon succumbed to the rigors of their circumstances.

De Aguilar remained in Xamanzana as Aquincuz's slave for the next eight years, hoping against hope that someday he would be rescued by his fellow countrymen. To make matters worse, Guerrero, however, was soon sent to serve a neighboring chief, called Nachan Can, who ruled a town that became the modern Mexican city of Chetumal, capital of the State of Quintana Roo. As it was well over a hundred miles to the south, near the border of what is today Belize, de Aguilar was effectively isolated from all contact with his native language and culture. Nevertheless, he did his best to remain true to his faith and to his identity as a Spaniard. By sheer luck, he had managed to hang onto his Book of Hours, which contained information about religious holidays and allowed him to keep track of the days and dates in the Christian calendar. (Indeed, he was only three days off when he was finally released in 1519.)

Given their circumstances, both men necessarily became fluent in the Yucatecan Maya dialect. However, other than that, their experiences diverged dramatically. While de Aguilar remained a true son of the Holy Mother Church, Guerrero went native. He pierced his ears, nose, and lip, dressed like his captors, was heavily tattooed, began worshipping their gods, and soon became a full-fledged — and free[11] — Maya warrior. Eventually, he became his lord's principal military advisor, and in 1517, when an expedition led by Francisco Córdoba attempted to land at Cape Catoche, near the site of what is today the world-famous resort city of Cancún at the northeastern corner of the peninsula, he fought against his fellow Spaniards and appears to have been instrumental in driving them off the beach.[12]

Guerrero also became his lord's son-in-law. Nachan Can's daughter, Xzazil Ha, bore him three children, two sons and a daughter, and he is often credited with siring the first *mestizos*, or mixed-blood offspring, in Mexico, if not the Americas per se.[13] He was later tasked with the administration of several temples in the vicinity of Ichpaatún (modern Oxtankah) a few kilometers north of Chetumal. In short, by the time Hernán Cortés arrived on the scene in 1519, Gonzalo Guerrero had become, in effect, a Mayan aristocrat — a far cry from his social standing in Palos, which, from all indications, was near the bottom of the Spanish heap.

Guerrero Rejects the Possibility of Rescue

When Cortés landed at the Island of Cozumel in February of 1519, en route to his eventual conquest of Mexico, he soon learned — probably via gestures and pointing toward the mainland on the part of the local Maya — that two "bearded men," who called themselves "Castilan," were being held captive by local chiefs. So he sent a letter by native courier to these chiefs, along with some emerald colored beads as ransom, demanding the return of his compatriots.

De Aguilar was ecstatic about the prospect of returning to "civilization" and the Catholic faith. It was the moment he'd hoped and prayed for during the eight long years of his captivity. His Mayan master released him from servitude, and he immediately sought out his former shipmate — apparently for the first time since they'd been captured — and begged him to return with him to Cozumel and his own kind.

But Guerrero demurred. According to Bernal Diaz del Castillo, de Aguilar recorded the renegade's reply as follows:

> Brother Aguilar; I am married and have three children, and they look on me as a *cacique* here, and captain in time of war. My face is tattooed and my ears are pierced. What would the Spaniards say if they saw me like this? Go and God's blessing be with you, for you have seen how handsome these children of mine are. Please give me some of those beads you have brought to give to them and I will tell them that my brothers have sent them from my own country.[14]

Like Jake Sully vis-à-vis the fictional Na'vi, he had become what amounted to a Mayan "avatar." Indeed, Diaz del Castillo, also reports that Guerrero's aristocratic wife, Xzazil Ha, haughtily exclaimed in her own tongue, "See this slave how he comes to seduce my husband!"[15] And according to other translators of Diaz del Castillo's account (for example, Maudsley 1928,), she added, "Be off with you!" to de Aguilar, thus, in effect, telling the apprentice friar to "piss off!" and leave them alone.[16]

In any case, de Aguilar said *adios*— which he probably meant literally as well as conventionally — to his former comrade and made his way to Cozumel. There, after proving to Cortés that he was in fact a Spaniard by indicating the nearly correct day and date (see above) and sharing his transcript of Guerrero's reply,[17] he happily joined the expedition. Subsequently, de Aguilar's fluency in the local Mayan dialect proved to be invaluable, especially in the early days of the Conquest. In Tabasco, Cortés took as his mistress an Indian woman, later known as La Malinche, "The Captain's Woman," who was bilingual in Nahuatl, the language of the Aztecs, and Yucatecan Mayan. La Malinche, whom Cortés christened (literally) "Doña Marina," would converse with Moteczuma, et al. and translate what was said into Mayan. Then de Aguilar would repeat it to Cortés in Spanish. Needless to say, Doña Marina soon learned Spanish in her Captain's bed. Nevertheless, in 1526 de Aguilar was rewarded for his service with a land-grant northwest of Mexico City.[18]

Gonzalo Guerrero Versus Francisco de Montejo

In 1526, the same year de Aguilar received his land-grant, one of Cortés' paladins, Francisco de Montejo, received a charter from the Spanish Crown to "pacify" the Yucatan Peninsula. Montejo had also been a member of the Juan de Grijalva expedition, which explored the Yucatán coast in early 1518, a year after Guerrero had helped prevent Córdoba and his Spaniards from establishing a beachhead at Catoche[19] and he had become obsessed with some-day conquering the Maya. And it is at this point that the parallels between Guerrero and Cameron's hero Jake Sully become most remarkable.

By June of 1527, Montejo had put together a fleet of four ships manned by several hundred fighting men plus a couple of cannon, at least three priests, and several Catalan merchants, who carried merchandise to trade with the Indians once "pacification" had been achieved. The expedition was well stocked with supplies of meat, cooking oil, wine, vinegar, and biscuits.[20] Curi-ously, even though Montejo had known de Aguilar and Doña Marina and realized that the Indians of the Tabasco region, now under Spanish domina-tion, could communicate with the Yucatecan Maya, he failed to bring along an interpreter.[21] This proved to be a major mistake, as he was unable to effec-tively interrogate captives.

After stopping briefly at Cozumel, where, like Cortés eight years earlier, they met little or no resistance from the local Maya, Montejo's fleet sailed to the mainland, landing just south of the village of Xelha. Although they man-aged to get ashore and establish a small settlement, from that point on the expedition suffered from constant and well-organized hit-and-run attacks. Within a few months, thanks to steady attrition from the attacks and the dwindling supply of food, despite raids on nearby villages, their numbers had been reduced by nearly two thirds. Eventually, after a long-awaited relief ship arrived, Montejo felt strong enough to mount a sortie southward down the coast toward the bustling Mayan port city called Chetumal. It was, of course, Gonzalo Guerrero's home base, and the frustrated Conquistador finally came to the realization that he was being stymied by his renegade fellow country-man, who was not only leading — or at least directing — the Indian attacks, but also teaching the Maya the tactics and military organization he'd learned during his youthful stint as a soldier during the Reconquista and later in Italy.

Indeed, writing some fifty-odd years later, Archbishop Diego de Landa observed that, "[Guerrero] showed the Indians how to fight, teaching them how to build fortresses and bastions."[22] In any case, in desperation, Montejo decided to send Guerrero a letter via a native courier, imploring him, as a Christian, to remember his duty toward God and the Spanish Crown and return to the fold. Much like Colonel Quartich offering medical aid for Jake's help in defeating the Na'vi, Montejo offers similar payment to Guerrero. His letter read in part:

> ... I beseech you not to let the devil influence you not to do what I say, so that he will not possess himself of you forever. On behalf of His Majesty I promise to do very well for you and fully to comply with that which I have said. On my part, as a noble gentleman I give you my word and pledge my faith to make my promise to you good without any reservations whatsoever, favouring and honouring you and making you one of my principal men and one of my most select and loved groups in these parts.[23]

Guerrero's reply, scrawled in charcoal on the reverse of Monjeo's letter, was short, sweet, and dripping with irony:

> Senor [sic], I kiss your Grace's hands. As I am a slave I have no freedom [to join you], even though I ... remember God. You, my lord, and the Spaniards will find in me a very good friend.[24]

As Inga Glendinnen remarks, "if Guerrero remembered God, his actions gave no hint of it," for his attacks continued unabated.[25] And he clearly hadn't been a slave for more than a decade.

Francisco Montejo and his diminishing band of Conquistadors hung on for several more years and had some success in the northwest part of the region. But in the southeast, where Guerrero led the resistance, it was another story altogether. In short, by 1535 there were no Spaniards left in the Yucatán Peninsula proper. Like Jake Sully and his Na'vi warriors, Guerrero and his adopted people had apparently triumphed over those who would despoil their culture, destroy their religion, and loot their precious resources.

Of course, that's where the film *Avatar* ends, on a note of triumph. But history keeps on going and has a way of becoming messier and nastier.

In 1533, before things totally fell apart in the Yucatán, Montejo received a royal patent that gave him permission to conquer several towns in Honduras. However, another of Cortes' stalwarts, Pedro de Alvarado, had received a similar patent the year before, and matters came to a head in 1536, when Alvarado claimed that he had already "pacified" the region. This has a direct impact on the denouement of our story.

As peace had come — at least temporarily — to the southeastern Yucatán, that same year the lord of Chetumal dispatched Guerrero and a fleet of fifty warrior-filled canoes to the Honduran coast to help Xicumba, a local Maya *cacique* with whom he was on friendly terms, to resist Alvarado's incursion. The expedition ended disastrously, at least as far as the Maya were concerned. After defeating a Maya contingent in a skirmish at Xicumba's town, Ticamaya, the Spanish discovered the nude and heavily tattooed body of a bearded European among the enemy dead. Ironically, he had been killed by a bullet from an arquebus, the same weapon he himself had carried as a Spanish soldier. Although Andrés de Cerezeda, one of Alavardo's officers, identified the corpse as that of Gonzalo Arocha,[26] most historians are convinced that the dead warrior was in fact Gonzalo Guerrero.[27] In any case, his luck had finally run out, although Guerrero had to have been well over sixty years of age when he died, a remarkably long life considering the era and the innumerable perils he had faced, both in Spain as a young soldier in the last days of the Reconquista and as a Maya warrior.

In 1540, the Spaniards regrouped under Montejo's son, Francisco Montejo "El Mozo," or the Younger, and once again attempted to conquer the Yucatán Peninsula. A small Spanish garrison had managed to hold on at Campeche in the northwest, and it was from there that the new campaign was mounted. As the Maya no longer had Guerrero to help them plot strategy, El Mozo was ultimately successful, although the renegade Spaniard's lessons were remembered, and it was not an easy task. Indeed, it wasn't until the late nineteenth century, after the so-called War of the Castes,[28] that the southeastern portion of the peninsula — that is, the area around Chetumal — was brought firmly under Mexican control. And as the modern statues of Guerrero and his family that have been erected in Chetumal, Mérida, and Akumal, all of which depict him clutching a spear and wearing the ear pieces, hairstyle, headdress, and loin cloth of an aristocratic Maya warrior, as well as a series of murals devoted to him and Xzazil Ha in the Governor's Palace and the *Ayuntamiento,* or city hall, at Mérida, clearly attest, memory of Guerrero and his impact on his adopted people still lingers in the popular culture of this region and elsewhere in the so-called *Mundo Maya*).[29]

Nevertheless, by 1579 Archbishop de Landa and his Franciscan friars had burned all but a handful of the Maya codices and had executed thousands of indigenous "heretics" for worshipping idols.[30] In effect, the Spanish had uprooted the equivalent of the Na'vi's sacred tree, and it would never rise again.

Embracing the Other

Several important questions remain: Why did Gonzalo Guerrero "go native" and embrace the other so wholeheartedly, while Geronimo de Aguilar did not? And, more broadly, what is the vicarious appeal of fictional characters, such as John Dunbar, Nathan Algren, and Jake Sully, all of whom, like Guerrero, eagerly defect to a simpler culture that is under threat either directly from their own or, in the case of *The Last Samurai*, from an industrial technology that has borrowed heavily from Algren's post–Civil War America?

In Guerrero's case, Clendinnen concedes that "What it was that held Aguilar to his Spanish and Christian sense of self, yet allowed Guerrero to identify with native ways, is mysterious."[31] She goes on to speculate that the fact that the renegade had been a sailor and had presumably visited a number of foreign ports before arriving in the New World may have conditioned him to accept non–Spanish — or, indeed, non–European — cultures, and that he must have had "an ear quick for foreign sounds." Yet Aguilar, although he probably had little or no experience with foreign cultures before he arrived in Darien, became equally fluent in Yucatecan Maya. I suspect that his early clerical training, which had to have been vastly different from Guerrero's upbringing on the streets of Palos, may have armored him against adopting the culture of his captors. One could perhaps argue that Guerrero was a hopeless "romantic" and that he eagerly embraced the exotic "other" into which circumstances had thrust him, while Aguilar learned the language simply to survive. However, and more realistically, the status Guerrero was able to achieve in the service of Nachan Can was almost certainly *far* greater than anything he could possibly have hoped to achieve within Spanish society, either at home or in the New World.[32] And the fact that he married what amounted to a "princess" must have reinforced this perception. All of this probably became obvious to him almost from the beginning, especially since I also strongly suspect that he was not in any way committed to the fanatical Roman Catholicism that was practiced in his homeland at the time. Indeed, it's not impossible to speculate that he had had a run-in of some sort with the Inquisition in his youth, and that it had caused him to reject — or at least seriously question — the "spiritual" values of the Spanish establishment. In fact, he may have come to hate them intensely, which might well explain both the ferocity and the tenacity with which he resisted both Córdoba in 1517 and later Montejo and Alvarado, to say nothing of the irony and, indeed, sarcasm in asserting to Montejo that he would "remember God."

Obviously, in the absence of *any* concrete information about Guerrero's formative years, we will never fully understand his motives. But the larger question still confronts us: why are people, real or fictional, who "go native" and resist attempts on the part of their compatriots to dominate and/or exploit an exotic culture with they've become enamored so compelling? To be sure, few go as far as Gonzalo Guerrero or Jake Sully in their support for their respective "noble savages," to use Rousseau's famous label. But over the years a number of my fellow anthropological fieldworkers have come pretty close. A well-known early example of such an ethnographer was Frank Hamilton Cushing (1857–1900), who, in the late 1880s and 1890s, became so engaged with the Zuñi Indians of Arizona that he became a Zuñi priest and refused to divulge, let alone publish, what he considered to be deep tribal secrets[33] Cushing, of course, didn't go so far as to encourage the Zuñi to rebel against the United States government, but he did identify with them to the point that he gave public performances dressed in Zuñi costumes.[34] At the same time, other early ethnographers, like the Anglo-Polish scholar Bronislaw Kaspar Malinowski (1884–1942), adopted what in this context might be labeled the "Aguilar stance." That is, they learned the local dialect and gained a great many insights into the exotic cultures they so assiduously studied, but always kept their distance.[35] Indeed, as Malinowski's private diaries, published in 1967,[36] clearly reveal, he was *not* enamored of the Trobriand Islanders and eagerly awaited the end of World War I, which had forced him, as an Austro-Hungarian subject and therefore an enemy alien, to remain in Australian-administered Melanesia for the duration of the conflict. Like Guerrero's onetime shipmate, he longed to return to the European civilization that had nurtured him.

Nevertheless, the persistence of the Guerrero story in Mexican popular culture,[37] as well as the popularity of films like *Dances with Wolves, The Last Samurai*, and, of course, Cameron's *Avatar*, tells us a great deal about contemporary Western culture. As I see it, the fact that American audiences find themselves rooting for the exotic *adversaries* of a contingent of former United States Marines underscores the extent to which vicariously embracing the other provides a form of catharsis in a society that in recent years has been marked by increasing poverty, political corruption, and economic exploitation fostered by nasty transnational corporations, both at home and abroad, and the hardening of social class distinctions, to say nothing of morally questionable wars against dark-skinned and culturally threatening communities in the Middle East and elsewhere.

As might be expected, this catharsis has raised the ire of a number of hardcore right-wingers. For example, in *Weekly Starndard.com*, John Podhoretz has asserted that, "The conclusion [of the film] asks the audience to root for the death of American soldiers at the hands of an insurgency. So it is a deep expression of anti–Americanism."[38] And right-wing blogger Debbie Schlussel has asked, "Why drive to the movies [to see *Avatar*] ... when you can just as easily read Noam Chomsky or the speeches of [Venezuelan president] Hugo Chavez in the comfort of your own home and couch?"[39] Cameron has effectively answered his critics by asserting that *Avatar* is indeed a political film. "This movie reflects that we are living through war," he remarked at a private industry screening in Hollywood in March of 2010. "There are boots on the ground, troops who I personally believe were sent there under false pretenses, so I hope this will be part of opening our eyes."[40]

As to the charge of "anti–Americanism," Cameron observed that "I've heard people say this film is un–American, while part of being an American is having the freedom to have dissenting ideas," which prompted a loud applause from the capacity crowd that had gathered at the ArcLight Hollywood to hear him comment on the film.[41]

But if in fact the filmmaker deliberately set out to make a political film, one that applauds Sully's decision to embrace the Na'vi and support them against the rapacious ambitions of his superiors, as well as his successful attempt to block the latter from carrying out these evil ambitions, there remains a fundamental albeit most unpleasant reality. Although Guerrero fought and died for his beloved Maya, "El Mozo" and the Spaniards eventually won, and a remarkable civilization, if not a people — there are today four to five million Maya speakers in Mexico, Belize, Guatemala, El Salvador, and Honduras[42] — was effectively destroyed. The sequels to *Avatar* might paint a different picture than the destruction of the Maya civilization, but Guerrero was an actual historical figure, while the Na'vi are merely creations of James Cameron's artistic imagination.[43] The end result, then, of the continuing comparisons to films such as *Dances with Wolves* is to hide the broader — and almost always nastier — realities of colonial conquests and provide a fictional "happy ending." And if the full story of Guerrero's career as a Maya warrior tells us anything, it is that such "happy endings" are very, very hard to achieve in real life.

NOTES

I would like to thank Professor RoseAnna Mueller, of Columbia College Chicago, for her most helpful comments and suggestions and for making a copy of her fascinating article on the evolution of Gonzalo Guerrero's popular image available to me. I also thank Matthew Wilhelm Kapell and Stephen McVeigh, for their most welcome support and encouragement, and my eagle-eyed wife, Mary Ann Littleton, not only for her perceptive suggestions, but also for her awesome skill as a proofreader.

1. E.g., Kirk Honeycutt: "He [Cameron] draws deeply on Westerns, going back to the 'vanishing American' and *Dances with Wolves*," "*Avatar*— Film Review," *The Hollywood Reporter*, December 12, 2009, http://www.hollywoodreporter.com/hr/film-reviews/avatar-film-review-1004052868.story (Access date, July 15, 2010); Tom Charity: "*Dances with Wolves* in outer space," "Review: 'Avatar' delivers on the hype," *CNN*, December 17, 2009, http://articles.cnn.com/ 2009–12–17/entertainment/avatar.review_1_avatar-sam-worthington-sacred-lands?_s=PM: SHOWBIZ (Access date, July 16, 2010); Steven Rea: "The gamer generation's answer to *Dances with Wolves*," "'Avatar' is an epic adventure — and great fun," *The Philadelphia Inquirer*, December 16, 2009,http://www.philly.com/philly/entertainment/movies/20091216_Avatar.html (Access date, July 16, 2010); Peter Keough: "[The film] should come as no surprise to anyone who has

seen *Dances with Wolves*," "Avatar: machine dreams: James Cameron plays games," *The Boston Phoenix*, December 18, 2009, http://thephoenix.com/boston/movies/94407-avatar/ (Access date, July 20, 2010); Ty Burr: "[It] is the same movie as *Dances with Wolves*, re-imagined as a speculative anthropological breakout," "Movie review, Avatar," *The Boston Globe*, December 16, 2009, http://www.boston.com/ae/movies/articles/2009/12/17/avatar_is_an_out_of_body_experience/ (Access date, July 16, 2010).

2. Dee Alexander Brown, *Bury My Heart at Wounded Knee: An Indian History of the American West*. New York: Henry Holt, 1991.

3. E.g., Bilge Ebiri: "Observers have ... remarked on how the eye-popping *Avatar* resembles other films — *Dances with Wolves*, *The New World*, and *Delgo*, among others. But the movie that most screams for a comparison is actually 2003's historical epic *The Last Samurai*, in which Tom Cruise played a troubled soldier going native in Japan and joining the rebels he was supposed to fight," December 21, 2009. http://www.filmcritic.com/features/2009/12/avatar-or-the-last-samurai/ (Access date, July 13, 2010). For a brief overview of this curious episode in the history of early modern Japan, often referred to as the Satsuma Rebellion, see John Whitney Hall, Japan: From Prehistory to Modern Times (New York: Dell Publishing Co., 1979), 283–284.

4. E.g., Richard Corliss, "It is said that just as [Cameron's] *Titanic* had themes of 'Romeo and Juliet,' *Avatar* has themes of 'Pocahontas,'" "Corliss Appraises *Avatar*: A World of Wonder," *Time Magazine*, December 14, 2009.http://www.time.com/time/arts/article/0,8599,1947438,00.html (Access date, July 15, 2010). Others have gone so far as to accuse the filmmaker of deliberately lifting the story from the 1995 Disney Film "Pocahontas." According to an anonymous review in *The Huffington Post*, "James Cameron worked on 'Avatar' for over a decade. That makes sense. It takes a long time to create the technology needed and to completely RIP OFF Disney's 'Pocahontas.' Sure movies borrow from movies all the time, but c'mon James, 'Avatar' might as well be 'Pocahontas in [*sic*] Space,'" January 4, 2010; updated March 18, 2010,http://www.huffingtonpost.com/2010/01/04/avatar-pocahontas-in-spac_n_410538.html (Access date, July 8, 2010). As we'll shortly see, this accusation is woefully incorrect; the stories are, in fact, very different in a great many important respects.

5. David A Price, *Love and Hate in Jamestown* (New York: Vintage Press, 2003), 182.

6. I've only been able to find been able to find two mentions (in English) of a comparison of Gonzalo Guerrero and Jake Sully. One was in a post by someone who calls him/herself "red pill junkie" [*sic*] on a website devoted to comparing *Avatar* to the story of John Smith and Pocahontas: "You think John Smith was the only white man to have 'mingled with the natives'? You guys should read the story of Gonzalo Guerrero, a Spanish conquistador that married a Mayan woman, had kids with her, pierced his ear lobes and fought against the European invaders alongside his new people. Gonzalo was more Avatarish than the Smith dude ever was"; red pill junkie, January 6, 2010. http://www.cartoonbrew.com/disney/pocahontasavatar.html (Access date, July 18, 2010). The second is by a blogger named Kate Elliott, who, in a comment on *Avatar*, states: "One of the more interesting stories that fall into the Dude Going Over is the story of Gonzalo Guerrero — Spanish sailor is shipwrecked, captured by a local Yucatec Maya group, eventually marries a chief's daughter and becomes part of the tribe and fights against the Spanish," December 4, 2009. http://kateelliot.livejoiurnal.com (Access date, September 20, 2010). As we shall see, "red pill junkie's" and Kate Elliott's assessments are pretty close to the mark. There are a couple of Latin American websites that also mention this possibility, e.g., Juan Miguel Company y Manuel Talens, "Reseña de la película Avatar, de James Cameron (USA 2009)," *Rebellion*, December 27, 2009. http://www.rebelion.org/noticia.php?id=99374 (Access date, July15, 2010). But the relevance of the Gonzalo Guerrero story to Cameron's film does indeed appear to have been missed by virtually all mainstream English-speaking film critics.

7. For a comprehensive overview of ancient Mayan culture, see Michael Coe, *The Maya* (4th ed.) (New York: Thames and Hudson, 1987). Cf. "Chetumal, in Search of Gonzalo" Guerrero, Father of the First Mestizo, *Chetumal, Quintana Roo*, no date.http://www.bicycleyucatan.com/gonzaloguerrerochetumal.html (Access date, July 14, 2010), and *Wapedia*, "Gonzalo Guerrero," no date. http://wapedia.mobi/es/Gonzalo_Guerrero. (Access date, July 14, 2010).8. *Wapedia*, "Gonzalo Guerrero."

9. *Wapedia*, "Gonzalo Guerrero."

10. Bernal Diaz del Castillo, *The True History of the Conquest of Mexico, Written in the Year 1568*. Translated by Maurice Keatinge (New York: R. M. McBride Company, 2 vols., 1927), 65.

11. It is said that Guerrero earned his freedom by killing an alligator that was attacking his master.

12. According to Diaz del Castillo, 64, when Cortés heard about this episode, he fatefully observed that he "regretted much his not being able to get him [Guerrero] into his hands."

13. See Michael C. Meyer and William L. Sherman. *The Course of Mexican History* (New York: Oxford University Press, 2006), 211. Indeed, as RoseAnna Mueller points, out Guerrero is widely regarded as the father (literally!) of *mestizaje*; Mueller, "From Cult to Comics: The Representation of Gonzalo Guerrero as Cultural Hero in Mexican Popular Culture," in *A Twice-Told Tale: Reinventing the Encounter in Iberian/Iberian American Literature and Film*, edited by Santiago Juan-Navarro and Theodore Robert Young, 137–148 (Cranbury, NJ: Associated University Presses, 2001), 138. See also *Chetumal, Quintana Roo*, "Chetumal, in Search of Gonzalo Guerrero, Father of the First Mestizo," no date. http://www.bicycleyucatan.com/gonzaloguer rerochetumal.html (Access date, July 15, 2010).

14. Diaz del Castillo, 62. The original Spanish is as follows: "*Hermano Aguilar, yo soy casado y tengo tres hijos. Tienenme por cacique y capitán, cuando hay guerras, la cara tengo labrada, y horadadas las orejas. ¿Que dirán de mi esos españoles, si me ven ir de este modo? Idos vos con la bendición de Dios, que ya veis que estos mis hijitos son bonitos, y dadme por vida vuestra de esas cuentas verdes que traeis, para darles, y diré, que mis hermanos me las envían de mi tierra.*"

15. Diaz del Castillo, 62.

16. A. P Maudsley, translator. Bernal Diaz del Castillo, *The Discovery and Conquest of Mexico 1517–1521*. (Mexico City: The Mexico Press [2 vols.], 1928), 91.

17. Why Guerrero didn't write his own reply to Cortés is unclear, for as we shall shortly see, despite his lowly origins, he was in fact literate in Spanish, if not Mayan; see. Diaz del Castillo, 62, who says that he read Cortés' letter. And as Mueller, 146–147, notes, Mexican journalist Mario Aguirre Rosas claims that Guerrero left behind a memoir, written on deer hides and velum supposedly obtained from the Montejo expedition; see Mario Aguirre Rosas, "Gonzalo de Guerrero: Padre del mestizaje iberomexicano." In *Prólogo de Alfonso Taracena* (Mexico: Editorial Jus, 1975). However, Mueller, 146, goes on to emphasize that the authenticity of this text, which is private hands, is extremely controversial.

18. Although de Aguilar clung steadfastly to his vow of chastity while he was Aquincuz's slave, like Cortés, he eventually took an Indian mistress and fathered two daughters. Because of his clerical status, de Aguilar's land reverted to the Spanish Crown after his death in 1531.

19. Inga Clendinnen, *Ambivalent Conquests: Maya and Spaniard in Yucatan, 1517–1570*. Cambridge: Cambridge University Press. 1987), 14–16.

20. Clendinnen, 20-21.

21. Clendinnen, 20.

22. Diego de Landa, *Account of the Affairs of Yucatan*, edited and translated by A. R. Pagden (Chicago: Philip O'Hara, 1975), 33.

23. Quoted from Gonzalo Fernández de Oviedo y Valdés by Glendinnen, 22.

24. Quoted by Glendinnen, 22; see also Robert S. Chamberlain, *The Conquest and Colonization of the Yucatan* (New York: Octogon Books, 1966), 63.

25. Glendinnen, 22.

26. The Spanish renegade was apparently known by several other names, among them Gonzalo de Aroca, Gonzalo de Aroza, and Gonzalo de Marinero, perhaps because he had once been a sailor. But most historians know him simply as Gonzalo Guerrero.

27. Chamberlain, 192–196.

28. See Reed, Nelson. *The Cast War of Yucatan* (Stanford, CA: Stanford University Press, 1964).

29. Mueller, 141–143. Indeed, as Professor Mueller has pointed out, Guerrero's image has steadily evolved over the centuries from that of a renegade Spaniard and an apostate Christian to a highly sympathetic Mayan — and indeed, Mexican!— icon. He has been the subject of

several recent novels, including Eugenio Aguirre's *Gonzalo Guerrero: Novela histórica* (Mexico City: UNAM, 1980) and Carlos Villa Roiz's *Gonzalo Guerrero: Memoria olvidada, trauma de México* (Mexico City: Plaza y Valdés, 1995), and even a comic book (Mueller, 139–141).

30. Clendinnen, 73–82, 133–134.

31. Clendinnen, 18.

32. Unlike the heroes of *Dances with Wolves* and *The Last Samurai*— respectively, Lieutenant Dunbar and Captain Algren — both Sully, with his twenty-second century version of an M16, and Guerrero, with his sixteenth-century arquebus, would today be called "grunts," that is, common, ground-pounding infantrymen at the bottom of their respective military heaps as well their social heaps. Thus, opportunities for advancement would have been few and far between across the board.

33. Curtis Hensley, "Ethnographic Charisma and Scientific Routine: Cushing and Fewkes in the American Southwest, 1879–1893." In *Observers Observed: Essays on Ethnographic Fieldwork*, edited by George W. Stocking, Jr., 53–69. (Madison: The University of Wisconsin Press, 1983), 56–63.

34. Hensley, 59.

35. George W. Stocking, Jr., "The Ethnographer's Magic: Fieldwork in British Anthropology from Tylor to Malinowski." In *Observers Observed: Essays on Ethnographic Fieldwork*, edited by George W. Stocking, Jr., 70-120 (Madison: The University of Wisconsin Press, 1983), 100-103.

36. Bronislaw K. Malinowksi, *A Diary in the Strict Sense of the Term.* Translated by Norbert Guterman. (Stanford, CA: Stanford University Press, 1967).

37. Mueller, 139–146. See also Note 28.

38. John Podhoretz, "Avatarocius: Another Spectacle Hits an Iceberg and Sinks," *Weekly Starndard.com*, December 28, 2009.

39. Debbie Schlussel, "Don't Believe the Hype: 'Avatar' Stinks (Long, Boring, Unoriginal, Uber-Left)," December 17, 2009. http://www.debbieschlussel.com/13898/dont-believe-the-hype-avatar-stinks-long-boring-unoriginal-uber-left/ (Access date, August 5, 2010).

40. Quoted by Brent Lang, "James Cameron: Yes, 'Avatar' Is Political," *The Wrap*, January 13, 2010. http://www.thewrap.com/movies/article/james-cameron-yes-avatar-political-12929 (Access date, August 5, 2010).

41. Lang.

42. http://www.csms.ca/maya.htm. Access date, October 7, 2010.

43. Whether the filmmaker was aware of Gonzalo Guerrero when he wrote the script for *Avatar* is at the moment a moot question. But the personas of the Spanish renegade and Jake Sully are so similar that I wouldn't be surprised to learn that Cameron had in fact run across this remarkable episode somewhere in the course of his background research for the film.

WORKS CITED

Aguirre, Eugenio. *Gonzalo Guerrero: Novela histórica.* Mexico City: UNAM, 1980.

Aguirre Rosas, Mario. "Gonzalo de Guerrero: Padre del mestizaje iberomexicano." *Prólogo de Alfonso Taracena.* Mexico City: Editorial Jus, 1975.

Anonymous. *The Huffington Post.* January 4, 2010; updated March 18, 2010. http://www.huffington-post.com/2010/01/04/avatar-pocahontas-in-spac_n_410538.html (Access date, July 8, 2010).

Bilge, Ebiri. December 21, 2009. http://www.filmcritic.com/features/2009/12/avatar-or-the-last-samurai/ (Access date, July 13, 2010).

Brown, Dee Alexander. *Bury My Heart at Wounded Knee: An Indian History of the American West.* New York: Henry Holt, 1991.

Burr, Ty. "Movie review, Avatar." *The Boston Globe.* December 16, 2009, http://www.boston.com/ae/movies/articles/2009/12/17/avatar_is_an_out_of_body_experience/ (Access date, July 16, 2010).

Chamberlain, Robert S. *The Conquest and Colonization of the Yucatan.* New York: Octogon Books, 1966.

Charity, Tom. "Review: 'Avatar' delivers on the hype." *CNN.* December 18, 2009. http://arti cles.cnn.com/2009-12-17/entertainment/avatar.review_1_avatar-sam-worthington-sacred-lands?_s=PM:SHOWBIZ (Access date, July 16, 2010).

Chetumal, Qintana Roo. "Chetumal, in Search of Gonzalo Guerrero, Father of the First Mestizo." No date. http://www.bicycleyucatan.com/gonzaloguerrerochetumal.html (Access date, July 14, 2010).

Clendinnen, Inga. *Ambivalent Conquests: Maya and Spaniard in Yucatan, 1517–1570.* Cambridge: Cambridge University Press. 1987.

Coe, Michael. *The Maya* (4th ed.). New York: Thames and Hudson, 1987.

Company, Juan Miguel y Manuel Talens. "Reseña de la película *Avatar,* de James Cameron (USA 2009)," *Rebellion,* December 27, 2009. http://www.rebelion.org/noticia.php ?id=99374 (Access date, July15, 2010).

Corliss, Richard. "Corliss Appraises *Avatar:* A World of Wonder." *Time Magazine,* December 14, 2009. http://www.time.com/time/arts/article/0,8599,1947438,00.html (Access date, July 15, 2010).

Diaz del Castillo, Bernal. *The True History of the Conquest of Mexico, Written in the Year 1568.* Translated by Maurice Keatinge. New York: R. M. McBride, 2 vols., 1927.

Elliott, Kate. "Avatar." December 4, 2009. http://kateelliot.livejoiurnal.com (Access date, September 20, 2010).

Hall, John Whitney. *Japan: From Prehistory to Modern Times.* New York: Dell, 1979.

Hensley, Curtis. "Ethnographic Charisma and Scientific Routine: Cushing and Fewkes in the American Southwest, 1879–1893." In *Observers Observed: Essays on Ethnographic Fieldwork,* edited by George W. Stocking, Jr., 53–69. Madison: The University of Wisconsin Press, 1983.

Honeycutt, Kirk. "*Avatar*— Film Review." *The Hollywood Reporter.* December 12, 2009. http://www.hollywoodreporter.com/hr/film-reviews/avatar-film-review-1004052868.story (Access date, July 15, 2010).

Keough, Peter. "Avatar: machine dreams: James Cameron plays games." *The Boston Phoenix.* December 18, 2009. http://thephoenix.com/boston/movies/94407-avatar/ (Access date, July 20, 2010).

Landa, Diego de. *Account of the Affairs of Yucatan,* edited and translated by A. R. Pagden. Chicago: Philip O'Hara, 1975, http://www.csms.ca/maya.htm; no date. (Access date, October 7, 2010).

Lang, Brent. "James Cameron: Yes, '*Avatar*' Is Political." *The Wrap.* January 13, 2010. http://www.thewrap.com/movies/article/james-cameron-yes-avatar-political-12929 (Access date, August 5, 2010).

Malinowksi, Bronislaw K. *A Diary in the Strict Sense of the Term.* Translated by Norbert Guterman. Stanford, CA: Stanford University Press, 1967.

Maudsley, A. P., translator. Bernal Diaz del Castillo, *The Discovery and Conquest of Mexico 1517–1521.* Mexico City: The Mexico Press (2 vols.), 1928.

Meyer, Michael C., and William L. Sherman. *The Course of Mexican History.* New York: Oxford University Press, 2006.

Mueller, RoseAnna. 2001. "From Cult to Comics: The Representation of Gonzalo Guerrero as Cultural Hero in Mexican Popular Culture." In *A Twice-Told Tale: Reinventing the Encounter in Iberian/Iberian American Literature and Film,* edited by Santiago Juan-Navarro and Theodore Robert Young, 137–148. Cranbury, NJ: Associated University Presses, 2001.

Podhoretz, John. Avatarocius: "Another Spectacle Hits an Iceberg and Sinks." *Weekly Starndard.com* 15 (2009), http://www.weeklystandard.com/Content/Public/Articles/000 /000/017/350fozta.asp, December 28, 2009.

Price, David A. *Love and Hate in Jamestown.* New York: Vintage Press, 2003.

Rea, Steven. "'Avatar' is an epic adventure — and great fun." *The Philadelphia Inquirer.* December 16, 2009, http://www.philly.com/philly/entertainment/movies/20091216_Avatar.html (Access date, July 16, 2010).

Reed, Nelson. *The Cast War of Yucatan*. Stanford, CA: Stanford University Press, 1964 red pill junkie, January 6, 2010. http://www.cartoonbrew.com/disney/pocahontasavatar.html (Access date, July 18, 2010).

Schlussel, Debbie. "Don't Believe the Hype: 'Avatar' Stinks (Long, Boring, Unoriginal, Uber-Left)." December 17, 2009. http://www.debbieschlussel.com/13898/dont-believe-the-hype-avatar-stinks-long-boring-unoriginal-uber-left/ (Access date, August 5, 2010).

Stocking, George W., Jr. "The Ethnographer's Magic: Fieldwork in British Anthropology from Tylor to Malinowski." In *Observers Observed: Essays on Ethnographic Fieldwork*, edited by George W. Stocking, Jr., 70–120. Madison: The University of Wisconsin Press, 1983.

Villa Roiz, Carlos. *Gonzalo Guerrero: Memoria olvidada, trauma de México*. Mexico City: Plaza y Valdés, 1995.

Wapedia, Gonzalo Guerrero, no date. http://wapedia.mobi/es/Gonzalo_Guerrero (Access date, July 14, 2010).

Conclusion: Seeing the Films of James Cameron Mythically

MATTHEW WILHELM KAPELL
and STEPHEN MCVEIGH

The American science-fiction writer Harlan Ellison had a unique reaction to viewing *The Terminator* in 1984. "I loved the movie. I was just blown away by it," he is reported to have said, adding "I walked out of the theater, went home, and called my lawyer."[1] Ellison's complaint was simple: he believed James Cameron had taken ideas he'd written for the 1960s television show *The Outer Limits* and plagiarized them. The episode Ellison pointed to, "Soldier," does bear an uncanny resemblance on some levels to Cameron's vision in *The Terminator*. "Soldier" involved time traveling soldiers from the future, taking their battles to the present day.[2] Eventually, Ellison received payment and credit on future prints of the film. It is fair to say, though, that any reader or viewer of science-fiction could readily pick dozens of other sources that Cameron had used in his creation of the T-800 cyborg killer. Malicious robots or artificial people, time travel, and saving-the-world narratives had been a staple of the genre for well over a century when Cameron wrote *The Terminator*. Indeed, Ellison's argument that Cameron had taken his ideas could as easily have been made by the 16th century Rabbi of Prague, Judah Loew ben Bezalel had he viewed *Terminator 2: Judgment Day*.[3] Rabbi Loew is a central person in many stories of the Golem, an artificial construct used to protect Jews during pogroms in stories from the Middle Ages. The differences between the Golem myths and the T-800 found in *T2* are actually quite minor. Like Schwarzenegger's character the Golem is artificial, programmed to protect, and very powerful.

The reason that prints of *The Terminator* had to carry a credit to Ellison, it seems, is that he had better lawyers than Rabbi Loew! Of course, there is another reason there is no credit offered to the obvious precursor of the many Golem myths in Cameron's Terminator films: the themes and motifs have been so prevalent, for so long, that they are part of the culture of the Western world. It would be as logical as the decedents of Homer suing Gene Roddenberry for so fully stealing ideas in *The Odyssey* and placing them in the final frontier of *Star Trek*, churches paying a licensing fee for their Christmas nativity scenes, or George Lucas offering credit to countless previous stories involving the hero myths he reused in *Star Wars*.[4] Yet credits are not provided for such use of common themes simply *because* they are so very common. And, at the same time, James Cameron has been continuously accused of lacking originality.

A major reason this book exists, however, is to examine the films of James Cameron because they have so artfully captured many of the themes, ideas, motifs and ideologies present in the contemporary world. Rather than confronting Cameron's work for lacking originality, we find his use of such themes to be central to his oeuvre. In other words, what Cameron has done time and time again is present contemporary ideologies in the narrative form of film. That phrase is not a mistake: "ideologies in narrative form," the religion and myth scholar Bruce Lincoln has said, is a very useful definition of what we mean when we say "myth."[5]

Thinking About Cameron Mythically: Seeing Myths

Myth remains a difficult term to define, however, beyond "ideologies in narrative form." The multiple ways in which the term "myth" is employed in the contemporary world is part and parcel of this issue. The term is employed to mean "a falsehood" as often as it is used to mean "a significant cultural story." Agreeing on a definition of the term remains quite difficult, and most scholars using the term spend a large amount of their time merely attempting to define it. The American scholar of myth, William G. Doty, has confronted this issue. For Doty the definitions fall into a wide spectrum, "from 'outright lie' to 'most important underlying source of cultural life.'"[6] Thus, a central issue when we offer the idea that the work of James Cameron can be seen as the presentation of myths is that, as Doty has noted, "myths can be made to mean whatever the myth teller wants them to mean, and their rhetorical power can be subjected to the prevailing modes of discourse of a particular era or power elite."[7]

If we accept Bruce Lincoln's idea that myth is an ideology in narrative form, however — that is, that all stories are myths on some level — then the films of James Cameron become easily seen as aspects of the "prevailing modes of discourse" of the period in which he wrote and filmed them. It is not a unique statement to suggest that films are among the prevailing modes of discourse in the contemporary world, and that primarily films are narrative as well. But this leaves open the next important question this book attempts to answer about James Cameron. The scholar of myth Robert Segal would add this simple fact: "myth accomplishes something significant ... but I leave open-ended what that accomplishment might be."[8]

The accomplishments of James Cameron's films are what each contributor to this volume has sought to discuss. This means that the essays collected here are examples of a critical exegesis of those myths presented by Cameron. Each contributor to this volume has examined the work of James Cameron from a perspective designed to add meaning to the original work. However, in another way, what each contributor has done is to encourage viewers to "think mythically" about James Cameron. By "think mythically" we follow the expla-nation of the American philosopher Robert Cummings Neville. Though, where Neville is primarily interested in religion, we would suggest that a sim-ilar perspective is useful in understanding film — and especially the work of James Cameron. As Neville would have it, "when people are 'thinking myth-ically' they are interpreting things, perhaps even the meanings of their own lives, within the coded contours of the narrative."[9] The contours of the nar-rative are precisely what allow Cameron's films to be received by audiences to such stunning success. And, where some critics see this as an indication of a lack of originality — that Cameron is co-opting the tropes of various genres, and little more — we see it as a strong indication that his films represent broad cultural understandings useful in contemporary societies.

Using myth, then, allows a centering of Cameron's narratives. As Doty has described it, myth is a "symbolic language useful for designating meanings within the everyday that are initially discerned in the realms of particularly heightened ... experiences."[10] As much as Cameron's films do precisely this, this volume is an attempt to break apart his "designated meanings" and exam-ine them with care. One designated meaning for Cameron is, of course, the political and McVeigh and Kapell offer a wide interpretation of all Cameron's films as ideological artifacts. The politics of Cameron's films range from the Cold War to the ecological speculation of *Avatar*. But all present "political myths" that, as Christopher Flood has put it in his definition of the term, offer "narratives of past, present, or predicted political events which tellers present to their audiences as truthful, intelligible and meaningful."[11]

James Cameron's mythmaking, then, does exactly what Flood describes, and Cameron spends much time in the present but musing about both past and predicted future. As a result, both Ace G. Pilkington and Andrew B. R. Elliott take pains to think through exactly what Cameron might mean when he approaches "history," "truth" and "historical truth." Both Pilkington and Elliott are concerned with some old questions about subjectivity, objectivity, and reality. And each really argue that Cameron has addressed these issues as well, but done so in a way that makes his films mythologically consistent, even if he is not always narratively consistent.

To accomplish this mythological consistency, Cameron uses all the tools available to him as a filmmaker. It is important to distinguish that a purpose of myth is, as Doty has noted, to *"provide symbolic representations of cultural priorities, beliefs, and prejudices."*[12] Examining exactly how this is done through spectacular filmmaking is what Bruce Isaacs examines in his essay here. The creation of the blockbuster is something that Cameron has been part of since his earliest filmmaking, and looking to exactly what such narratives really endeavor to provide filmgoers is, Isaacs suggests, a significant cultural undertaking. That process is one of increased technological sophistication and Cameron has long been a leader in such advances in filmmaking. It might be surprising, then, that such a seeming technophile as Cameron would, in the end, actually provide a far more negative view of technology. Like the Prometheus myth about humanity's acquisition of fire, however, Cameron has presented both the positive and negative, leading to the end result of a very ambiguous view of technology. As Elizabeth Rosen notes, the irony in Cameron's use of cutting-edge technology to make his contemporary myths is that, those myths tend to see the negative effects of technology as easily as the positive.

It is perhaps an indication of how strongly important mythological concepts resonate in Cameron's world-view that gender has remained central to his oeuvre. Three chapters here confront Cameron's take on gender in different ways, but all agree with William G. Doty that the term, itself, "can no longer remain an apparently simple social science term that merely reflects the passing impact of culture upon one's biological constitution."[13] Thus, Dean Conrad sees in Cameron the explicit use of traditionally heroic archetypes to forward strong female characters, Narminio and Kapell trace Cameron's work through the lens of academic, institutionalized feminism, and Roger Kaufman looks for underlying gay themes from the perspective of Jungian psychology. Cameron's work traditionally examines what gender means in cultural terms, and each of these three chapters examines the significance of his examination. If myth is, indeed, an "ideology in narrative form," then Cameron's films have traditionally examined the "gender ideology" dominant at the time he made those films.

Yet, as much as women have remained an important part of Cameron's films, he has also confronted — repeatedly — what it means to be "the other" in ways different than gender. Between the humans and the Terminators, the West and Islam, the classes on board the *Titanic*, or the aliens — be they in *Aliens* or on Pandora — Cameron's narratives all revolve around the confrontation between world-views. As such, John James and Tom Ue offer a carefully post-colonial reading of *Avatar* while C. Scott Littleton offers a pre-colonial examination of *Avatar*'s precursors. Both chapters offer a mediation of the colonial, and that mediation is what Cameron, himself, seems to call for in his films. Thus, both chapters and Cameron's films are in line with Homi K. Bhabha's "demands [for] an articulation of forms of difference."[14]

The chapters here are thus a kind of "thinking through myths" in the work of James Cameron. Each offers further insight into Cameron's attempts to "present models *of* our society and present models *for* our society." This, it should be noted, is a definition of the use of myths from William G. Doty.[15] But it is also a very real statement about what James Cameron's films offer as well: a way to *see* contemporary myths as well as a way to *think* about them. Thus, each contributor here has attempted — each from their own perspective and in their own way — to provide a way to think about the films of James Cameron. The result we desire from such thinking is the purpose of this collection. Cameron's mythic visions have been successful precisely because they are in constant dialog with the more general myths of today. And, in thinking through the myths retold by James Cameron it is our hope that readers will then be able to revisit those films and see them anew, as if for the first time.

NOTES

1. Quoted in Christopher Heard, *Dreaming Aloud: The Life and Films of James Cameron* (New York: Doubleday, 1997), 77.

2. "Soldier," Written by Harlan Ellison, *The Outer Limits* (American Broadcasting Company: Original Air Date September 19, 1964).

3. Information on the Golem myth is drawn largely from Emily B. Bilski, *Golem! Danger, Deliverance and Art* (New York: The Jewish Museum, 1988); Rabbi Loew did not create the Golem myth, but for the purpose of argument his claim to the idea seems as reasonable as Ellison's.

4. See Matthew Wilhelm Kapell, ed, *Star Trek as Myth: Essays on Symbol and Archetype at the Final Frontier* (Jefferson, NC: McFarland, 2010), for *Star Trek*'s use of mythological themes; and see Matthew Wilhelm Kapell and John Shelton Lawrence, eds., *Finding the Force of the Star Wars Franchise: Fans, Merchandise and Critics* (New York: Peter Lang, 2006) for Lucas's use of such themes.

5. Bruce Lincoln, *Theorizing Myth: Narrative, Ideology and Scholarship* (Chicago: University of Chicago Press, 1999), 207.

6. William G. Doty, *Myth: A Handbook* (Westport, CT: Greenwood Press, 2004), 11.

7. William G. Doty, *Mythography: The Study of Myths and Rituals* (Tuscaloosa: University of Alabama Press, 2000), 25.

8. Robert Segal, *Myth: A Very Short Introduction* (New York: Oxford University Press, 2004), 6.

9. Robert Cummings Neville, *The Truth of Broken Symbols* (Albany: State University of New York Press, 1996), 38.

10. William G. Doty, "Myth and Postmodernist Philosophy," in Kevin Schilbrack, Ed., *Thinking Through Myths: Philosophical Perspectives* (New York: Routledge, 2002), 146.

11. Christopher Flood, "Myth and Ideology," in Kevin Schilbrack, Ed., *Thinking Through Myths: Philosophical Perspectives* (New York: Routledge, 2002), 178.

12. Doty, *Myth: A Handbook*, 18, emphasis in the original.

13. William G. Doty, *Myths of Masculinity* (Edmore, MI: Crossroads Press, 1993), 16.

14. Homi K. Bhabha, *The Location of Culture* (New York: Routledge, 1994), 96.

15. Doty, *Mythography*, 454.

About the Contributors

Dean **Conrad** teaches courses in creative writing for film, theater, television and radio at the University at Hull, England, where he earned his Ph.D. with a dissertation on women in science fiction cinema. He was first published with a critical analysis of *Star Wars* (Valis Books, 1996) and his recent work includes essay contributions to the British journals *Foundation* and *Science Fiction Film & Television*. He is guest-editing a double-edition of the American journal *Post Script*— on cinema distribution and exhibition — and completing a book on women in science fiction film.

Andrew B. R. **Elliott** is a senior lecturer in media and cultural studies at the University of Lincoln, U.K., where he teaches a range of courses in film and television studies. His research focuses on the representation of history on film, the notions of adaptation, authenticity and truth across the media. He has published on a variety of topics ranging from Vikings and violence to authenticity and television detectives, and his recent book *Remaking the Middle Ages* (McFarland, 2010) analyzes the semiotic reconstruction of the medieval period. He is writing a second book on the portrayal of history in film and media, and his conference, Rethinking Epic, seeks to examine the role, function and influence of the present-day new epic.

Bruce **Isaacs** is a lecturer in film studies at the University of Sydney, Australia. His research and teaching focus on film aesthetics and history, as well as various intersections of film and popular cultural practices. He has published widely in the field, including the monograph *Toward a New Film Aesthetic* (Continuum, 2008). He is contracted to publish a second book with Continuum in 2012, examining the aesthetic evolution of American High Concept Cinema.

John **James** holds a B.A. in English from Bellarmine University, and is finishing an M.A. degree at Columbia University in New York. In 2008 he was a scholar of the English Speaking Union, whose funds allowed him to study at Exeter College, Oxford. He has won awards for both poetry and criticism, including an Academy of American Poets Prize, and his work has appeared or is forthcoming in *Columbia Poetry Review* (Chicago), *DIAGRAM* and *The Los Angeles Review*, among other publications.

Matthew Wilhelm **Kapell** has edited books on *The Matrix* (with William G. Doty) and *Star Wars* (with John Shelton Lawrence) and, most recently, *Star Trek as Myth* (McFarland, 2010). Trained as an historian and an anthropologist, he works in the war and society and American studies programs at Swansea University in Wales, U.K. He has taught at the University of Michigan–Dearborn, and began his study of film as a way to enliven his lectures on anthropological theory. His publications include work on the press coverage of the 1943 Detroit "race" riots, the utopian fiction of Mack Reynolds, and Christian romance novels, and coauthored works on the genetics of human development and the effects of poverty on human growth.

Roger **Kaufman** is a founding member of the Institute for Contemporary Uranian Psychoanalysis, the first organization devoted to gay-centered psychoanalytic theory and practice. He is an adjunct faculty member for the M.A. degree in clinical psychology at Antioch University, Los Angeles, where he received his M.A. in 1999 following a B.A. from Brown University in 1983. His writings on gay-centered archetypal psychology and film have been published in several anthologies and periodicals, including Kapell's *Star Trek as Myth* and Kapell and Lawrence's *Finding the Force in the Star Wars Franchise*. His work has also appeared in *Jung Journal, Journal of Analytical Psychology, Los Angeles Times, White Crane Journal,* and the *Gay & Lesbian Review Worldwide*.

The late C. Scott **Littleton** was a professor of anthropology emeritus at Occidental College in Los Angeles. Littleton received a Ph.D. in anthropology from the University of California–Los Angeles, in 1965, and taught at Occidental until his retirement in 2002. Specializing in Japanese religion, the legends of King Arthur, and comparative Indo-European mythology, his *New Comparative Mythology* was one of the first books to bring the work of French comparative mythology into the English-speaking world. His *From Scythia to Camelot* (with Linda A. Malcor) and *Shinto* cemented his reputation as a scholar at ease in both Western and Eastern traditions. He died shortly after finishing his essay for this book.

Stephen **McVeigh** is a lecturer in war and society at Swansea University in Wales, U.K. His teaching and research explores American political culture and military history in literature and film. He is the author of *The American Western* (Edinburgh University Press, 2007) and his essays have appeared in the *Journal of War and Culture Studies*, Engel's *Clint Eastwood: Actor and Director*, Kapell and Lawrence's *Finding the Force in the Star Wars Franchise*, Kapell's *Star Trek as Myth*, and Moffitt and Campbell's *The 1980s: A Critical and Transitional Decade*. He is writing an article on the connections between the life and fiction of Ernest Hemingway and Raymond Chandler, and a monograph tentatively titled *George W. Bush, 9/11 and the American Western*.

Elisa **Narminio** recently completed an M.Sc. degree in international relations theory at the London School of Economics, focusing on international law as well as women and children in conflict and post-conflict situations. She holds an M.A. in comparative literature from the Sorbonne (Paris), where she specialized in European literature, contemporary mass-mediated film, and gender studies. Her research interests include pop culture, gender studies, women in conflict, and processes of conflict and peace in Africa and the Middle East.

Ace G. **Pilkington** has a D.Phil. in Shakespeare, history, and film from Oxford University and is a professor of English and history at Dixie State College. He is the author of *Screening Shakespeare from Richard II to Henry V*. He is an active member of the Science Fiction and Fantasy Writers of America, and his work has appeared in *Astounding, Asimov's,* and *Weird Tales.* His essays on film have appeared in *Literature/Film Quarterly, The Yearbook of English Studies, Shakespeare and the Moving Image, Shakespeare from Page to Stage,* Robert Kahn's *Movies: The Ultimate Insider's Guide,* and Kapell's *Star Trek as Myth.*

Elizabeth **Rosen** is the author of *Apocalyptic Transformation: Apocalypse and the Postmodern Imagination* (Lexington, 2008). She has most recently contributed chapters to the Modern Language Association's *Approaches to Teaching the Graphic Novel; Spoiler Warnings: Critical Approaches to the Films of M. Night Shyamalan;* and *Reel Revelations.* She teaches at Lafayette College, and is the nonfiction editor of the webzine *Ducts.*

Tom Ue is a doctoral candidate in the Department of English Language and Literature at University College London, where he researches Shakespeare's influence on the writing of Henry James, George Gissing, and Oscar Wilde. Ue's publications include "'How Is She to Blame?' The Woman Question and Narrative in Mary Elizabeth Braddon's *Lady Audley's Secret* and George Gissing's *Eve's Ransom,*" published in *Eve's Ransom: George Gissing e le sfide del romanzo tardo-vittoriano* (Aracne Editrice, 2010); he has essays forthcoming on Harriet Beecher Stowe, Thomas Hardy, Oscar Wilde, and co-written with John James, Sherwood Anderson and James Cameron.

Index

The Abyss (film) 6, 16, 20, 28–30, 45, 47, 49, 54, 56, 57–58, 62, 63, 65, 84, 110, 112–114, 117, 125, 138, 146, 175–176; and filmmaking technology 6, 110, 112, 117; as gendered film 131–133
Afghanistan 19; *see also* Iraq; Middle East
Aguilar, Geronimo 11, 201–210
Alice in Wonderland (film) 194
Alien (film) 16, 53, 54, 75, 76, 79, 85, 127, 128, 129–130, 138, 149, 174
Alien film franchise 77, 129
alien queen (character, *Aliens*) 28, 56, 78–79, 115, 125, 130, 131, 149, 153–154, 174–175
Alien vs. Predator (film) 77
Alien Woman: The Making of Lt. Ripley (Gallardo-C. And Smith) 129–130, 148
Aliens (film) 9, 16, 20–26, 45, 53, 54, 55, 58, 62, 72–79, 82, 85, 102, 112, 114–118, 125, 129–131, 132, 133, 137, 139, 146–147, 148–151, 152–154, 155–157, 159–163, 168, 173–175; and gender 146–151, 152–163; and homosexual archetypes 172–175 and Vietnam War 20–26, 53
Aliens of the Deep (documentary film) 47
Anderson, Barbara 1
Anderson, Joseph 1
anima 169, 178
animus 169
apocalypse 19, 22, 44, 48–49, 112–113, 134
Apocalypse Now (film) 190
Apone, Sgt. (character, *Aliens*) 55, 152, 153
L'Arrivée d'un Train à La Ciotat (film) 95
Asimov, Isaac 53–54
Astounding Science-Fiction (periodical) 124
Augustine, Dr. Grace (character, *Avatar*) 63, 64, 119, 139, 153, 157, 159, 186, 189, 206
Avatar (film) 6, 7, 8, 9, 10, 11, 15, 16–19, 20, 28, 30, 37–40, 44, 54, 56, 61–63, 72, 82, 92, 93, 94, 98–103, 109–112, 117, 118–119, 125, 130, 139, 140, 146–147, 148–163, 167, 176, 177–183, 186–195, 200–210, 218, 219–220; as colonialist film 186–195, 200–210, 219–220; and filmmaking technology 6, 61, 92, 98–99, 100–103, 109; and gender 82, 139, 146–163; as homosexual narrative 176–181, 182, 183; as political film 15–16, 17–19, 30, 37–40, 44, 218
Aziz, Salim Abu (character, *True Lies*) 30, 31, 33, 38

Barthes, Roland 146
Battle Angel (film) 141
Battle Angel Alita (manga) 141
Battle Beyond the Stars (film) 5, 126
Bay, Michael 90, 93, 94, 101
Bazin, Andre 83, 99–101, 102–103
Benjamin, Walter 83, 91, 112
Berlin Wall 39
Bhabha, Homi K. 220
Bhagavad Gita 50
The Birth of a Nation (film) 32
Bishop (character, *Aliens*) 54–56, 117
Blackmore, Tim 25
Blade Runner (film) 99
Blomkamp, Neill 187, 194
Bond, James (character) 31, 48, 135
Brigman, Lindsey (character, *The Abyss*) 57, 113–114, 118, 131–133, 138
Brigman, Virgil "Bud" (character, *The Abyss*) 29, 57, 58, 176
Brin, David 44, 56
Britannic (*Titanic* sister ship) 47–48
Brooks, Ann 149
Brooks, David 190–191, 194
Bukater, Rose DeWitt (character, *Titanic*) 35, 48, 54, 59, 61, 72–74, 80–82, 85, 86, 118, 137–138, 141
Bukatman, Scott 92, 94, 98
Burke, Carter J. (character, *Aliens*) 25, 27, 54, 55–56, 77, 85
Bush, George W. (U.S. president) 194

Calypso (sea vessel) 47–48
Cameron, James: as auteur 3–4, 8, 90–91, 96, 101, 168; and colonial narratives 186–197, 200–210; as filmmaker 1–12, 44–45; as film technician 6–7, 90–103; and gender 124–141, 146–163; as historical filmmaker 44–65, 72–87; and homosexual themes 167–183; as political filmmaker 15–40; and technology 109–120; *see also* individual film titles
Campbell, Joseph 126–128, 134, 138, 140
Camus, Albert 152
Canada 19, 20, 46
Canadian Women's Army Corps 20
Castillo, Bernal Diaz 202, 204
CGI (computer generated image) 84, 96, 110, 133, 141

Chacon, Trudy (character, *Avatar*) 139
Chavez, Hugo 209
Chetumal 203, 205, 206, 207
Children of Men (film) 103
Chomsky, Noam 209
The Clash of Civilizations (Huntington) 30–33, 34
Classical Hollywood 72, 73, 82, 90, 93, 99, 101; *see also* Hollywood; post–Classical Hollywood
Coffey, Lt. Hiram (character, *The Abyss*) 28, 58, 113–114
Cold War 16, 20–21, 25, 28–30, 33–36, 39, 113, 218
Colonial Marines (*Aliens*) 25–27, 55–56, 77, 79, 82, 102, 115, 118, 149–150, 154
Colonialism 10, 186–197, 200–210, 219–220; *see also* post-colonialism
Connor, John (character, *Terminator* franchise) 23, 52–53, 57, 114, 115–116, 134, 135, 171–173, 182
Connor, Sarah (character, *Terminator* franchise) 9, 23, 49, 50–52, 54, 114, 115, 118, 126–128, 129, 131, 133–136, 138, 147, 156, 171–173
Cook, David A. 1
Coppola, Francis Ford 4, 101
Corliss, Richard 35, 147
Corman, Roger 5–6, 83, 126
Costner, Kevin 44, 191, 200
Cousteau, Jacques 44, 46–48, 56, 59
Cozumel 11, 202, 204, 205
Crimson Jihad (fictional terrorist group, *True Lies*) 30–31; *see also* War on Terror
Cuban Missile Crisis 19, 49, 57
Cyberdyne Systems (fictional corporation, *Terminator* franchise) 23, 24

Dances with Wolves (film) 11, 63, 191, 200–201, 209, 210
Dargis, Manohla 186
Dark Angel (television series) 44, 62, 111
The Dark Knight (film) 90
Dawson, Jack (character, *Titanic*) 35, 59, 80, 86, 137, 138, 141
The Day After (television film) 21
The Day the Earth Stood Still (film) 57, 136, 139
DeMille, Cecil B. 72, 90
DePalma, Brian 4
Derrida, Jacques 34, 36
Digital Domain 6, 93, 110
District 9 (film) 187, 194, 195–196
Doty, William G. 6, 217, 218–219, 220
Dreaming Aloud (Heard) 3, 44
Dyson, Miles (character, *Terminator 2*) 23–24, 114, 134, 135
Eden 62, 113
Egyptian Myth 171–172
Eisenhower, Dwight (U.S. president) 21–23, 37

Eisenstein, Sergei 72
Ellison, Harlan 216
The Emerald Forest (film) 63, 190
Emmerich, Roland 90, 93
The End of History and the Last Man (Fukuyama) 16, 33–36, 39
The Enemy Below (film) 57
ET: The Extra-Terrestrial (film) 98
The Extinction Syndrome (play) 61
Eytukan (character, *Avatar*) 158–159, 193
Eywa (deity/life force, *Avatar*) 63–64, 140, 151, 158, 179, 186

Faisil (character, *True Lies*) 32, 33
Fanon, Franz 188–189, 191
feminism 9–10, 130–131, 132, 134, 139, 146–163, 219; *see also* gender
FernGully: The Last Rainforest (film) 191
filmmaking technology *see* individual film titles
Fincher, David 77
Ford, John 90, 101
Foucault, Michel 155, 156, 157
Fukuyama, Francis 34, 36; see also *The End of History and the Last Man*
The Futurist (Keegan) 3, 19, 127

gay sexuality 10, 161, 167–183, 219; *see also* gender; homosexuality; same-sex romantic love
gender 9, 10, 25, 28, 81–82, 112, 134, 146–163, 169, 176, 219; *see also* feminism; gay sexuality, homosexuality, same-sex romantic love; sexuality
Ghosts of the Abyss (documentary film) 47, 110
Glendinnen, Inga 206
"go native" 207–208
Goldwyn, Sam 40
Griffiths, D.W. 72
Guerrero, Gonzalo 11, 201–210
Gunning, Tom 95

Haggard, H. Rider 63
Hall, Stuart 191–192
Heaven 112–113, 171
Heinlein, Robert A. 52, 53
The Hero with a Thousand Faces (Campbell) 126
Hicks, Dwayne (character, *Aliens*) 27, 55, 56, 77, 78, 130, 153–154
Hitchcock, Alfred 90, 91, 101
Hockley, Caledon "Cal" (character, *Titanic*) 35, 80
Hollywood 2, 4, 8, 10, 11, 12, 17, 40, 47, 72, 90, 95, 97, 99, 101, 103, 112, 117, 125, 126, 127, 141, 195, 210; *see also* Classical Hollywood; post–Classical Hollywood
Hometree (*Avatar*) 186, 191–192, 193
homosexuality 10, 167–183; *see also* gay sexuality; same-sex romantic love
How to Train Your Dragon (film) 194

Huntington, Samuel 32–33; see also *The Clash of Civilizations*
Hurd, Gale Ann 126, 133
The Hurt Locker (film) 194

Imperialism 17, 18, 31, 38, 82
Inception (film) 90, 94
Indiana Jones and the Kingdom of the Crystal Skull (film) 187, 194–195, 197
Industrial Light and Magic 6
Inside the Actor's Studio (television show) 46
Invaders from Mars (film) 21
Invasion of the Body Snatchers (film) 187, 194, 195, 197
Iraq 17, 19, 38, 44, 63, 190; see also Afghanistan
Irigaray, Luce 154

James Cameron's Expedition: Bismarck (documentary film) 47, 110
Jaws (film) 4–5, 98
Jeunet, Jean-Pierre 77
Jorden, Rebecca "Newt" (character, *Aliens*) 25, 28, 55, 56, 78, 117, 130, 149, 150, 153, 174–175, 182
Jung, Carl 10, 126, 140, 168–170, 179, 182
Jurassic Park (film) 5, 97, 98, 100

Keldysh (Russian sea vessel) 15, 48, 59, 61
King Kong (film) 127
Kipling, Rudyard 63
Kristeva, Julia 157
Kubrick, Stanley 5, 91, 92, 93, 102, 141
Kurzweil, Ray 119

Landau, Jon 109
Last of the Mohicans (film) 190
The Last Samurai (film) 11, 191, 200–201, 208, 209
Lebow, Richard Ned 146, 157, 160, 162
Lincoln, Bruce 217
Lord of the Rings (film franchise) 10, 84, 167
Lucas, George 4–6, 25, 91, 93, 101, 110, 126, 141, 217
LV-426 (fictional planet, *Aliens*) 25, 26, 75, 76, 129, 132, 146, 149, 151–152, 154, 174

Malinowski, Branislaw 209
Maslin, Janet 35
The Matrix (film franchise) 90, 91, 95
Maya (Native American culture) 11, 200–210
Memento (film) 72
Messiah Complex 187, 190–191, 194
Middle East 32, 33, 72, 209
Midsummer Night's Dream, A (play) 63
Military-Industrial Complex 16, 18, 20, 34, 37–38; in *Aliens* 24–25; in *Terminator* films 20–24; see also Cyberdyne Systems; Multinational United; Weyland-Yutani
Milius, John 4
Mills, C. Wright 2

mise-en-scène 79, 102
Montana (fictional US submarine, *The Abyss*) 28
Montejo, Francisco 205–208
Multinational United (fictional corporation, *Avatar*) 195, 196
Mulvey, Laura 90
myth 6, 63, 65, 83, 98, 99–100, 124–141, 152, 171, 172, 173, 176, 177, 190, 192, 216, 217–220; see also Campbell, Joseph; Lincoln, Bruce; Segal, Robert

Nachan Can 203, 208
Na'vi (fictional species, *Avatar*) 10, 11, 37, 38–39, 62, 63, 64–65, 72, 118–119, 140, 150, 151–152, 153, 158, 159–160, 162, 167, 177, 178–181, 186–190, 191, 192, 193–194, 195, 200, 201, 204, 206, 207, 201; as colonized culture 186–190, 193–194, 200–201
Neville, Robert Cummings 218
"Newt" see Jorden, Rebecca
Neytiri (character, *Avatar*) 9, 63, 64, 72, 126, 138, 139–140, 141, 146, 147, 150–151, 153–154, 155, 157, 158–161, 178, 179–180, 181, 189, 192, 193
Niagara Falls 20, 46
A Night to Remember (film) 60
9/11 15, 19, 30, 31, 37, 38–39, 40; see also War on Terror
Nolan, Christopher 90, 93, 94, 97, 101
Nolte, John 17
Nostromo (fictional space vessel, *Aliens*) 25, 76, 117
NTIs (Non-Terrestrial Intelligences, *The Abyss*) 28, 29, 58
nuclear war see apocalypse

O'Bannon, Dan 128, 130
Olympic (*Titanic* sister ship) 60
Orientalism 188
The Outer Limits (television series) 216

Pandora (fictional planet, *Avatar*) 2, 10, 11, 37, 38, 62, 63–65, 72, 83, 91, 139, 146, 151–153, 157, 158, 162, 177, 179, 180–181, 183, 186–189, 190, 191, 193, 197, 200, 219
Piranha II: The Spawning (film) 4, 49
The Planet of the Apes (film franchise) 128
Platoon (film) 27
Pocahontas (film) 11, 191
Pocahontas (individual) 140, 200–201
Podhoretz, John 17, 209
post–Classical Hollywood 90–92, 97; see also Classical Hollywood; Hollywood
post-colonialism 10, 187; see also Colonialism
The Postman (film) 44
postmodernism 8, 45, 72, 73, 87, 130, 131–132, 162, 168
Prince, Stephen 18

Quaritch, Colonel Miles (character, *Avatar*) 38, 152, 153–154, 159

Rabkin, Eric S. 132
Rambo: First Blood Part II (film) 15, 17, 26, 28, 53, 125
Rashomon (film) 72, 82
Reagan, Ronald (U.S. president) 27
Reese, Kyle (character, *Terminator* franchise) 25, 49–51, 52–3, 54, 82, 128, 134, 171
Ripley, Lt. Ellen (character, *Alien* franchise) 9, 25, 26, 27, 28, 54, 55–57, 72, 75, 76–78, 79, 82, 85, 86, 102, 115, 117, 118, 125, 127, 128–131, 132, 133, 134, 137, 141, 146–161, 174–182; and gender 128–131, 146–161; as homosexual archetype 174–182
Roddenberry, Gene 216
Rorty, Richard 36
Rosenstone, Robert 72
Rossellini, Roberto 72
Routledge Film Guidebook: James Cameron (Keller) 3, 32, 36, 51, 90, 91, 93, 101
ROV (Robotic Operated Vehicle) 15, 19
Run Silent, Run Deep (film) 57
Russia *see* Soviet Union

Said, Edward 188, 189
same-sex romantic love 167, 168, 181, 182; *see also* gay sexuality; homosexuality; same-sex romantic love
Sartre, Jean-Paul 188–189
Sawicki, Jana 155, 162
Scholes, Robert 132
Scorsese, Martin 4, 101
Scott, Ridley 16, 24, 72, 77, 78–79, 99, 127, 128, 129, 130, 131, 138, 174
Secular Steeples (Ostwalt) 112
Segal, Robert 217
Sharman, Leslie Felperin 125, 136
Skynet (fictional defence computer system, *Terminator* franchise) 21, 23–24, 52, 114, 134, 140
Skywalker Sound 6
Smith, Captain John 200
Soviet Union 21, 28, 30, 39, 57, 194, 195
Spectres of Marx (Derrida) 34
Spielberg, Steven 4–6, 72, 91, 97–100, 101, 103, 187, 194–195
Star Trek (media franchise) 10, 167, 170, 217
Star Wars (media franchise) 5, 6, 10, 26, 98, 126, 127, 129, 141, 167, 170, 178, 217
Starship Troopers (Heinlein) 53
Stone, Oliver 27, 72
Strange Days (film) 3, 31, 111, 125
Stringer, Julian 74
Sulley, Jake (character, *Avatar*) 9, 10, 11, 37, 63, 64–64, 69, 91, 100, 101, 118, 138, 139, 150, 151, 153, 154, 158, 159–160, 161, 162, 177–179, 180–181, 182, 186–187, 189–190, 193–194, 195–197, 200, 201, 204, 205, 206, 208; as colonialist character 189–190, 193–197, 201, 204–205 as homosexual archetype 177–179, 180–181

T-800 (cyborg, *Terminator* franchise) 92, 53,

54, 57, 115–116, 118, 133, 134, 135, 171, 172–173, 182, 216, 219
T-1000 (cyborg character, *Terminator 2*) 2, 92, 100, 103, 110, 115, 118, 133, 171, 172, 219
Tasker, Harry (character, *True Lies*) 30–33, 76
Tasker, Helen (character, *True Lies*) 76, 125, 136–137
The Terminator (film) 4, 16, 18, 20–24, 25, 38, 44–45, 48–53, 54, 55–57, 62, 63, 82, 86, 91, 92, 100, 112, 114, 115, 118, 124–125, 127, 128–129, 131, 133, 134, 136, 138, 146, 147, 170–173, 177, 182, 216; and homosexual patterning 170–173, 177; as political film 20–24
Terminator 2: Judgement Day (film) 16, 20, 22–24, 31, 45, 51, 54, 75, 91, 92, 100, 110, 112, 114–116, 118, 125, 133, 134, 133–137, 146, 170–173, 175, 177, 182, 216; and filmmaking technology 91–92; and gender 133–134, 135–137; and homosexual patterning 170–173, 177; as political film 20–24
Terminator 2: 3-D (attraction) 92
Terminator 3: Rise of the Machines (film) 135
Them! (film) 132
3-D filmmaking 6, 16, 62, 65, 92, 98, 99–103, 110–111, 141, 177, 178
Titanic (film) 4, 16, 18, 19, 33–36, 44, 45–46, 47, 48, 54, 59–60, 61, 62, 72, 73, 74, 79–82, 84, 85, 86, 91, 92–93, 97, 110, 111–113, 118, 125, 137–138, 141, 146, 147, 170, 219; and filmmaking technology 79–82, 85, 110, 113; and gender 137–138, 141, 146–147; as political film 33–36
RMS *Titanic* 2, 15, 19, 72, 74, 80, 93, 97, 111, 112, 118
La Totale (film) 31
Transformers (film) 90, 94
True Lies (film) 16, 30–33, 34, 36, 38, 76, 86, 111–112, 125, 135–137, 138; and gender 125, 135, 136–136; as political film 16, 20, 30–33, 34, 36; *see also* Cold War
2001: A Space Odyssey (film) 5, 91, 92, 102, 141
2012 (film) 90

Unobtanium (fictional mineral, *Avatar*) 146, 151, 187–188
USSR *see* Soviet Union
The Usual Suspects (film) 72
Utopia 113, 114, 116, 118, 120

Vasquez, Pvt. (character, *Aliens*) 77, 78, 115, 131, 139, 151, 157
Veyne, Paul 74
Vietnam War 20, 24–28, 29, 30, 39, 53, 190
Vogler, Christopher 127, 137

Walker, Mitch 168–169, 171, 176
war *see* Cold War; Vietnam War; War on Terror
War on Terror 19, 190

WarGames (film) 21
Weinraub, Bernard 44
Weyland-Yutani (fiction corporation, *Alien* franchise) 25, 75
What Is History? (Carr) 45
Whelehan, Imelda 154, 162
Williams, John 98
Wisher, William 124, 171
The Wizard of Oz (film) 63, 127

World Trade Center 15, 31; *see also* 9/11
The Wreck of the Titan (Robertson) 59

Xamanzana 203
Xenogenesis (short film) 5, 124, 125–126, 128, 135

Yucatán Peninsula 11, 201, 202, 205, 206–207